From the two-time Grammy-nominated singer-songwriter behind the groundbreaking album Exile in Guyville comes a haunting memoir in stories in the tradition of Patti Smith's *M Train*

It's hard to tell the truth about ourselves. It opens us up to being judged and rejected. We spend so much time hiding what we're ashamed of, denying what we're wounded by, and portraying ourselves as competent, successful individuals, that we don't always realize where and when we've gone missing. In that, I don't think I am alone.

When Liz Phair shook things up with her musical debut, *Exile in Guyville*--making her as much a cultural figure as a feminist pioneer and rock star--her raw candor, uncompromising authenticity, and deft storytelling inspired a legion of critics, songwriters, musicians, and fans alike. Now, like a Gen X Patti Smith, Liz Phair tells the story of her life and career in this haunting memoir that reveals the moments that have stayed with her. For Phair, horror is in the eye of the beholder - in the often unrecognized universal experiences of daily pain, guilt, and fear that make up our humanity. Illuminating despair with hope and consolation, tempering it all with her signature wit, Horror Stories is immersive, taking readers inside the most intimate junctures of Phair's life, from facing her own bad behavior and the repercussions of betraying her fundamental values, to watching her beloved grandmother inevitably fade, to undergoing the beauty of childbirth while being hit up for an autograph by the anesthesiologist.

Horror Stories is a literary accomplishment that reads like the confessions of a friend. It reveals the high stakes and hidden beauty in life's most haunting moments, and gathers up all our isolated shames, bringing us together in our shared imperfection, uncertainty, and cowardice, smashing the stigma on not being in control. But most importantly, the uncompromising precision and candor of *Horror Stories* transforms these deeply personal experiences into tales about each and every one of us.

HIGH PROFILE PROJECTS UPCOMING: Liz will be releasing her first album of new materials in 8 years, and embarking on a Worldwide Tour for 2019.

REEMERGENCE OF A TRAILBLAZER: EMI is re-issuing Phair's albums with updated materials in conjunction with a major marketing campaign for inclusion in the Rock and Roll Hall of Fame to commemorate 25 years since her groundbreaking album, *Exile in Guyville*.

NEW DOUBLE ALBUM: Her first album since 2010 is due this fall, and is intended to pay homage to her debut.

NEVER BEFORE SEEN PHOTOS: Liz will be including black and white photos throughout primarily as chapter heads, that will give a behind-the-scenes look on her life.

Horror Stories • Liz Phair
Random House • Hardcover • 10/08/19 • $28.00/$37.00C • 9780525511984

horror stories

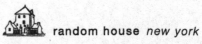

random house *new york*

LIZ PHAIR

horror stories

a memoir

Published in the United States by Random House, an imprint and division of Penguin Random House LLC, New York.

RANDOM HOUSE and the HOUSE colophon are registered trademarks of Penguin Random House LLC.

Hardback ISBN 978-0-525-51198-4
International edition ISBN [insert]
Ebook ISBN 978-0-525-51199-1

Printed in the United States of America on acid-free paper

randomhousebooks.com

987654321

FIRST EDITION

Book design by Simon M. Sullivan

[dedication TK]

[epigraph TK]

contents

horror stories

prologue

'␣ve been writing songs for thirty years. From the beginning, my songs have been stories. Every time I recorded an album, I was writing my memoirs. When I listen to the music I created in my twenties and thirties, I instantly travel back in time to inhabit those moments again: how I felt, what I thought, what hurt me, what I longed for. I wrote straight from the heart so the truth would ring like a bell, and resonate in the listener's heart as well.

Every time I pick up a guitar and start to strum, I hear a melody forming in my head. It dances along with the chords I'm playing, bouncing up and down as it tests the boundaries of the key. I feel like I'm playing with a wish that wants to get out, or anger that needs to be released. Sometimes I don't even know how I'm feeling, until I start singing and it all comes tumbling out. It's almost like dream interpretation, except I'm awake. I don't know how I'd navigate the world if I couldn't write about it.

My manager called me the day Prince died. I was on tour with the Smashing Pumpkins, opening for them as a solo act in opera houses across the country. My manager and I had other business to discuss, but naturally our conversation turned to Prince, and to all the other artists we'd lost in 2016. It seemed like a year in which a disproportionate number of fixed stars in the musical firmament were extinguished. At one point, we joked that this was the Rapture, and God was starting an all-star band. But beneath our levity, a sense of urgency thrummed.

He spoke with uncharacteristic candor. "Liz, you need to think about this next record. Nobody knows how much time they have. You might be gone, and you gotta ask yourself: Are you making the album you'd want to leave behind if it were your last?"

I thought about my son, and what I'd like him to know if I weren't there to guide him. I would bequeath him the courage to face his fears, the vision to see opportunities for connection and love in even the darkest times. I'd pass on my faith that there's a brilliant story in each and every moment of our lives if we pay attention. I'd draw out the poison of thinking that faults and failures make someone unworthy, and instead I'd reveal how bad decisions are just equal and opposite manifestations of great gifts and abilities. I'd leave him with the power to hope.

Horror Stories is my effort to slow everything down and take a look at how we really become who we are. It's more than just my personal story. It's about the small indignities we all suffer daily, the silent insults to our system, the callous gestures that we make toward one another. Horror isn't necessarily the big, ghoulish creature waiting to pounce on you in the dark. Horror can be found in brief interactions that are as cumulatively powerful as the splashy heart-stoppers, because that's where we live most of our lives.

In the stories that make up this book, I am trusting you with my deepest self. We spend so much time hiding what we're ashamed of, denying what we're wounded by, and portraying ourselves as competent, successful individuals that we don't always realize where and when we've gone missing.

How foolish we feel in those rare instances when the fog dissipates, the path is clear, and we see our hapless footprints wandering around all over the place. Those are the resolute moments, the sober morning-after reflections when we plant our feet facing in the direction we wish to go and vow never to deviate from honesty, empathy, and inspiration.

It's hard to tell the truth about ourselves. It opens us up to being judged and rejected. We're afraid we will be defined by our worst decisions instead of our best. Our impulse is always to hide the evidence, blame someone else, put the things we feel guilty about or that were traumatizing behind us and act like everything is fine. But that robs us of the opportunity to really know and care about one another. It closes a door that could lead to someone else's heart. Our flaws and our failures make us relatable, not unlovable.

I learned this when I released my debut album, *Exile in Guyville*, back in 1993. I wrote those songs during one of the hardest periods of my life. I had no money, and I was lonely, confused about the future and angry about the past. The lyrics reflected my reality in an unflinching, unapologetic, and sometimes explicit way that people deeply connected with. Fans came up to me at my concerts expressing gratitude and admiration for my bravery in telling the truth, because it made them feel a little less isolated and overwhelmed about their own difficulties. They heard themselves in the music, not me.

My motivation for writing this book is to articulate those experiences that people may not always want to recognize, but describe them in a way that makes them worth the effort. By taking situations that are disempowering and then finding a way through the maze, I find that examining the weaker moments in our lives makes us stronger. In that, I don't think I am alone.

Come walk down some dark and mysterious paths with me. Once your eyes adjust, you'll see that monsters are only mirrors. There is music in the creaking trees. Deep beneath our workaday world, we are all dreaming.

ART TK

one

SHE LIES

We left her there. That's the part that haunts me. We saw her need, and we ignored it. The bathroom was crowded. It was hot. I was waiting for my turn at the mirror to put on lipstick. I don't know why I only see the scene from two angles: looking down out of the corner of my eye while I do my makeup, and waiting with my back against the wall for my friends to finish washing their hands.

I don't know if she was a blonde, a brunette, or a redhead. I know that she was at the party. I think she was wearing an olive-green jacket, but actually, I might have made up that detail. I seem to be assembling her outfit partially from fact and partially from fiction, as if I'm trying to dress her the way I used to dress my old Barbie dolls, make her look presentable, give her that dignity. My conscience is a fantastic prosecutor. After so many years, only the damning evidence remains. I was there. I saw it. I did nothing.

Fear is an exhausting emotion, and I was scared so often that first semester in college. It was overwhelming trying to find my class-rooms in a maze of unfamiliar buildings. I was afraid to ask the other students what the professor meant when she said our reading was reserved in the library. I was too scared to use my zip card in the cafeteria line, in case there was a trick to it. Trying to look like I knew what I was doing was my constant priority.

Looking back, I feel compassion for my younger self. I was just trying to get by. I was only eighteen, and my brain was still forming. I have to have something to say to the jury in my defense. The truth is, I was happy that night. I had met some girls I liked, finally. They all knew each other from a private school in Manhattan. They smoked clove cigarettes and smelled like patchouli. They had boy-friends and were trying to set me up with a guy from their group. One by one, they each took me aside and whispered something nice he'd said about me. They raised their eyebrows when they spoke about him, like I was lucky.

He wasn't my type. He was okay. I went to a movie with him a week later, and we sat silently in the theater waiting for the lights to dim, having nothing to say to each other—just breathing slowly, acutely aware of the proximity of our limbs. He was nervous, I re-member, because he blurted out, "If you'd ever hit somebody over the head with a baseball bat, you'd never forget it." I agreed.

I've linked these memories together because, after I turned down the chance to be his girlfriend, my new friends looked for someone else to fill the vacancy and round out the octet. I didn't see them much after that, which was probably for the best. Though we never discussed it, I blamed them for not taking responsibility just as much as I blamed myself. How could we, how could any of us who were there, have turned a blind eye to what was happening? We can be monsters, we human beings, in the most offhand and cavalier ways.

It reminds me of those sociological experiments that expose how fundamental cruelty is to the establishment of society. A family, a clan, a nation, can't be described without drawing a line around those who are included and leaving others outside the boundary. When researchers ask a group of students to single out and ostracize a member of their pack, someone always brings up William Golding's *Lord Of The Flies*, that story of shipwrecked children who devolve into a primitive tribe. But the shunning instinct doesn't require isolation on a desert island or captivity in a science lab to find expression. It's much, much closer at hand. Scratch the right tender spot and people turn savage.

It's instinct, and that's that. Not everyone regrets the unkind things they do. Guilt is the poisonous flower that springs up after a selfish act. In order to grow, there has to be soil present to begin with. The most impressive blooms get pressed into your book of recollections, and every time you go back and reread a chapter, their dry, skeletal remains drop out and fall into your lap. Decomposition marks the pages, and when you've interred too many bad memories, the book itself begins to smell.

We dig our disgrace by inches. Some of the meanest things I've done have been fleeting, momentary offenses. I only recognize their malignity once they've lingered overlong in my imagination. The painter Ed Paschke used to say, "They're the bugs that get stuck in your grill." I'd call them aftershocks of missiles lobbed from a safe distance. I've been carrying around for decades the tiny, toxic shards of souls I've casually shattered.

Late at night on a train, for instance, a man smiles at me, and I sneer—like he's the most disgusting thing I've ever seen. I'm scared. I'm nineteen, and I don't want to get raped. But as his face falls, I know instantly that he meant instead to reassure me that everything was okay. He was there. I was safe. If you think that's the bad part, it isn't. Everybody makes mistakes. My culpability begins the moment I turn my face away and stare out the window, pretending that I am better than he is. I let him think that he is repellent, allow him to sit there in shame and dwell on how poorly he was perceived. When he gets off the train, he looks as downcast as any man who hates himself will be. Wondering what kind of day he'd had, what situation he was going home to, what cares and worries weighed on him, this is my burden to bear for as long as I have a memory.

"If I Had Only" is the hit song I'll never release. When quantum physicists talk about entanglement, I know exactly what they mean. When Einstein calls a phenomenon "spooky action at a distance," I want to leap up out of my seat and shout, "Amen, brother! Preach!" It's a lonely universe, and the void takes up so much of it. Why are we surprised to find dark matter residing within ourselves? Emptiness is filled to the brim with anti-starlight. Spread out a towel, lie down, and bleach beneath the not-done, the not-said, the not-redeemed.

A famous comedian left his dog on the back porch of his Mulholland Drive aerie. He lived in New York and rarely made it back to Los Angeles. His assistant would drive up twice a day to feed the crippled old Newfoundland and walk him for ten minutes along a dusty arroyo where no grass grew, on a bare gravel path along the scrubby side of a mountain. I visited him three times. I didn't know the owner, so I just stood there beneath the tiny deck where this big dog lay all day, panting from the heat. I said nice things to him, like Romeo wooing Juliet. He had the sweetest, gentlest disposition despite being, for all intents and purposes, abandoned.

I had the chance to adopt the dog, but he was too big and too old for my narrow house, and he'd have had trouble climbing up and down all the stairs. I asked around up at the stables where I rode horses. Nobody was interested. Many months later, after I'd given up hope, I got a call from someone who knew of a farm for Newfies that might be able to help. I didn't respond. I never called back. I was on tour, I was busy, it fell through the cracks. And now I carry this dog around with me forever. He comes back and visits me like a ghost, that sweet face of his, to remind me that I am forging chains like Ebenezer's, and they grow heavier as I go.

So who was the girl in the bathroom? I'll never know. What were her dreams? Why was she there? What made her get so drunk? She was dressed the same way we all were, in a frilly miniskirt and ankle boots. She looked like she'd be a nice person to meet on another day, under different circumstances.

I could tell by her shape and the quality of her skin that she was pretty. But she had to be lonely, because where were her friends? Where were the people who were supposed to keep track of her? Where was the roommate or the boyfriend who was supposed to make sure she could stand up and get home again? She must have come alone to that party. It must have taken courage, a lot of liquid courage, to stand around not knowing anybody. Her unconscious body on the floor was proof of just how nervous she'd been.

Her legs were sticking out of the stall. We stepped around and over them. It reminded me of that scene in *The Wizard of Oz* when the Wicked Witch of the East lies prone after Dorothy's house lands on her. People coming into the bathroom tittered and pointed at first, then gasped. Then they shut up.

The line right inside the door was still lively, still revved up from the party atmosphere outside, but as you moved deeper into the inner sanctum of the lavatory, it got silent. People went about their business with a grim, thin-lipped efficiency. Eyes darting, cheeks pale. Faucets turning on and off. Nobody saying anything. Nobody doing anything about it.

She was lying face down, passed out, her head resting on the floor next to the toilet, a big smear of excrement extending out from between her sprawled legs. I'd never seen someone who'd shit themselves before, let alone publicly. The humiliation of it was extreme.

As I waited with my back against the wall, I had a clear view of her soiled underpants. I don't remember what I was thinking. I was just uncomfortable. We all were. Whether I was aware of how dangerously close to death a person would have to be for their body to forcibly expel alcohol from their anus, I couldn't say. It also didn't occur to me that she could be drowning in her own vomit. When one end excretes, generally, so does the other. It's the body's late-stage response to poisoning. No one thought to check if she was breathing, at least while I was there. No one wanted to go near her.

It wasn't just the mess that repelled us. What was it about her behavior that we were rejecting? If she'd crashed her car while speeding, would we walk past the smoking wreck, averting our eyes? Would we shrug and say, *That's what you get for engaging in reckless behavior*? I'm certain we wouldn't. We would rush to the vehicle and do our best to save her. In fact, I can't think of another instance in which we would judge instead of helping. What we were judging was how easily that could have been us.

Let me paint another picture for you. Let me describe a better world to live in: Four girls enter a bathroom and find one of their classmates collapsed and in distress. Quick! Get help, they shout. They try to revive her, they check to make sure her air passages are clear. One of them takes off her sweatshirt and covers the girl to preserve her modesty. Don't let anyone else in! Has someone called nine-one-one? Hurry, we need help! Oh my God, I hope she's going to be okay. Please, God, please let her be all right! But that's not what happened. And that's what I have to live with.

There's something relentless about hindsight. It chips away at the unimportant details, leaving just the guilt, just the unfinished business. I cannot exorcise her from my conscience or purge her from my past. She will always be lying in that bathroom in my soul, waiting for me.

ART TK

two

BELOW

I t's one of the first authentic days of summer, when the glittering sunshine erases all winter doubt; the kind of day that is exhilarating. The sky is such a deep shade of blue that it takes my breath away. We are standing on top of a massive sand dune, 130 feet above the eastern shore of Lake Michigan. I shield my eyes, trying to see the tip of the Sears Tower poking up out of the water as I look back across the vast expanse toward Chicago. If it were nighttime, I would see the red lights on its broadcast towers blinking incongruously above the horizon, as though the rest of the building and skyline were submerged. I squint, but it's no use. The curvature of the earth has swallowed up my life.

I turn back to make sure the kids are all right. They're clambering over dead wood and streaking down the sandy mountain, arms waving, hair flying, until one of them face-plants. The other two fall backward onto their rumps. Only the adults can make it any distance without careening off balance. The dads show off in a race to the bottom, their legs scuttling to stay ahead of their accelerating torsos. They're not so much running as falling with resistance.

Alberto attacks the slope chest out, like he's expecting his wings to catch the wind and lift him up into the air. Jim keeps his back perfectly straight, running down an imaginary staircase. When the gradient levels out, they slow, shifting gears into a trot. Mallory and I watch our husbands' tiny figures come together and start making the arduous climb back up to the top.

It's not yet eleven o'clock. We left so early in the morning, to get here while the sand was still cool, that her children are still wearing their pajamas. Olivia is bending down and peering into the maw of an old tree trunk that has fallen on its side. Adam and Nick are throwing twigs and handfuls of sand at each other.

This hilltop was once home to a stand of black oaks, sixty to eighty feet tall. The dune is moving inland so rapidly that the trees have been buried alive, their topmost branches still sticking up above the ground, a few remaining leaves fluttering in the breeze. Most of them have already died, their limbs twisted and dried out like those bleak trees in old western movies. Mallory and I sit in a patch of shade and enjoy a moment of silence. I run my fingers through the sand, making wavy patterns that I smooth away and redraw. Mallory has that look on her face like she's contemplating existence. We've been friends since fourth grade, and I am fluent in her mannerisms.

"Do you think," she begins, and immediately I know she's about to ask a philosophical question, "that you could live out here? I mean, imagine if you grew up in some small town in Indiana. Like, just a normal, average town. Do you think you'd care about the same things? Would you even want to live in the city?"

I think I know where she's going with this. She's always lobbying me to move back out to the suburbs.

"For instance, if you hadn't been adopted, do you think you'd still be an artist? Or would you be someone totally different?"

I'm wrong. She's talking about her own life and wondering if she's made the right choices.

"I don't know." I look out at the wide green surface of the lake and see a canvas. "Probably. I think I'd always be creative."

"Huh." Mallory always says "Huh" when she disagrees with something you've said. She cocks her head to the side and looks at me as if to say, You don't know yourself as well as you think.

One of the children starts wailing, a shrill cry of outrage. We jump to our feet to referee. Olivia has a triumphant look in her eyes, and an insouciant saunter. She's stolen Adam's branch away. Nick stands by, not sure whose side to take.

"Come on, you guys!" Mallory rallies the troops with a whoop of delight. "Let's go see Daddy! Come on, Nickel." She holds out her hand to my son. "Don't you want to go see your dad? Then we can get burgers and fries!"

The men are still only halfway up the hill. They're not out of shape; they're talking. When you have children this age, you take any chance you can get to grab a little peace and quiet. I watch Mallory and the kids zigzag down the incline, kicking up puffs of sand with every bounding footfall. My heart clenches with joy. It is a perfect day.

I take off my glasses and clean them with the bottom of my T-shirt. I feel ridiculous wearing these wire-rimmed spectacles, like the spinster schoolteacher in *Little House on the Prairie*. Normally, I wear contacts, but I'm getting LASIK surgery tomorrow and need to let the natural shape of my eyeball spring back, so the ophthalmologist will have more meat to work with. He's going to slice off a thin layer of my cornea. He'll do it while I am still awake and able to see the knife. Then he'll pick up the partially severed flap and fold it over to one side, leaving it there to hang by a hinge, while he aims a laser directly at my pupil and starts pulverizing tiny bits of my lens until the curvature of my meniscus approximates twenty-twenty vision. He'll ask me to stare straight into the red laser beam, and I'll hear the rapid *bang, bang, bang* of the weapon firing, but I won't feel the explosions.

I dig my toes down into the sand, picturing the trees buried beneath me. What must it be like to have grown up in the sunlight and the rain, to have groaned and swayed under the storms bearing down on this coastline, only to be entombed and immobilized, cut off from all sensation, suffocated? In tree time it must have happened very fast. They live so slowly that the roving dune must have seemed like an alarming advance. There are a lot of ways an oak tree is prepared to die: infestation, disease, fire, saw blades; but I'll bet drowning in silica dioxide wasn't something they anticipated.

It reminds me of a terrifying scene I saw in a film once, when I was a child. A dead pharaoh was being laid to rest in his underground burial chamber. One of the priests who'd helped prepare his body for the afterlife turned traitor and betrayed the rest of the royal family, trapping the pharaoh's heir and his relatives inside the tomb. Huge limestone blocks came down outside the chamber, blocking off all the exits. A dreadful confusion ensued as small channels opened up in the ceiling and released torrents of sand, which began filling up the vault. The young heir, distraught, looked to his mother for help, but she knew there was nothing they could do. They would all die together in a matter of minutes, when there was no more air to breathe and grit choked their lungs. I can't bear to think about those trees anymore.

Mallory and the kids have met up with Alberto and Jim. Adam, Nick, and Olivia are scampering up the side of the sand dune on all fours, their energy undiminished. I try to remember whether or not I reapplied Nick's sunscreen. His little blond head bobs along as he powers up the hillside, sticking close by his dad. He looks like me around the face, but his coloring is his father's. The group stops. They are almost to the top, but the exhausted adults need a rest and stand with their hands on their hips to take in the spectacular view.

I notice more people arriving on the beach, far below us. It looks like a father and three children. It's nice to see another family out enjoying the day. Judging from the father's mullet and mustache, they probably live in one of those small Indiana towns Mallory was just waxing nostalgic about. The older girl and boy stand back from the water's edge while the father and the youngest son wade out up to their ankles. The little boy is no more than five years old, slight of build and excitable. The dad lights a cigarette.

All of a sudden, the playful boy loses his balance and falls face-first into the water. He jumps right back up again, but the front of his clothes are soaking wet. Enraged, the father backhands his son off his feet. His tiny body arcs backward through the air, landing five feet away from where he started. I gasp, going completely rigid. My heart starts thumping in my chest. The father walks over and picks the little boy up by the arm and kicks him in the ribs. This man is beating his child like a dog. I make a guttural sound that starts deep in my throat. My hands fly up to my chest, one on top of the other. Mallory, Alberto, and Jim have all frozen, watching. And then it stops. Like a sudden squall, it is over.

Nobody moves. We don't call out. They wouldn't hear us; they're too far down the slope. So far below, in fact, that they look like miniature dollhouse figures, almost unreal. I am shaking. The man's other children don't react at all. It's clear from their body language that this is an everyday occurrence. I want to run down there and smash this asshole's face in with a rock, watch the lake water turn red around our desperately grappling bodies. I can see his mouth spluttering, his eyes wide with surprise, as I drown him in the shallow water.

I have another split-second vision in which I take this boy home with us and care for him and raise him as part of our family. I see myself tucking him into bed after he is combed and clean, smoothing out his anxious brow with a tender touch, explaining to him that his daddy loved him, but some people are just angry and sad. They hit the closest thing to them.

I take this scenario forward in time to his college graduation, when he is a fine, strapping young man with competitive athletic ability and no abusive tendencies. I do all this recalibration of his destiny in a matter of seconds. I've raised an entire human being in my mind. He's fine. He's safe. Do my thoughts make any difference? Does prayer make a difference? Can powerful intentions start a separate timeline of events in another dimension of reality? Are we linked now because of our emotional intersection? Have we ricocheted off each other in a way that means anything?

Nothing's changed, I realize. Nothing's different. This brave little child picks himself up and walks back to the shore to join his siblings while the dad continues to stare out at the lake, smoking. The whole revolting cycle of love and violence starts to play out in my mind. The same guy who just hit his kid will be the one tucking him into bed—if not tonight, then tomorrow. Sometime. What kind of horror is that, to be five years old and to know that the person you have to accept love from could at any moment be the person who ends your life?

The single mercy is that none of our children witnessed it.

Mount Baldy is closed to the public now. You can't go there anymore. A freak accident exposed a hidden danger lurking beneath the soft quartz sand. In 2013, six-year-old Nathan Woessner and his family were visiting the dunes on a summer holiday camping trip. Nathan and his friend Colin decided to race up the face of the dune, starting from the bottom. With the emerald water of Lake Michigan sparkling at their backs, the two young boys dug their feet in and scaled the mammoth sandpile.

Nathan was climbing right by Colin's side, until he wasn't. Colin said Nathan went to investigate an open hole, but when he lowered himself in, the dune swallowed him up. By the time his parents reached the spot of his disappearance, all that remained was a shallow depression. They started digging frantically with their hands, but whatever sand they managed to displace quickly filled back in again. A local geographer who happened to be there studying dune movement assured them that it wasn't possible for any subsurface cavities to exist. The pressure of the surrounding sand was just too great. But Nathan's parents were adamant. He was there. They wouldn't abandon him.

Emergency services came with a back hoe and dug down eight feet. The rescue was described in the December 2014 issue of *Smithsonian* magazine. "They began noticing odd features in the sand: pipe-like cylinders, eight inches in diameter and a foot or two long, of what looked like old bark. Brad Kreighbaum, 36, a third-generation firefighter, soon came across a six-inch diameter hole that shot deep into the sand: 'You could shine a flashlight and see 20 feet down.'

"When he scooped Nathan's body out of the sand at 8:05 p.m., Kreighbaum noticed other patterns in the cavity cocooning the boy. Its inside wall was sandy and soft, but bore the imprint of bark, almost like a fossil. It was as if the boy had wound up at the bottom of a hollowed-out tree trunk, except not a bit of tree was there."

The ancient stand of oaks had rotted away so slowly that their sturdy bark kept the weight of the sand at bay. Nathan Woessner was revived, and he walked out of the hospital two weeks later, perfectly fine. I hope that while he was unconscious underneath the dune, Nathan could hear the muffled cries of his family promising to save him. I like to think that the old trees made a collective decision that no child would ever again be hurt on their watch, and that our earlier prayers for that poor beaten boy reached them, the silent sentinels of eastern Lake Michigan.

ART TK

three

SURF THERAPY

Rory and I have gone for a swim. It's late in the afternoon, but the air is still hot and languid. We can cool off and get out before sunset, when the sharks come in. I love that my boyfriend will do spontaneous things with me. He's strong and brave and handsome. I love being out in the water with him, far from shore, just the two of us. He spins me in a slow circle, creating a shallow wake. I throw my arms around his neck, and we kiss.

"We should swim that way." Rory points back toward the Manhattan Beach pier. The current has pulled us fifty yards further up the coast. I didn't even notice that we were drifting. I do the sidestroke, keeping my eyes on my man. As long as Rory's there, I feel safe. He stops and circles back to me, sliding his hand down to my ass. I rest my chin on his shoulder, treading water, out of breath. The open ocean looks intimidating from out here, alien and unconquerably vast. It's overwhelming. I turn my gaze back toward the shore.

We're almost in line with our favorite beach house, the multi-million-dollar property Rory and I have picked out as our future residence once we're married and strike it rich. It's a fun game to play, imagining, What if? He's so confident about us as a couple that it makes *me* optimistic. We've met each other's families. We've gone on trips together. His sister even threw us a big party to introduce me to all their friends. Rory's the first guy in a long time that I could really make a life with.

He snags a yard of seaweed that's floating nearby and tosses it away. There was a red tide a couple of weeks ago, a poisonous algae bloom that kept us out of the water. We watched from my balcony as the rust-colored plumes choked and muddled the sandbar. Dead fish and birds washed up along the trash line. One night, we took flashlights down to the beach to view the bioluminescence. At first, we didn't know what we were looking for. Then a wave crested, and a streak of ultraviolet light shot down the length of its barrel. It was so beautiful I wanted to swim in it. How could anything that dazzling be toxic?

A large swell takes us by surprise, and Rory and I break apart—tilting our faces up to the sky to breathe as the surge rolls through. With my ears submerged I hear the underwater kingdom clicking and scraping. I'm up to my neck in a world that I'm usually unaware of. It's merely a distraction, an interruption in the lovely evening I'm having with my boyfriend. I don't want to think about the unknown or the unknowable. We're in love, and that's all my soul has room for.

It's not like there haven't been warning signs. My subconscious has been trying to tell me something, knocking on the door of my awareness with symbols and metaphors that spring to mind spontaneously; but when you're holding your hands over your eyes, it's hard to read signs. At a weekend wedding in Napa, one of Rory's friends accidentally spills red wine on me at the reception. One minute I'm a vision in a cream-colored Stella McCartney dress, and the next, I'm Carrie from Stephen King's imagination, covered head to toe in blood. People gasp in horror and back away as I stand there dripping. We wash my dress out in the sink and laugh about it, dancing late into the night, but the stain lingers. Life doesn't do the math for you; it simply supplies the data. All I've done on my computation sheet is doodle our initials inside little hearts and arrows.

Minor problems are easy to ignore. His mother doesn't like me. Her sphinxlike eyes follow me around when I'm in her house, sizing up the competition. And my mother only sort of likes him. Nobody really gets us. It's not a relationship that my friends embrace. They're happy I'm happy, but our two worlds never quite fit. He's smart, and funny as shit, but I'm the bookish one. He's athletic and stylish. In that way he's got me at a disadvantage, and he knows it.

One time we're playing tennis and I tell him not to go easy on me in the next set. His forearm turns into a laser-guided weapon, and I can't return a single hit. I burst into tears and am inconsolable. I'm devastated by how much of his skill he's been suppressing. We've played casual matches for months, but the gap in our ability was never so evident. I can't express it, but some part of me recognizes how it symbolizes the ways in which we hold each other back. Another part of me senses the danger in how seamlessly he can fake it. The truth is, although we spend half of every week together, I don't really know this man.

On the surface, Rory and I get along well. We have a natural rapport that is playful and instinctual. He's charming and adept in social situations, and I'm finally in step with my married friends. If he's selfish or cold occasionally, I rationalize it as the prickly ego of an alpha male, and if I'm being strictly honest, I take a little bit of pride in it. But my judgment is clouded by the thrill of this role-playing. I'm keeping more and more of my thoughts to myself. I long to slip into that life that I see everyone else living, that looks so easy and appealing from the outside.

I have no idea how to be that type of woman. I've been reading online dating advice, trying to be the perfect girlfriend. I don't ask him where he goes when we're apart, or when I'm going to see him next. If he hurts my feelings, I don't get angry; I just get busy with other priorities. It seems to be working, because he treats me like a princess. He spoils me. I think I'm being feminine and paying him respect, but what I'm actually doing is not listening. There's a lack of intellectual discourse between us that is totally uncharacteristic of me.

Which is ironic, because I'm more than happy to communicate in other ways. We make love all the time. I complain to my therapist that we fuck three or four times a night on the weekends and I'm so tired, but really I'm bragging. Our sex life didn't start out this fevered. In the beginning, it was awkward and stilted. But the whole getting-to-know-each-other part and subsequent deepening of appreciation all happened on the physical plane, while our emotional life is still stuck in adolescence.

I dip my head back in the ocean, slicking the hair off my face. The houses along the strand look like stock photographs, their windows glinting gold in the fiery light of the sunset. Our bodies float through warm and cold pockets. I feel Rory's strong arms suddenly lift me high up out of the water as a rogue wave breaks over our heads. He's laughing as he lowers me back down, his blue eyes shining. He's so goddamn magnificent, all tan and broad shouldered. How did I get so lucky? I don't even have to look out for myself. He does that for both of us.

The sun is sinking lower in the sky, but I don't want to go in just yet. We're the last ones left out in the water at this hour, apart from some surfers still bobbing on their boards farther up the beach. The lifeguard is locking up his tower, a pickup truck idling on the sand waiting to take him back to the substation. He knows we're good swimmers. We come down here often. We're planning to be back in the morning, actually.

Tomorrow, Rory has his girls, but I don't have Nick—which is kind of nice, because when it's all five of us, my son ends up helping out with the childcare more than he'd like to. Hadley and Avery won't leave him alone. They go into his room and coax him out to play. I love Rory's daughters like they are my own. He and I met on a blind date, set up by a mutual friend. I couldn't believe I'd found an attractive single father of two beautiful babies. I thought God had granted my wish. I thought that, because I'd been working so hard to become a better person, I'd finally earned the right to have a family.

Looking back, I've been thinking about the paper snowflakes I cut out to decorate Rory's tree that first Christmas. We hadn't been going out for very long, but it was important to me that his bachelor pad look festive for the girls. This was Hadley and Avery's first big holiday since their mom and dad split, and I wanted to make their time with their father feel as homey as possible. It's funny how women start marking their territory. I wonder now if *she* saw them, and if they fought about it.

Hadley, Rory's eldest, was a tough nut to crack. She was only two and a half when I came into their lives, and she tested me mercilessly. It took a solid year of consistent love and loyalty before she trusted me. I wouldn't let her push me around. She and I butted heads in the beginning, but we ended up bonding the most deeply. More so than Rory and I, even.

I was there at night when she was sick. I sang the girls to sleep and carefully untangled their hair after bath time. I kept them busy on airplanes with books and games. I made Hadley wear her sweater when it was cold outside. I wouldn't let her torture her little sister, even when Avery started it. I believed in her, and I think she knew that.

I got a lot of things wrong with Rory, but I did a pretty good job with his kids. One time, the girls and I got stuck in the stairwell of their building when the power went out. We were on our way up to the pool when it suddenly went pitch black, and I mean *lightless*. The girls were screaming and going crazy, of course, and I had both of them by the hand. They refused to move, either up or down. Some-how, I managed to convince them that we could make it all the way up to the exit. I picked up Avery and carried her in one arm while Hadley and I talked our way up the twenty-seven steps to the top. After that, we were inseparable.

I wonder what kind of young women they are now. I wonder if they remember me, or if their parents ever told them about our time together. Most likely, it's all been erased and filled in again with *her* memories, because that era must have been painful for her. Sometimes it's easier to plaster over old wounds and not stir up the past. I know Rory wouldn't want his daughters to know the role he played in our breakup, and I don't blame him. If I had to guess, I'd say Rory's a sociopath.

"I'm going to take this wave," he says, letting go of me and positioning himself in the water. He checks over his shoulder a couple of times, then executes three perfect freestyle strokes as the wave starts to front-load and bear down toward the shore like a freight train. Before I know it, he's gone. I don't see him again until his head pops up in the whitewater, seventy feet away. I can't believe he's just left me out here. I tread water for a minute, feeling the familiar sting of disappointment behind my eyes. I swallow a lump in my throat, vowing not to take it personally. No matter how many times this happens, I never get used to his sudden shifts in personality.

Almost to be a dick about it, I don't swim in immediately. I lie back and look up at the sky, feeling my body gently rise and fall on the swells that carry me aloft like Rory had done just a few minutes ago. My allegiance has switched to the sea. She, at least, is dependable, sort of. Rory's not even watching me. He's walked back up the beach to where our clothes are and is drying off with a towel. He says he loves me all the time. He's asked me to marry him more than once. But something in the back of my mind keeps nagging me to be cautious. There's something I already know but don't want to see.

"But what is his character like? What are his values?" my best friend asks after she meets him.

I don't understand what she's talking about. "Look at him, Anne! He's perfect. Can't you just be happy for me?" I'm frustrated that it's not totally obvious to her how amazing he is. Why do I need to explain what I see in him?

It's a fragment of a conversation from an uneventful day. And yet I've gone over it a hundred times in my mind, trying to glean what I missed about Rory in the first place.

I'm careful. I wait a long time before I introduce Rory to my son. I know Nick will like him, and I don't want to risk either of our hearts until I'm sure it's serious. After six months, I arrange for them to build a rocket ship together for Nick's fifth-grade science project.

The other students gather around as Rory and Nick huddle together on the schoolyard blacktop. Rory holds the directions in one hand, helping Nick stabilize the launchpad with the other. They light the fuse and jump back, but nothing happens. Then, in a burst of flame and smoke, the rocket shoots skyward, ascending several hundred feet into the air, disappearing from view. The other kids cheer and congratulate Nick, running out onto the soccer field to scavenge the fallen capsule. It's an unequivocal success.

I walk with more confidence in the school pickup line after that, especially when Rory is with me. Nick seems proud, too, in his own quiet way, like we have a unicorn on a leash or something. I'm grateful to be able to shed the label of "single mother" for a while and imagine that the other women envy me rather than pity me, the way I fear that they usually do. It's impossible to express the sense of relief I feel having the protection of a man in my life again.

That tension between independence and security is churning inside of me as I float here, alone in the water. I feel colder without Rory, but also more real. I'm aware that I've been acting like those superficial girls I was jealous of in high school. I'm surprised at myself. I didn't realize I'd been harboring such a deep-seated need. It's clear to me now that Rory represents a once-in-a-lifetime opportunity for a do-over.

I'm on the verge of an epiphany, when I suddenly get that tingling feeling, that dreadful sensation that I'm being watched, and it's not by my boyfriend. My awareness flips upside down, and I can see myself as I appear from underwater: pale limbs dangling down from above. My subconscious is trying to tell me something, knocking on the door of my awareness with symbols and metaphors from the murky deep. I turn around and see that the sun is gone. There's nothing left but an orange smear on the horizon. I need to swim in.

I catch the first wave, but it's a dud. I keep paddling. The second one moves me forward a few feet. For some reason, I'm panicking. I have a vision of a solitary great white shark gliding in the gloom, its black eye darting, curious snaggleteeth aching to investigate. I put my head down and start pulling hard in a flat-out crawl, breathing only when necessary. I keep my kick powerful and neat, no splashing. I'm good at this. But I forget that I'm inside the surf break, and before I know it, I get caught up in a massive dumper that pounds me down to the ocean floor. I let the wave take me and spin me around in a washer cycle. I know that when it's done I'll be scooting into shore.

Things change after that. It's as if the unseen threat has followed me out of the water and is chasing me around everywhere I go. I start to second-guess Rory's judgment. He notices the briskness in my tone of voice. Several times, when we're driving home from dinner, we find we have nothing to say to each other. I stare out the window of the car, watching the streetlights flash by, wondering where the happiness went. I tell myself that we're in a difficult phase, that we're both stressed out from work. He complains that I'm dismissive of his opinions, impatient with him. I can't deny that I am distant, critical of his choices, no longer in awe of my fine, strapping boyfriend. Suffice to say, we're fighting more. Rory gets short with me, and I deserve it. I've become increasingly insecure. But he's still pushing for total commitment, as though catching me like a wave could magically transport him over the trouble and let him outrun the consequences of his mistakes. In romantic moments, he lobbies to get me pregnant. I still believe that he loves me, that we love each other. I've never had any reason to doubt it.

He breaks up with me, finally. We go on this terrible vacation, and I'm a sullen, uncooperative bitch. Maybe I want to push things to a head, because nothing is making sense anymore. Something is pulling the puppet strings of our interactions and making him act crazy.

He writes beautiful love letters, pledging his life to mine, then gets blackout drunk and is barely able to lift his head the next morning. For two weeks he doesn't speak to me. Then he comes over and cries like a baby on my couch, holding my face in his hands as he weeps, saying that we can never be together. It's so weird. I'm like, But I'm right here. He says he wants to make love one more time, so we do, on the floor in front of my fireplace, but I don't feel anything. Somehow, I feel irrelevant to the drama in my own relationship.

I need to get out of town. Rory is exhausting me. I drive to Arizona and meet my friend Kim, who is attending a Greenbuild conference in Phoenix. We ride around the city in rickshaws and stop at three or four bars. We go to a NASCAR rally and have a blast. It feels so good to be myself again, free from anything having to do with Rory. I'm not sure I fully realize yet that this is the end.

On the drive home, over the phone, he finally tells me what's been happening. He's never completely stopped seeing the girl he was dating right before me, a trainer who works at his gym. She got pregnant, and two months ago she gave birth to his son. I'm thinking, Two months before this conversation? You mean the son that you kept pestering me to have this summer, you jackass? The imaginary son you named and joked about and tried to impregnate me with, but I wanted to wait? Jeeeeezus fucking *Christ*.

"Well, that explains a lot," I quip. I'm in shock. I get off the phone and start laughing. Catastrophes this big unfold in slow motion. Kim keeps asking me if I need to pull over, but I want to get back to Los Angeles. I have to see him in person. This whole thing feels totally insane.

As we drive back through the cactus-dotted mesas of the Mojave Desert, I keep thinking about what Rory knew and when he'd known it. I pry open all our old memories to see what's really going on below the surface. Beneath our picturesque life together, a separate timeline has been running. Two realities, parallel but distinct. I will admit that, for one surreal moment, it feels electrifying to be a part of something so fiendish, so calculatingly dishonest. I could book a spot on a daytime TV talk show, with his baby mama and his ex-wife and me pouring our hearts out to Maury Povich. It's tabloid-level awful, but it's happening to me.

I go straight to his apartment. He looks terrible, really bad. He seems to be expecting me to rage, but I feel strangely compassionate. I'm numb, as though I were going through some kind of dissociative episode. How can the person standing in front of me, whom I trust and admire, be a liar and a common cheat? I struggle to connect the dots. It seems clear that no matter what he'd done, it's worse to be him than me. A person would have to be really broken to run a game like this; to deceive himself and everybody else so effectively.

He's despondent. He says he'll do anything I want. He tells me how much he loves me, and he begs me to forgive him. He says we can do everything my way from now on, that he will be completely honest. Inexplicably, I'm entertaining the idea. This is surreal, and I'm not thinking rationally. My reality has been blown apart, and all the pieces are flying around everywhere. I'm lost in the middle of the chaos, floating in the eye of a storm. I'm also really, really calm. I know one thing: I want to have sex with him.

His face is open and hopeful as we lie on his bed together. The shades are drawn, and the room is filled with that soft blue light that only happens on certain stately afternoons. He looks so vulnerable as he fucks me, so real and present. I really feel him this time, after months of us being disconnected from each other, and I'm grateful to have this experience again. There were no more secrets poisoning the space between us.

I lie across his back afterward, breathing in the scent of his skin. I curl my finger around the soft tendrils of hair at the nape of his neck, whispering that I want to do it again. "This could be the last time I ever get to touch you," I tell him, and I mean it. I get choked up when I hear myself say it out loud. He flips over, and we have sex again. We get up and shower.

Things get hazy after that. There's some missing time. Looking back, I can only recall the two most traumatic incidents before I get out of there for good.

We're sitting in his living room talking. I'm listening to him tell me more lies about his affair. My plan is to ask him every question I can think of, because I'll never have the chance again, and I'm going to need some kind of narrative to try to make sense of our relationship. I stand up at one point to go to the bathroom, and while I'm gone he apparently checks my phone, because when I get back, he says, "Who's this?" He's pointing to a text I just received from a man I recently had coffee with.

"Is this a date?" He's accusing me.

"It was coffee, in the daytime, and we were broken up, remember?"

His demeanor has changed completely. He's irate, seething with jealousy. He's so upset that he's visibly shaking. "I can't believe you would do this. I'm not even ready to start dating yet," he says, drawing himself up to his full height. His tone is imperious. "You need to leave now." His eyes flash as he points toward the door.

I can't believe what I'm hearing. I look closely at his expression to make sure he's serious. The man who's just told me he's had a *baby* with another woman while we were together is furious that I'd go for coffee with another man. Suddenly, I'm not looking at my shitty boyfriend anymore; I'm scanning the situation through the lens of vital statistics. I'm alone in an apartment with a six-foot-two-inch male weighing approximately 220 pounds who has lightning reflexes and is enraged, and possibly crazy. At least crazy enough to scare the hell out of me.

Again, the event path goes haywire. I have no idea what happens next, or why I choose to stay in his apartment. I wish I could tell you now that I laughed in his face and walked out the door. I wish there'd been a limo waiting to take me back to my fabulous life and skyrocketing career. I hate letting you see how much I needed him, how invested I'd become in a person who didn't even exist, really. There's no good explanation. It's *Twilight Zone* all the way.

Somehow we get it together enough to function, and the girls come back from their mother's house. I'm trying to act normally, for their sakes, but I'm shattered inside, because I know I'll never see them again. They'll never understand why I left, because the person responsible for this tragedy will never admit his guilt to that extent. He lies. That's been demonstrated. Hadley and Avery will think I abandoned them. In my heart, they're my daughters, and hurting them like this is unbearable. I want to die, and that feeling will last for a very, very long time. But I can't keep seeing them right now. I can't walk through the fire of Rory's new circumstances with them. We're not getting out of the stairwell this time. We're not going to reach that exit. It's going to stay dark for a very, very long while. I know what it's going to do to them psychologically, after I leave, when they realize I'm gone for good.

Believe it or not, that fucker isn't even finished yet. He drops one last bomb, just to make sure every part of me is dead. His mom and sister are arriving in twenty minutes to meet the new member of the family. They're bringing gifts and rallying around the new mother. I've been cut cleanly out of the picture. The ramifications are starting to pile up around me until I think I'm going to suffocate. The numbness has worn off, and I am sobbing as I get into my car and drive home. I don't stop crying, in reality, for six months straight.

I try to stay sober for my son, but it doesn't always work. It's December now, the festive season, and everyone I run into who hasn't seen me for a while asks me when we're getting engaged. I'm unable to date. I'll be unable to date for the next year, and—if you want to know the truth—for the next ten. I don't trust my judgment anymore, and I'm afraid of being manipulated. I'll miss my innocence, but I've come to terms with the reason that this was my fate. There was a time when I didn't care how my actions affected other people. I was unhappy, and I didn't let myself feel enough to connect with anyone else's pain. Everybody has to pay for their sins, and Rory will, too—eventually. The scales of justice have a funny way of balancing.

The winter drags on. And then it's spring. I don't rebound as well as expected. There are days when I sit in my living room and look out at the sea until the sun goes down, nursing a drink, letting the house go dark around me. I feel so worthless. The man I loved has stabbed me in the back, pushed me out of a moving car and left me in a ditch by the side of the road.

I can't go back to therapy after this. I can't talk about it. I feel hollow, emotionally vacant. My therapist is worried. He calls every couple of weeks to check in. I keep putting him off, saying I'm not ready to see him yet, but I'm scaring myself. I'm behaving recklessly, taking unnecessary risks—indifferent to my personal safety. Making my adrenaline spike is the only way I can feel anything. I know my therapist is training for the Catalina Classic paddleboard race, so the next time he calls, I sarcastically suggest, "I'm not coming back to therapy, but you can teach me how to surf if you want to."

I never dreamed he would take me up on it. But that fine man, that therapeutic pioneer, says, "Sure."

"I can't charge you for it," he clarifies, "but if that will help, I'd be happy to do it."

Within a week, I'm back out in the waves, this time straddling a big, buoyant foam board, my therapist treading water beside me. Part of me wants to give up. Depression has sapped my will to try. But the physics of the sport won't let me. I'm on the board, and the waves are coming in. A surfboard is designed to catch the column of water, whether you're on it or not. Your weight is what drives you forward—faster, if you lean into the momentum. Sometimes I crouch, wobbling to keep my balance, and sometimes I kneel, like I'm proposing to the shore. Learning to surf is hard work, and I have to actively participate.

He teaches me how to count waves in sets. He shows me how to turtle under a crumbling crest. He moves my board into position and pushes me forward until I drop down into the wall of the wave. If I'm lucky enough to catch a ride all the way in, I scream like a lottery winner, trust-falling into the foaming whitewater while my board shoots up onto the beach. Given what I've been through, I refuse to wear a leash. He doesn't cringe when our fellow surfers smirk at my antics. He stays right beside me, and he never leaves.

One time, during our lesson, I look over at him and feel a shiver of recognition. My therapist is the one submerged up to his neck in deep water, waves threatening to break over his shoulder, nothing to hold onto. As soon as he thrusts me forward, I will be leaving him behind. He will wait out there alone as I barrel in towards the shore. This is the sacrifice he makes to try to heal me, to fix the pain that can't be stitched up with words.

He brings his own board, eventually. Some mornings we just sit out there, stroking the glassy surface with our hands, our feet pickling in the brine. I see dads I know from Nick's school paddle by, and we say hello. Slowly, my confidence returns—simply by getting up early and getting into water that's unpredictable and much too cold. At work, when I'm composing music for television shows, seawater trapped in my sinuses suddenly pours out my nose and splashes onto the keyboard. It's pretty funny, and I'm able to laugh at my own foibles again. I no longer feel like an exposed nerve everywhere I go.

Being in nature is a gift. The dawns we witness are so heavenly, so pastel and peaceful, that the sky and the sea appear to merge. It's just layers of pink and purple, smoke and orange, blue and gold. Even when it's overcast and drizzly, the water turns this velvety, viscous green that is indescribably luxurious. There's a zen to surfing that comes from the environment itself. You're betwixt worlds, removed from the hustle and bustle of civilization but not so far out of your element as to be in danger. You exist in this narrow zone of grace that feels ephemeral and ancient.

The rhythm of the waves crashing on the beach is hypnotic. You watch shorebirds flock in great wheeling arcs across the sky. Pelicans skim the shoals in a single-file line, coasting on their gargantuan wings. Occasionally, a pod of dolphins cruises through the surf-break, so close you can almost touch their silken gray backs, their placid, piston-puffing exhalations just another sound in one big glorious symphony.

Sometimes we talk about how I'm doing, but mostly we just bob in the water, intermittently catching waves. There's an unspoken affirmation in our surf sessions that I desperately need. He isn't my doctor in these moments; he's my friend. I don't know what an ethics board would make of his decision to help me, but I know that, through his willingness to climb into my nightmare and take that risk, he's showing me how to trust men again.

My eyes still occasionally drift over to that mansion Rory and I wanted to buy, only now I see it very differently. It's just a box of metal and concrete with a couple of well-placed windows. There's no dream, no future in it. The people who own those big houses on the strand never live in them anyway. They stand empty and dark eleven months out of the year, a stage set for tourists to gawk at. The owners come back and throw extravagant parties during the holidays, but it's all for show. A poignant reminder that a house is not the same thing as a home.

Imagine for a second that you're standing inside one of those rooms right now, looking out at me through the UV-tinted windows. The sea sparkles, distant and flat, like an image on the screen of a muted television. Feel the silence, the stillness around you. Taste the stifling air that's been circulating for months without a breeze in this four-story mausoleum. Inhale that factory-floor new-carpet smell. Pass by the beds that are never slept in, the chairs that are never used, the dishes that are never set around a table. Hear the dampened *tick*, *tock* of a mantelpiece clock. You're alone, where furtive ghosts like to dwell. It's a monument to life abandoned, to purpose thwarted. How could anything that toxic be dazzling?

I unzip my shorty wetsuit and strip off down to my waist. The sun is rising, and it's getting hotter. I adjust the straps on my bikini top and make sure that my baseball hat's on tight. I've dipped it in the water to keep it cool, and now my eyes are stinging as I squint into the light. My wet thighs squeak against the epoxy resin as I shift my weight on the board. The sun's rays pierce the surface of the water, splaying out like shimmering searchlights. I catch a flash of silver swimming three feet down, possibly a perch or a California halibut. I would love to know what kind of fish are around here. Maybe I'll buy a snorkel mask and come out here next week.

"Liz!"

"Huh?" I snap out of my day dream.

"See that next set coming in? That second wave looks pretty good."

"I'm ready. Let's go."

ART TK

four

MAGDALENA

'm sitting in the makeup chair, one of those canvas-backed director's thrones that are awkwardly tall and feel like they could fold inward at any moment. There's too much air circulating around me—on my calves and the small of my back, across my naked shoulder blades. I'm restless and anxious about the photoshoot, frustrated to be sidelined here in the beauty department while the rest of the crew discuss the setup. You'd never know it to look at me, though. I'm frozen in place, holding absolutely still.

A petite woman with red hair and perfect features is lining my lips. I have my mouth open in an obliging O shape, and she has her pencil in her hand, squinting at my vermilion border like a forensic scientist trying to trace the outline of a missing piece of evidence. We met fifteen minutes ago, and we are literally breathing into each other's mouths. I try to conserve oxygen, exhaling slowly, off to one side. My eyes flick between hers, the pencil, and the large vanity mirror on the wall. I no longer recognize myself.

The incandescent globes give off a warm glow that is both comforting and vaguely incriminating. I feel X-rayed, displayed in flat white light with all my flaws magnified. The process of transformation is always the same, but the results vary considerably, depending on who the artist is and what look they're going for. I never get used to the precision of professionally applied makeup on my already angular face. It seems like we're doubling down where we should be compromising. But I let my glam squad do their thing, because the only outcome that matters is what the camera captures.

The pictures we're taking today will run in a hip New York teen magazine, alongside a feature promoting my latest album. We're down in the Meatpacking District at somebody's friend's loft, and the photographer is pregnant. It's all very avant-garde, but I have to protect my upcoming record launch. I want to see the references for the concept they're pitching. I need assurance that it'll come across in print the way they say it will. I've been doing a lot of photo shoots lately, and I feel like my identity's being robbed. I have no idea that I'm about to take some of the best pictures of my entire career.

When I first arrive at the loft space, they parade me around and introduce me to everyone on the team. We thumb through a rack of clothes as the photographer explains her vision. She wants to do something provocative, something that will push people's buttons. I see a lot of bondage gear. If a man had suggested we explore S&M narratives, my hackles would have risen immediately. But the sight of this heavily pregnant woman directing a staff of eight while wearing combat boots, tight leather pants, and a concert T-shirt that barely covers her enormous belly completely disarms me, and I agree to go along with her inspiration.

What I'm itching to say now, as I sit here getting cosmetic powder pressed into my pores, is that I've changed my mind. I've had a few minutes to think about it, and I want to back out. I'm afraid the pictures will look tacky, or like porn, or—worse—like I'm desperately trying to convince people I'm still sexy. I call my manager again, but he's half way to Midtown and not answering his phone. If I want to stop this train, I'll have to speak to the conductor myself.

But there's something else that's preventing me. The makeup artist, whose face is hovering mere inches from my own, is crying. Not just weeping but sobbing uncontrollably. She doesn't make a sound, but she's obviously overcome. It's a drama that's unfolding between the two of us, since no one else has noticed anything. Each time she sniffs, her eyes clear temporarily. Then the tears well up and spill out again, running down her cheeks, along with what's left of her mascara.

She's also wet, soaked through from the rain that's started pouring down outside. Somebody sent her out to buy cigarettes and tape from Duane Reade, and when she got back she was in pieces. She hasn't even bothered to dry off. Whatever upset her is so grave that her own comfort is inconsequential. My first impression of her was positive. She was polished and friendly, an elfin Goth girl of twenty-two or twenty-three whose own makeup was immaculately applied and flattering to her complexion.

I can't imagine what has happened to her in the interim. I wonder if her boyfriend called to break up with her, or if she bumped into an ex on the street. Maybe someone in her family died. I ask her if she's all right, and she brushes off the question. "Yes, I'm fine." If we were anywhere besides New York City, I'd press her further. But residents of this crowded metropolis have to construct a sense of privacy out of thin air and determination, and it's not always nicer to pry.

The tip of her tiny nose is red. She's working kohl pigment into my lash line, smudging it repeatedly with a beveled brush. She has to support one arm with the other, because her diaphragm is heaving, making her hand wobble. She doesn't have time to take a break and calm down. I showed up late, and we're behind schedule. Maybe I've caused her to miss an appointment, I think. But she seemed happy and relaxed before she went out.

I run through scenarios in my mind. Maybe she's broke, and she just found out she lost a job that she was counting on. Maybe she's recently sober, and it's all become too much for her. Maybe her dog got hit by a car, but she can't leave work, because she's broke and recently sober. Conjecture is starting to scramble my brain like eggs. I have to focus on my own situation and figure out a way to salvage this photo shoot without sapping the inspiration from my photographer.

"You look amazing." The hairstylist comes over and stands behind my chair, running his fingers through my shag. I glance in the mirror. I do look remarkable. The makeup artist has given me beautiful red lips and a bold, dark eye. The stylist continues to play with my hair, coaxing it up into a tousled, windswept texture until I feel wild and daring to match. The makeup artist smiles for the first time since her breakdown. I can tell she's proud of her creation. I don't want to disappoint any of them. I rotate my head from side to side, pulling expressions that I would never normally try, watching myself disappear inside a character.

And, just like that, we're on the move. They rush me over to wardrobe, where I strip behind a flimsy curtain—swapping my street clothes for the outfit they've selected. I'm so thin from all the work I've been doing that everything fits me like a glove. I emerge to gasps of delight. Despite my earlier qualms, even I get caught up in the fantasy. I'm a biker bitch. I'm Olivia Newton John in *Grease*, after she turns bad at the end of the movie. I impulsively grab a red cowboy hat, and somebody lends me a cigarette. Now I'm Ponyboy from *The Outsiders*. It's all a game of dress-up.

I step in front of the camera and strike saucy poses against the oilcloth backdrop. They've got good music playing, and we're going wherever the moment takes us. The shots look incredible. Everybody leans over the photographer's shoulder to admire her test prints. She lets me keep a few of the Polaroids. I feel uninhibited and free. But this journey has a destination, and the photographer has a road map for how to get us there. Each subsequent setup is more psychologically intense than the last, until we reach the boundary of my comfort zone. She wants me make a bold statement about the subjugation of female power, to inhabit a role that makes me feel truly vulnerable. She wants me to embrace bondage. The hesitation in the room tells me that this fork in the road was anticipated. It's up to me to say yes.

In the end, I do it for Magdalena. I put on a low-cut dress that accentuates my breasts. One of the assistants ties my arms behind my back, crisscrossing my body with a rope that he loops twice around my neck. My mouth is duct-taped. The only way I can communicate now is through my eyes. The makeup artist comes on set to smudge my eyeliner and administer glycerin drops to make it look like I'm crying. She stands in front of me, her cheeks dry as she makes mine wet. She's had time to fix her own makeup, and she looks like a different person. She's done a shimmery pastel look on herself, going for a completely different aesthetic.

That's when it dawns on me that there was never any crisis. She got caught out in the rain and her face came off; that's all that happened. Her beauty-armor disintegrated, and without it she felt vulnerable and exposed—naked in a way she hadn't chosen to be. I pity her, thinking how sad it is for such a bright and talented girl to place so much stock in her appearance. Which is hilarious, considering that I'm working my good angles while trussed up like a glitter-basted chicken, wearing designer clothing under tungsten halogen lights, surrounded by a team of professionals hired to make sure I look stunning, and I'm still not convinced that it'll turn out all right.

She inspects my makeup one last time, touching up any blemishes. Then she looks directly into my eyes, checking to see if I'm okay in here, inside this abduction-victim disguise. It catches me off guard, because I can tell she's looking at me; not the recording artist who came in for a photo shoot, not the businesswoman who's worried about her marketing, but the fragile, insecure person I think I'm fooling everybody into not noticing. "You look great," she whispers. I nod, since I can't speak, but I know that she'll be there if I need her, if it all gets too much for me, if I can't leave because I need this spread in the magazine—along with a dozen other things that I rely on every day in order to feel in-control and safe.

We're taking a risk by glamorizing suppression, but our gamble pays off. This shot of me bound and gagged will be chosen as the cover of the 1990s volume of Getty Images' Decades of the Twentieth Century series, representing a whole wave of indie feminism. A strong female artist with a bold voice shown silenced and constrained. Only a woman could have taken this photograph, and maybe only a pregnant one would have conceived of it in the first place. In depicting the loss of freedom, the image calls attention to the bravery of the survivor. It's the antithesis of my first album cover, in which my arms are flung apart, my mouth is open, I'm naked, natural, and lascivious. Oh, women are dolls! Let's play with them.

By the time we're done shooting, the rain has stopped. I get a round of applause, and everyone congratulates the photographer. It's a wrap. The crew switches off the big studio lights, and the room is suddenly bathed in the lavender shadows of a stormy afternoon. The show's over, the illusion undone. I step out of my borrowed clothes feeling a little let down, like Cinderella back in the ironing cupboard after dancing all night at the ball. I wander out into the kitchen and marvel at how quickly I've gone from being the star attraction to being somebody no one pays any attention to. The grips are busy packing up their equipment. The makeup artist zips up her bags.

It feels weird to hang out, now that everything is back to normal. I want to leave, but my limo is stuck in traffic down by the Battery, and it's rush hour, so I'll never be able to catch a cab. The photographer is sharing her favorite shots of the day with her husband, the two of them huddled together in a touching pose of intimacy. They're looking at pictures of me, but the girl in those photographs is someone else, someone who'll never exist in quite the same way again; an amalgam of everyone who collaborated on the shoot. That's the hardest part about being your own product: It's difficult to know what's you and what isn't.

I decide to head out. I'm not sure where I'll go, but I can walk around the block if I have to. As soon as I push open the big industrial door and step out into the freshly cleansed air, I feel a weight lift from me. It's six o'clock, and the streets are jammed. Financiers in business suits and office workers in silk blouses crowd the sidewalk, moving rapidly, with single-minded purpose. Horns, sirens, and shouts punctuate the city soundtrack. I fall in step with the foot traffic, traveling east. I can feel people glancing at me as we pass each other. Though no one would mistake me for a model, I walk a little taller, with a little more swagger, exhilarated to have a secret occupation that makes me interesting. I stop in at a bodega to buy some health bars and a bottle of water. The man at the register can't take his eyes off me. I smile demurely, counting my change, feeling as gamine as Audrey Hepburn in *Roman Holiday*.

As I'm leaving, I catch sight of myself in the mirror behind a display case. I look like a deranged zombie prostitute. My makeup, which was so striking in the photographs, is a frightening mess in natural daylight, caked on and settling into the creases. My eyeliner is smeared half an inch below my lashes. I'm horrified, the shame triggering old insecurities about my face.

When I was twelve, an age at which everyone else was starting to date, I had to wear glasses and braces. For a couple years, I struggled with a persona that didn't feel like my own. While other girls were moving ahead, I was stagnating.

Once the braces came off and I got contacts, I wasted even more time trying to prove to myself that I was attractive. I'd pick out the hottest guy at a party and see if I could get him. We'd sneak off somewhere to fool around, but in the middle of it, I'd leave. Some of them called me a tease, but that wasn't what I was doing. I was like a person suffering from OCD who keeps flipping on a light switch to make sure the electricity still works. And inside, I felt worse and worse. The mask I put on myself was far more distorting than a couple of pieces of metal and plastic.

That's the thing they never tell you about looks. They matter; of course they do. But they weigh nothing compared to actions. You can change your looks easily if you have the right attitude, but bad patterns of behavior are like weeds: Once they take root, they are incredibly hard to eradicate.

I remember one photo shoot I did at the beginning of my career, maybe my first or second ever. Some newspaper in Chicago commissioned it and threw a party for themselves during the session. They laid me out on a fur carpet, wearing nothing but trousers and suspenders over my nipples, while anonymous guests—strangers—sipped cocktails and watched me from the periphery. It was disturbing, like the orgy scene in the film *Eyes Wide Shut*. I could hear the spectators commenting, but I couldn't see them very well, because I was under bright lights while they were in the dim candlelit recesses of the studio.

Some of my lyrics are explicit, so I'm sure they expected me to dance around and be outrageous. But I couldn't move. I just lay there, a photo-shoot virgin, dull eyed and mute. I was so freaked out that I retreated inside of myself, disconnecting mentally from my surroundings. They were left with an empty shell of a person to work with. It was like bad sex. No one knew what to do about it. I didn't know how to say no back then. I didn't have a manager. I had no concept of what was normal for my profession.

The funny thing was, although I felt exploited and I hated it, it was the way my makeup looked that made me cry afterward. The makeup artist was the nicest, sweetest man, and my only ally in this upsetting situation, so I didn't have the heart to tell him that his heavy bronzer, nude lips, and spidery fake eyelashes made me feel clownish and ashamed, like a dog wearing a cone collar or one of the last kids to be picked for the PE team. I kept thinking about how many people in the city were going to see me looking like this, and I was devastated.

What exactly are we evaluating when we think about our looks? Is it what's actually there or how people respond to us that shapes our opinion of ourselves? Can you describe someone's looks without picturing the way they move, the sound of their voice, or their personality? If you break it down into parts, just the physical attributes—brown hair, brown eyes, round face, short, fat, pigeon-toed—is that really how they look, or is it just shorthand for your much more nuanced and complex way of identifying them? Like skimming the title page and chapter names without reading the book. Even something as objective as a photograph shows the bias of whoever was holding the camera. And as a viewer, you add your own reaction to the image.

So what are looks? Seriously, what are they?

I'm sitting in the back of a convertible car. Five of us are crammed in here together, plus three in the front seat, squeezing sideways or balanced on each other's laps. I remember somebody perched on the back of the vehicle like the grand marshal in a parade. It's well past midnight, and the wide suburban streets are deserted. We're driving under the speed limit, because we're drinking. I look up at the deep maroon sky, crisscrossed by vaulted tree limbs. I can smell their new summer leaves on the wind.

We're on our way home after a party. Everybody's getting dropped off one by one, and no one wants to be the first to go. Whoever is driving is loosely following the directions of whoever's next, but really, we're just cruising. School is out, and our summer jobs haven't started yet. The future feels infinite. Maybe we'll go down to the lake later and drink beer and wine coolers. Maybe we'll drive to Evanston and see what dive bars we can sneak into.

I don't remember what year it is. Probably '84 or '85. I'm at least a junior in high school, and tonight I'm the property of a boy I've just started dating, the friend of my friend's brother. We've all known each other since grade school, except for this one girl who's sitting on my left. I don't know how she got here, but she's welcome.

We're an uncomplicated group of revelers. Life is pretty good. There are the usual bummers—stuff like college applications, nagging parents, and break ups. But everybody's family is more or less the same. This area is big on conformity. Dads commute downtown or fly off on business trips. Moms stay home and cook, clean, drink, decorate, and entertain. Everybody plays sports on the weekends. Our stories are largely interchangeable. Except when somebody goes and does something stupid, like tells the truth about themselves.

I would never. Not in a million. Total buzzkill.

"Come here." My new boyfriend drapes his arm around my neck and pulls my face toward his. He's pretty drunk. We kiss for a while, our tongues circling lazily. He tastes like the sweetness of beer. The smell of his cologne, mixed with the warm scent of his skin, makes me dizzy, crazily turned on. I snake a few fingers between the buttons of his oxford to feel the novelty of his chest hair. I'm impressed with how strong his muscles are. He's got a firm grip on my inner thigh, and he moves his hand higher, surreptitiously slipping it up under my skirt until the side of his index finger presses into the groove of my pussy. He starts rubbing it up and down, kissing me deeply. No one's ever touched me like this before. My back arches involuntarily, and I push my breasts against him.

Suddenly, the car swerves, making our teeth click together. Somebody's cigarette has fallen onto the upholstery, and we all hitch up out of our seats so the boys can swat it out. Sparks fly off the smoldering cherry as they chase it around the floorboard.

"What the fuck." The driver pulls over. "Will you guys please be careful? Did it leave a burn?" Everybody settles back down as the car picks up speed again.

"Bro." My friend's brother hands my guy a beer from the minicooler in the front seat. They start complaining about their summer football-training schedule. I turn to the girl that nobody knows. She's very pretty, with long, fair hair and cut-glass cheekbones. I don't remember how she met us. All I know is that she needed a ride, so we're giving her one. She looks young. She might only be a freshman.

"So, are you psyched for this summer?" I twist my earring in my ear, feeling like a sophisticated older sister.

"No," she says nervously. It's such a weird thing to say that it takes me a few seconds to process it. Everybody around here says "Are you psyched for" about everything, and the appropriate response is always "Totally." You don't have to mean it; it's just an opening bid. But it's literally the most common phrase spoken on the North Shore. I'm kind of sorry I started talking to her.

I can tell she wants me to ask her more, but I don't say anything. Finally, she offers timidly, "Are you?"

I shrug. "Totally. I'm working at Ravinia with a couple of my friends. It's going to be awesome. I don't know, we'll probably just party the rest of the time. Then I'm going away in August."

"Oh, cool! Where are you going?" She shifts up onto her knees, manifesting the correct girl cues, so I'm comfortable speaking with her again. There's a proper rhythm to banter between strangers, which must be observed in order to keep the chi flowing.

"We go to a house in Lakeside, Michigan, right around the lake? My cousins come every year, and it's so much fun. It's, like, right on the water. It's so beautiful. I can't wait."

She has a couple of options here. She can say "Oh my God, how cool" or "Like, I'm so jealous" or even "We go to Wisconsin." But she doesn't say anything normal. She just looks wistfully off to the side and sighs, "I wish," without finishing her sentence.

This is exhausting. I want my boyfriend to rescue me, but he's leaning forward talking to the people in the front seat. All I can do is stroke his back, craning my neck around to see if there's a conversation I can join on the other side of him.

"I'm sorry I'm being so depressing." She turns to me, her brow furrowed. "I'm just scared."

"Of what?" I strike a balance between polite and noncommittal.

"This is my last night." She stares at me, her eyes searching mine. "I have to have an operation tomorrow," she continues. "They're removing part of my nose and my jaw, and the doctor says I'll never look the same again."

At first I think she's joking, or lying to get attention. But then I see that she's genuinely frightened.

"What's going to happen to me?" She is begging me for consolation, looking at me as if I know what the fuck to answer, as if we're already in the hospital ward waiting for the anesthesiologist.

"I don't know." I have no clue what to say. "That's terrible," I add, because I mean it. She's one of the prettiest girls I've ever seen. I can't imagine what it would be like to be confronting disfigurement at her age, before anything has even happened to you; before college, before marriage, before everything. I'm paralyzed, standing on a high wire, halfway between what I thought reality was a minute ago and what she's asking me to contemplate. It's too much.

"I don't want to go home," she announces to nobody in particular. It's like her thoughts are just spilling out of her mouth and she can't stop them.

I don't know how to react, so I just sit there, enduring the awkwardness. By some miracle, I manage to stay present. Looking back, I've always been glad that I did. She needed someone to confide in.

"Do you think I'm pretty?" Her voice quavers. It's the query of an eight-year-old, desperate for validation. She obviously doesn't want to be alone in her misery, but I can't save her. I didn't set the clock that's ticking down. Her parents probably let her go out tonight because they wanted her to have a taste of all that she'll be missing out on in the future, all the exciting wildness of being young. It breaks my heart that this boring car ride is her last big adventure, her last carefree experience as a teenager, with no one staring at her and a lot of guys who would kill to ask her out.

"You're beautiful," I tell her. "Seriously. I wish I looked like you."

It's the right thing to say. She smiles, authentic pride breaking across her face, a vision of adolescent splendor. But her melancholy returns, like a cloud that steals the warmth of the sun on a brisk autumn day, bringing with it the chill of winter. She knows she has to let go.

"I wish I had taken more pictures." She looks down at her fingernails. "I used to hate how I looked in photos."

I wish this had never happened. I wish I'd never heard her story.

I wish she'd never been here. But I can't just wish her away.

"Will you remember me? Will you remember how I look right now?" She pleads with me, reaching for my hand.

"I will," I say. I don't know what else to do to make her feel better.

And I do, Magdalena. Even to this day.

ART TK

five

RED BIRD HOLLOW

My brother, Phillip, wants me to climb the tallest pine tree on our grandparents' property. It's the big one he points out from our bedroom window, the broad, stately conifer poking its head up above the canopy. Granddad says it's nearly two hundred years old, almost as old as the Declaration of Independence. When we run down the hill to the barn and look back up toward the house, its spire reaches higher than the roof. Phillip considers it his personal Everest, a challenge to be met and conquered before the end of the summer. He's afraid to climb it alone, so he's trying to persuade me that there's something magical hidden up there, like butterflies or fairies.

I've been reading a lot of illustrated books about elves and folklore lately. There's so much flora and fauna in the woods around Red Bird Hollow that I'm convinced the forest is enchanted. Winnie and Granddad's renovated farmhouse sits on fifteen acres of woodland in Indian Hill, a small municipality outside Cincinnati. It's horse country, with lots of winding trails and long driveways. When Granddad bought the place in 1952, my mother called the move "social suicide." She was in college at the time and refused to join the family this far away from the cultural attractions of downtown.

To Phillip and me, it's a wonderland that we explore every weekend while my parents have some time to themselves. We spend all day outdoors, roaming the woods, wading through the creek, or venturing across the road to the spring-fed pond. Winnie rings the big bronze bell when it's time for us to come home and get cleaned up. There's always somebody coming over for dinner. Red Bird Hollow is a gathering place for the extended family, the type of household that encourages neighbors to drop by unannounced. Each day is an adventure, yet the landscape exudes an atmosphere of peace and tranquility.

Granddad enjoys his country living. He's acquired the habits of a gentleman farmer. He drives a small tractor, shoots clay pigeons, and has his cocktails on the patio every evening at dusk. His booming laughter fills the air whenever we're all together, scaring the sparrows from the eaves. He stables some of the neighbors' horses in the barn, and I like to visit them and feed them oats. They lip the grain from my open palm while I stroke their noses, fascinated by the way their velvety skin lays over their sturdy skulls.

Phillip isn't too interested in the animals. Normally he plays war with our cousins, but today he only has his little sister—and I'm not tempted to take up BB guns and bows and arrows. He thinks it's the perfect opportunity to tackle the massive pine tree without the Voss boys around to make fun of him if he fails. If he succeeds, he'll be able to claim the distinction for all time, and they'll be sorry that they didn't think of it first. He climbs up the ladder into the rafters of the barn and sits on the edge of a hay bale, shaking handfuls of straw down onto my head. He can be a real pest when he doesn't get his way.

We hear the screen door slam up at the house, and the dogs come streaking down the hill toward the barn, the tags on their collars jingling. The horses stamp impatiently in their stalls, ears twitching, tails swishing the flies away. The brown mare extrudes a steaming volley of manure, and the smell propels us back out into the yard. Phillip follows me around, harrying me, suggesting that at the very least there'll be colorful eggs in all the birds' nests scattered among the branches.

I collect the robin-egg shells that fall down onto the thick carpet of pine needles on the forest floor. I use them in my spells. Their wondrous blue-green color has nothing to do with the parent birds' plumage. Still, Phillip sells me on the logic that cardinals lay red eggs, goldfinches lay golden ones, and blue jays' eggs are azure. Phillip could sell snow to an Eskimo. He beguiles me with his argument that this tree is the largest for a reason, that it's the gateway to a mythical realm—and, just like Jack with the beanstalk, we'll find treasure at its pinnacle.

I trudge up the driveway in my Keds and bellbottoms, listening to Phillip chatter excitedly about how far we'll be able to see once we reach the top. He says I'll be able to look into my friend Tiffany's house next door and wave to her. I don't want to play with Tiffany right now. She has more Breyer model horses than me. What I want are some live pixies or some iridescent black raven eggs. I really need magic to be real, and I live in a state of quasi denial where flowers have faces and inanimate objects can communicate. Everything I know I glean through signs and symbols. I think thunderstorms can see me.

On the material level, though, I'm very practical. I have survival skills, or at least a survival instinct. Phillip's tried his best at times to kill me, but he hasn't yet succeeded. For my part, I have pondered the odds of his survival if, say, our station wagon came to an abrupt stop and he flew through the front windshield. These kinds of accidents can and do happen to kids our age. Our friend Scott Carroll ran right through a plate-glass door during a game of tag at his birthday party, and I couldn't take my eyes off the long, jagged shard sticking out of his arm. Childhood is a time of curiosity and peril, and nobody comes out of it unscarred.

Phillip takes us on a detour to the toolshed. I assume it's his way of hazing me, since he knows I'm afraid to go in there. Granddad keeps his rakes, hoes, and hedge shears hanging on the walls. They look like implements of torture, and I feel much safer in Winnie's kitchen with her mixers, frying pans, and chopping knives. Phillip pockets a strip of firecrackers from our father's Fourth of July stash and looks through the drawers of Granddad's work table for a box of matches. Luckily, he doesn't find any. As we're leaving, I notice that the weather vane on the roof has spun around and is pointing south-west.

We walk back behind the house and a little way up the second ridge to the forest's edge. A hundred yards further in is the clearing where Winnie and I pick wildflowers. One time, we encountered a full-grown buck with towering antlers, standing stock still, silently watching us. Fungi sometimes grow between the tree roots, and I've found toadstools that look exactly like the ones in fairy tales: bright red caps with white polka dots. Purple nightshade also grows back there, which Winnie warns me is poisonous.

Phillip dares me to eat unknown berries all the time. I've watched him pop things into his mouth that I would never touch let alone taste, only to see him drop them to the ground behind his back in a diabolical sleight of hand. The only wild berries I trust are the ones growing in the blackberry thicket. I've stood amongst the brambles and darting honeybees eating them by the handful until my finger-nails turned black from the juice.

There are so many things to do at Red Bird Hollow. I wish Phillip would give up on his quest to impress our cousins. It'll only lead to more taunting and abuse. It's not that I'm afraid of heights. Young though we may be, Phillip and I are both experienced climbers. I crawled across our jungle gym before I could even walk steadily. My dad nearly had a heart attack when he came home from work one day to find my mother watching me from the screened-in porch. She put her finger up to her lips and shushed him. "Elizabeth can do it," she whispered.

We hang out in trees a lot. Especially me; it's my favorite way to disappear. If you want to win a game of hide-and-seek, just haul yourself up into a tree. You'd be amazed how few people ever think to look up. It's relaxing to lie back among the branches, bathed in dappled sunlight, listening the sound of the rustling leaves. I feel safe up there.

But I'm used to climbing the groomed yews and maples that grow in our neighborhood. The white pines on Winnie and Granddad's property are generations older and twice as wild. There's no city forester out here removing dead branches or marking hollowed-out trunks for felling with a big orange X. If Phillip's tree is diseased, we won't know until it's too late. One of the boughs could give way. Or the soil around the roots might be eroded, and the whole thing could topple over from our weight.

Phillip shields his eyes, gazing up between two pines, trying to gauge which trunk belongs to the tree we want to climb. He can't tell unless he can see the tops of them. He instructs me to wait here while he goes back down to the house to check our position. I pat the bark of the one I'm standing beneath. It sounds pretty healthy.

The truth is, now that we're here, I'm intimidated. Not just by their size and coarseness but by the worry that we ought to ask their permission first, as if they can feel us eyeing them, and they haven't decided whether or not we're trustworthy. It's an unfortunate fact that every Christmas, Granddad gets out his chainsaw and cuts down one of their young to prop up in the living room and decorate.

I love my grandfather. He's very patient, and encouraging of us kids. But he has a rural attitude toward the stewardship of the natural world that is anathema to my delicate sensibilities. My mother and uncle tell a gruesome coming-of-age story about Red Bird Hollow, and how a calf they raised and named Mooey wound up on their dinner plates the next year.

I touch my forehead to the tree trunk, silently transmitting my good intentions in case there really is a tree sprite or woodland guardian listening. My life is filled with spiritual rituals at this age. Phillip thinks I'm a witch, but I'm only a pagan. At church, I scribble "help" on backs of the suggestion cards they stock in the pews next to the hymnals. Years later I'll be confirmed as an Episcopalian, but right now I belong to the woolly faith of my imagination.

Phillip shouts for me to move over to the tree to my left. He comes running back up the hill, out of breath. He looks a little nervous, too, and I pray that he's about to change his mind. It's not a great day for climbing. Dark clouds are looming on the horizon. We stand flush with the trunk and look up its central artery, calculating the best route. It's a handsomely shaped tree with a uniform number of offshoots, spaced evenly and tapering gradually. I can hear the great branches swaying in the wind overhead. Every time the boughs creak, my stomach crumbles with queasiness.

The dogs are racing back and forth across the lawn, chasing a ball that they keep running up the hill and dropping at our feet. Phillip picks it up and throws it in a high arc down the hill, to distract them. Then he boosts me up onto the lowest limb. I'm only six, so I can't reach it by myself. We have to hurry. If Winnie or Granddad sees us through the windows, they'll come out and tell us to get down. Once we ascend past the sparse lower branches, we'll be hidden from view in the dense foliage. Diana, our cowardly springer spaniel, squirms and whines at the foot of the tree. She points her nose up at us, barking loudly. Phillip snaps his fingers angrily and tries to shoo her away.

I move slowly and deliberately. The twigs scrape my skin every time I hook a leg over a branch and pull myself up. Phillip overtakes me and nearly knocks me off balance in his determination to be first. I grab hold of some sturdy greenery to reestablish my footing. My hands are covered in the sticky sap that oozes out of tiny woodpecker gashes in the bark. It's pretty cluttered up with dead sprigs in here. I start breaking them off like a bushwhacker as I go.

It smells wonderful, though. Pine is my favorite smell in the world besides tomato leaves. We're about thirty feet off the ground, but because we're on a hill, it feels higher. I stop to take in the view. Phillip was right. The surrounding landscape is spread out before me in a glorious expanse. I can see the wind rippling through the grass in the field behind the barn. The pond is ruffled by gusts that sweep over its surface, changing the color from silver to black and back again. Our tree sways ever so gently. Something colorful catches my eye on the slanting gray roof of Winnie and Granddad's house.

"Phillip!"

"What?"

"It's your parachute!"

Phillip climbs back down to see. Sure enough, it's the missing paratrooper from the Roman candle he shot off last Fourth of July. He thought it was a dud, because we could never find the toy that was supposed to be inside. He was bitterly disappointed at the time; he was only nine. I know I've scored points by finding it, but I also know that he'll never give up until we've gotten it off the roof somehow. It's lying right above the false fireplace.

The original farmhouse at Red Bird Hollow was built in 1849. It was just a simple five-room plan. Over the following century, several owners added on to it, including my grandparents, who constructed an additional two-story wing. They made other improvements as well, widening the dining-room and living-room areas to make space for bookshelves—and a longer dinner table, since they like to entertain. In the process, the architect discovered a discrepancy between the measurement of the outside of the house and the inside perimeter of the rooms they were renovating. There was about three and a half feet of missing space.

When they broke through the wall next to the fireplace, they discovered a secret chamber that we would later find out had once been used to hide men and women fleeing slavery. In the 1850s and '60s, Cincinnati was a major stop on the Underground Railroad. Kentucky had some of the harshest laws of any state in the South, and it was just across the river from the emancipated territory of Ohio. You could push off in a boat and make it to the shores of freedom in less than an hour if the weather favored you. Unfortunately, the Ohio River valley was also crawling with bounty hunters. People weren't immediately safe from captivity once they set foot in the North; they could still be caught and returned if one of the mercenaries found them.

Once our family realized that an abolitionist had built the farmhouse, the whole layout suddenly made sense. No one ever used the front door, because it faced a relatively steep drop-off overlooking the valley. You had to approach the front porch from a side path, whereas the back door opened out onto flat land and a gently sloping driveway, which looped around past the barn and down the hill before intersecting with the main road. It was almost as though someone had built the house backward.

But now it all made sense, because safe houses always hung lanterns out front to signal their hospitality. Fugitives traveling by foot across the dark valley would have been able to see the lamp on that front porch from miles away. The farmhouse at Red Bird Hollow was sited and built specifically with this purpose in mind. It was a humbling and inspiring realization that sent a shiver through your bones. There might never have been any other purpose to the house at all. There's certainly no farmland beyond Granddad's small field. Thoughtful details, like how the hidden room would have stayed warm from the back of the heated bricks in the fireplace and how the chimney had two separate shafts to allow fresh air to get in, speak to the convictions of the builder.

Whoever those men and women were who came seeking sanctuary for a night or two, or more, they must have successfully made it farther north, or the secret room would have been found and destroyed long before my grandfather's time. There's a strong likelihood that the house itself would have been burned to the ground if the hideaway had ever been discovered. Imagine how much fear and disquietude, relief and impatience, that windowless three-by-six-foot refuge had known. Imagine the stories this tree could tell if it could speak. The evergreen I'm dangling in was alive through it all. It saw and heard everything.

A faint rumble of thunder echoes across the valley. I look up at Phillip, who is ten feet above me already, and wonder if he's more likely to be struck by lightning since he's up the highest. I start climbing again, but slowly, so I can maintain a safe distance between us.

The back of my hand itches. I brush something crimson off my wrist. Now my forearm itches. I inspect my skin and spot two microscopic red spiders crawling on me. I hate spiders more than anything, but these arachnids don't look dangerous. They're no bigger than pinheads. Still, I frantically shake my clothing, flipping my long hair over to make sure there's nothing in it. The branch I'm standing on bounces a little bit too freely, and I hop onto the next one quickly. We're up very high now. Almost twice as high as the roof of the house. I can see Tiffany's über-modern glass home through the trees—a multilevel, multicolored architectural experiment.

I hear Phillip's foot slip off a branch overhead, and he scrambles to save himself. Some loose material falls around me as a result of his misstep. "Go back!" his panicked voice suddenly urges me. "Libby, go back down! Hurry!"

"What's wrong?" I start to scoot along the limb, gingerly reaching a toe down to the branch below me. It's a lot trickier climbing down than climbing up.

"Just go! Hurry!" Phillip lets out a shriek, and a string of swear words the likes of which I've never heard—which is impressive, considering how much our father likes to curse. It's an introduction to a brand-new area of the English language.

"What is it? Tell me," I wail. His fear is contagious. I'm slipping all over the place. I try to maneuver my weight toward the center of each branch, but I'm suddenly clumsy and can't find my balance.

"It's a spider's nest. Don't look up, Libby! Just go! Faster!"

"What?!" Of course I look up. At first I don't see anything. Then, slowly, my eyes adjust to make out the familiar eight-legged shapes splayed out on all the branches, motionless, camouflaged perfectly. They're huntsmen, huge, bigger than the size of my hand, and they're everywhere. Everywhere. Everywhere.

I burst into tears. "Phillip!"

"It's okay, Libby. Go down! Please!" He's begging.

"I can't! They're going to fall on me!"

"You can do it." Phillip knows spiders are my number-one fear, the only thing that absolutely incapacitates me. I reflexively jump and scream whenever I see one. And these are the biggest goddamn spiders in the world.

"It's okay! I'm going stay above you, okay? I'm going to stay right above you, Libby. They won't fall on you; they'll fall on me." I know Phillip is almost as scared as I am. His gallantry in this moment is something I'll never forget.

I'm trying to move quickly, but I'm terrified they're all going to start running toward me. I know if they do, if even one of them zips closer, I'll let go and free-fall to the ground. There's no way I can stop myself. I hold my breath, moaning with misery as I squeeze past a spider that's resting vertically on the trunk. At the last second it darts around to the other side, and the motion of its legs is enough to make my knees buckle. I shudder with revulsion, emitting little squeaks and whimpers. I can't believe they were here the whole time we were climbing up.

It feels like an eternity before we're out of spider territory. I'm shaking so badly by the time we get down that I can't even hold on to the last branch, and I fall the final six feet onto my back. Winnie is there, picking me up in her arms, asking us what happened and pushing the dogs away as they jump all over us trying to lick our wounds. My skin is covered in nasty scratches that will take weeks to heal, because they're infected from the sap. My face is smeared with tears and dirt. I have pine needles and broken twigs tangled in my hair.

Phillip gives me a big hug as the first raindrops start to fall, saying, "I'm proud of you, Libby. You were really brave up there." I hang my head down as we walk inside the house, letting my hair close around me like a veil. I just want to look at the ground, and at my feet in my red sneakers, and at the small, familiar things that don't overwhelm me.

Winnie washes us off in the kitchen sink with her rough, gray Lava soap, which she thinks can cure anything. Lightning flashes outside the window, followed by a close crack of thunder. A gust of cold wind blows the curtains up. Winnie rushes around the house closing all the windows while Phillip and I change clothes. The thunder doesn't even make me jump anymore. My adrenaline is utterly depleted.

Downstairs in the living room, Phillip switches on the TV, and we watch *I Love Lucy*, sitting cross-legged on the carpet. The rain beats against the windowpanes as lightning freeze-frames the sky and thunderclaps vibrate throughout the walls and floor, but we're safe inside our sturdy old farmhouse. Winnie brings us bowls of Honeycomb cereal with milk. Poor Diana is hiding beneath the couch, trembling, because she's the most cowardly dog ever and always dives under the bed during thunderstorms or fireworks. I get on my hands and knees and crawl to her, squeezing in to fit my body around hers, stroking the side of her ribcage to stop her shaking. "It's all right, girl," I whisper in her silky ear. "You're safe."

Granddad comes into the living room and gives a whoop, invigorated by the storm. "It's raining cats and dogs!" He lights a roaring fire in the fireplace, then settles into his wing chair to do the crossword. Winnie brings him a Scotch on the rocks, singing, "It's raining, it's pouring, the old man is snoring" for our benefit. She's got dinner going in the kitchen, and I can smell beef and potatoes browning in the oven.

Diana's stopped shaking, now that she's warm. The violent part of the storm has passed over us. I lay my head down on my arm and stare into the dancing flames, feeling drowsy. I spot my favorite Barbie-doll shoe silhouetted against the firelight. I thought I'd lost it months ago. And there's the blue agate marble from our 3-D tic-tac-toe game. I rake my fingers through the carpet, snaring half a dozen more beloved lost items amidst the loose fuzz and dust bunnies: treasure I put in my pockets and don't tell Phillip about. He doesn't believe in magic. He'd call it junk and take it from me or toss it into the underbrush. I'm the keeper of the sacred rituals and. it's my job to make sure the universe stays on track.

I take my job very seriously. I don't want the fairies to get mad at me or the trees to complain. But mostly, I don't want to live in the flat dull world of reality. I need more than that. And I know it's out there. There's always something precious hidden at Red Bird Hollow. These woods are enchanted. After all, they contain my childhood.

ART TK

six

HOLD THIS FOR ME

The plane's engines change pitch as we begin our descent into Heathrow airport. I look out my window, disappointed not to see any of London's historic landmarks beneath the dense cloud cover. I can feel myself getting anxious about leaving the security and privacy of first class. No one's pushing or shoving, there are no surprises, things run smoothly. I've become a virtual recluse in my off hours, Howard Hughesian in my phobic avoidance of germs and people.

At heart I'm an introvert, an avid observer of the quirks and contradictions in people's behavior. I like to be alone, to dream, to muse on the human condition and then turn it into art. But as soon as I got famous, my life turned upside down. I'm never alone anymore. In the mornings, I visit radio stations and play songs live on air. In the afternoons, we sound-check for a group of two dozen contest winners. Then there are the concerts, where I confess my private thoughts and feelings in front of thousands of people. I sign CDs after the show and shake even more hands. Throughout it all I'm being photographed. When work is over, I climb onto a tour bus with eleven dudes, or head right back to the airport.

I need more personal space. Lately, everywhere I go, I get ambushed. There were fans waiting for me at the airport this morning, and I can't figure out how they knew what flight I was taking. Paparazzi and professional autograph-collectors waited outside of my hotel in Paris, so I had to use the back entrance, and check in under an alias. I can't move around freely by myself anymore.

A little over a year ago, when I had graduated from college but hadn't found a job yet, I was unable to pay for the bare necessities—like rent, or a haircut. I took the bus and the train everywhere or, whenever possible, walked. I bought thrift-store clothes and rationed beans and rice throughout the day, hoping someone would invite me over to their house for dinner. I was the definitive starving artist. I lived in an apartment that was in the process of being torn down. One time, when I was using the toilet, I looked to my right and saw a workman staring up at me through a hole in the floor.

Now I have no more financial worries. My circumstances have changed dramatically in a short space of time. Hotels regularly upgrade my room to the penthouse, and limousines pick me up and drop me off wherever I need to go. I have more offers to attend social gatherings and VIP events than I know what to do with. I put all the beautiful invitations in a pile on my desk and hope that someday I'll have time to answer them. If I don't, I can always paste them in a scrapbook.

I still feel like the same person inside, but I'm frightened by the things that I'm supposed to embrace. The trappings of celebrity amount to a defensive wall behind which I can hide. Sometimes, during photo shoots, I get downright hostile because I think the photographer is trying to expose me. They say they want to capture the real person, but I don't know who that is, so how can *they*? My persona is so fragile it tears like tissue paper in the rain.

"Pardon, Miss Phair?"

I turn to see the Air France flight attendant standing in the aisle, smiling down at me. Her colleague has come forward from the aft cabin, whispering something before disappearing back into economy.

"There is a passenger on board who would like to say hello to you after we land." She bends down, speaking softly, "a Mr. Jake Papua? He says he knows you, that you grew up together. Would that be all right?"

I'm stunned. I nod automatically. I haven't seen Jake since we were kids. We might have been in a few of the same classes in high school, but I don't remember us talking much. Certainly not since his accident. Now I think about him whenever I drive by his house on Hawthorne Lane. His story has become part of the lore of my hometown. I suppose the same could be said about mine.

I was walking past our old elementary school, in fact, when my friend Mallory told me what had happened to him. I remember thinking how low and oppressive the clouds looked at that moment. I could hear the shouts and laughter of children running around at recess, and my heart clenched in nostalgic pain. Were we ever that innocent? I seem to recall us being fairly tribal and savage from the start.

In that respect, not much has changed. Just a few months ago, I read a passage from 1 Corinthians 13 at my best friend's wedding. I was fresh off tour, hoarse from having flown in on a red-eye after playing a gig the night before. One of the bridesmaids pulled me aside and gave me some unsolicited advice before I went up to the pulpit: "Speak up, because people in the back of the church are having trouble hearing." It didn't occur to either of us until it was too late that she and I had very different expectations of what it meant to project into a microphone.

"'If I speak in the tongues of men or of angels'"—I got my mouth right down on that thing—"'but do not have love, I am only a resounding gong or a clanging symbol. If I have the gift of prophecy and can fathom all mysteries and all knowledge, and if I have a faith that can move mountains, but do not have love, I am nothing. If I give all I possess to the poor and give over my body to hardship that I may boast, but do not have love, I gain nothing.

"'Love is patient, love is kind. It does not envy, it does not boast, it is not proud. It does not dishonor others, it is not self-seeking, it is not easily angered, it keeps no record of wrongs. Love does not delight in evil but rejoices with the truth. It always protects, always trusts, always hopes, always perseveres.'"

My brother said my reading sounded like the voice of God coming down from on high to warn the pious and the wicked. He couldn't stop laughing about my overblown delivery. He thought some of the older guests might have suffered heart attacks.

The reception was held at Indian Hill Club, one of the most traditional and buttoned-downed institutions on the North Shore. At the end of the meal, the bride and groom fed each other slices of chocolate cake with a raspberry swirl. My friend's new husband got a little cheeky in front of photographers and slipped her some tongue when they kissed. I'll never forget Mary, enveloped in a giant white explosion of tulle, plopping down on the toilet in the powder room stall—too furious to bother closing the door. "Oh my God, Liz," she moaned, "I married a dick!" They're one of the happiest couples I know.

But back out in the drawing room, beneath the oil paintings of hunting scenes the lined the walls, I was confronted by a pack of matriarchs who'd gotten a little too cozy with the open bar, all wanting to know what manner of infidel I was.

"Why didn't you play at your best friend's wedding?" one steely-eyed golf widow growled. "Are you too good to sing for your friend now?" She swirled ice around her hatch rocks glass, determined to force a confession out of me.

"She didn't ask me." My face flushed crimson. I saw my mother talking to some friends across the room and prayed for her to come save me.

Another coifed matron in a Chanel bouclé suit loomed over me, brandishing her wealth and power. "What's wrong with you? Do you have a split personality? You're dressed so prim and proper, but I've read about you."

I don't know, goddamn it, I want to scream. I don't know what's wrong with me! But something is definitely wrong with me, because I can't stand to keep my thoughts and feelings bottled up like you ruthless doyens of propriety. Maybe I overshot the mark. And, yes, I expect to be run out of town, tarred and feather, a crimson letter stitched across my chest, for saying "fuck" and "cunt" and talking about my sex life in public. But, lady? I'm only twenty-six years old and I've known three friends who killed themselves, a dozen girls with eating disorders, seven guys who went to rehab, and more people than I can count who've been sexually assaulted and never talk about it. I want to hear the truth. I want to feel solid ground beneath my feet.

The wheels touch down on the runway with a bump, and my head dips forward as the co-pilot applies the brakes too suddenly. Dignity is worth fighting for in this land of fences and locks. It feels awful to be singled out, to be rejected or pitied. I have a vision of Jake in fourth grade standing by the schoolyard steps, his nose perpetually running, waiting to join one of the popular all-boy kickball games. This will be good, I think. I can be generous and try to help a vulnerable person feel better about himself. It's got to be hard for him. I have nothing like his challenges, and I'm riddled with anxiety. Poor guy. I hope he's not massively depressed.

We pull up to the gate and wait for the flight attendants to unlock the doors. There's a delay with the gangplank operator, and everyone gets stuck standing up by their seats, their heads bent at odd angles under the low ceiling. No one is talking. Their eyes dart around the interior of the aircraft, or they simply stare at their feet. I start planning what I can do to make this a quick and positive experience for Jake. We'll get somebody to take our picture, and then he can dine out on the story for the next couple of weeks. I'm pretty well-known at this point, so bumping into me ought to net him an eager audience. He probably doesn't get out that much and it'll be a boost to his self-esteem.

There's a commotion in the back of the plane. Everybody's heads come up, straining to see around their neighbors as we hear someone storming up the aisle. "Excuse me, pardon me, coming through." A young man on crutches hurtles into the first class cabin, and there he is: Jake from the playground. He has the same freckles, the same long nose and unruly hair that I remember, except now he's well over six feet tall, with a rangy athleticism that seems comically out of place in the plane's narrow corridor.

"Hey, Liz! How's it going?" He greets me loudly, like a true Chicagoan. I feel myself shrink with embarrassment. "This is pretty crazy, right? I couldn't believe it when I saw you were on this flight." He accidentally knocks the person next to him off balance. "What were you doing in Europe? Playing some shows?" Everyone around us is listening. They have nowhere else to go. Jake's enjoying himself, voluble and smiling. He shifts his weight on his crutches, perfectly at ease as the center of attention. It's kind of endearing, or inspiring, especially considering he was such an annoying kid.

"I read about your record in *Rolling Stone*! Congratulations—that's awesome. I've been meaning to catch one of your gigs, but I've been competing on the wheelchair-tennis circuit. The training schedule's nuts, and I have to do a lot of interviews. Listen." He leans in. "Can you do me a favor? I need to make a tight connecting flight, and as you can see"—he looks down at his crutches—"I have my hands full. Can you carry my leg for me to the gate?" He braces against his armpit support and lifts up an enormous pink prosthetic limb, handing it over to me before I've even had a chance to answer.

"Sure." I take the artificial leg from him, pitching forward slightly under its weight.

"When I saw you I thought, Man, that's a lucky break!" We're finally moving, filing out of the airplane one at a time through the galley and onto the Jetway. "It's kind of awkward asking a stranger to help," he calls over his shoulder. He's taking long, loping strides on his crutches, and I have to hustle to keep up.

"You still living in Chicago?" He keeps his eyes trained forward, navigating the mass of moving bodies inside the terminal.

"Yeah, um . . ." I scurry around the outside of his wake. "I live over in Bucktown. Do you know that area?"

"Not really." He stops to read the overhead signs so he knows which direction to head. "Okay, we're going this way!"

He's coming from Prague. He makes the Czech capital sound so romantic, all Gothic spires and medieval vaults. He says it was the only city in Europe that escaped destruction during World War II— that you can trace a thousand years of history in its architecture. For some reason, I keep picturing vampires sitting in coffee shops along meandering cobblestone roads. I'm doing my best to pay attention to his anecdotes, but I'm distracted by the giant plastic appendage I'm carrying. The first issue I have to grapple with is the sheer size of the thing. I'm only five feet two, and Jake is well over six feet, most of it below the waist. That means that his artificial limb is almost two-thirds my height if you stand it upright. It isn't heavy, exactly, but it sure isn't light.

I try different conveyance methods as we make our way rapidly through the terminal. There's the soldier-marching-with-a-musket approach whereby I grip the lower shin and rest the thigh in the groove of my shoulder. Every time I turn my head, though, my cheek presses against the hard-baked flesh-colored plastic. The horizontal-two-handed-log-tote is unworkable in a crowded environment. I'm too narrow, and the leg is too wide. With harried air-travelers rushing past me, I have to continuously swivel my body left and right like a turnstile, apologizing profusely.

The best solution, ultimately, is to hold it like a jousting lance. I can switch arms when one of them gets tired, and guide the prosthesis through oncoming traffic with only minor course corrections. At first I point the toes out in front, thinking that will streamline the effort. But the fulcrum turns out to be farther back on the leg than I realized, so I flip it around and aim the socket forward, letting the foot stick out behind me. The only drawback to this position is being downwind of the contact zone. I have no doubt it's clean, but Jake *is* an athlete.

By the time we reached his gate, I've worked up a sweat and am out of breath and frazzled. "Thanks a lot," Jake says, taking his leg back. "It's great to see you. Have a good trip! I'll check out one of your shows. You should come watch me play tennis sometime! We have games every weekend when we're not on the road." Since his hands are full, he can't wave, but he flicks his chin in the air as a farewell gesture before slipping through the other passengers waiting to board—moving right up to the front of the line. "Excuse me, sorry, look out, coming through."

I watch him for a second longer, then wander off, somewhat dazed and feeling like I've just been through a car wash. I make it onto my next flight without incident, taking a seat in business class and preparing for the long haul back to Chicago. As we are taking off, I realize that neither of us even mentioned the fact that he'd lost his leg, even though I hadn't seen him in years. He correctly assumed that, being from the same hometown, I already knew. I've heard his story multiple times: how he tried to cross the street in Boston but misjudged the speed of an oncoming trolley car. He's famous, and he accepts it.

I have a long time to think about that—why I feel like a victim, a captive to my celebrity in need of velvet ropes and special treatment. Sometimes I look at my friends and family and think, You just don't get it. You don't understand what I have to deal with. But there's no way I have it worse than Jake does. I begin to wonder if it's all an excuse, a way of blaming my loneliness and antisocial tendencies on the scapegoat of fame. While I've been folding myself up into a pity-party picnic basket, Jake has willed himself to be more capable, less careful, less isolated. Maybe all I need to do is stop thinking about myself for five minutes.

In the darkness and privacy of my cubicle, midway over the Atlantic Ocean, I even shed a few tears about it. I've done all the polite rituals—brushing my teeth, putting in earplugs, pulling on the thin, dark socks they give you in your overnight kit—before curling up beneath my not-clean blanket on my mostly flat reclining seat, listening to the loud thrum of the jet engines through the upholstery.

At some point in the journey, the flight attendants bring me a drink, and as I sip it, I can feel my resolve to be less self-centered weakening. I like being in the comfort of these premium digs. I like feeling pampered and catered to and cosseted. I enjoy complaining about my problems to people I can see are impressed and envious. Hell, give me twenty years and I might turn into another hard-drinking dame at the country club, demanding that you make the same choices as me. It's easier to believe in limitations than it is to take responsibility for your fate.

By the time they're serving us breakfast, I'm over it, ready to get home and be done with this promotional trip. One by one the passengers sit up, raising their window shades to let the strong morning sun stream in, golden and blinding. I smile at the man next to me, who's brought along a second dress shirt, still in the dry cleaner's bag, so he'll look crisp and fresh when we land. My experience with Jake will become a funny story I'll tell my future boyfriends that will make me seem unaffected and compassionate. But a small kernel of self-awareness has taken root in my brain, and I can't pretend that it hasn't. I know exactly what's wrong with me, I just don't want to do anything about it.

They say radiation dissipates at an exponential rate the farther away from the source you move, but if you focus those waves into a beam, it can travel with integrity an almost infinite distance. That's what Jake's example will become for me: a tightly compressed, enduring insight. It won't stop me from making a gazillion more mistakes, but it continues to be a guiding principle that changes my mentality in barely perceptible increments. If Jake can see himself the way he does, I can choose to look at myself differently, too. It's up to me.

The pilots begin our final approach into O'Hare. Everybody fills out their disembarkation cards and packs up their belongings. I'm proud to be among these good-looking Americans. We are the elite, the educated, the sophisticated upper class, back from our international business trips. We are the first ones off the plane, given priority over the regular fare customers.

As I step onto the Jetway, the men walking ahead of me pick up speed. I do, too, thinking there must be a logical reason for it. As I round the corner and enter the hallway marked "Arrivals," several men in gabardine suits push past me and start running.

A strange thing happens when people around you panic. There's a primal instinct to stay with the rest of the pack. It must be some ancient survival strategy. Nonetheless, I find myself racing down an airport corridor behind a group of grown men in suits, jostling and elbowing each other out of the way to be first in line at customs and immigration. That's all they're fighting over: who gets to proceed directly to the first available passport agent, and who has to wait his turn. I witness their silent, desperate grappling as they round a corner, their shoulders bumping into each other, their dress shoes slipping and sliding over the polished floor. It's white-collar blood sport. I'm surprised they don't hit one another over the head with their briefcases.

It isn't civilized, it isn't generous, and it isn't normal. These professionals are just a bunch of savages. They're not winners; they're ridiculous. There's no level to which I can aspire that will guarantee safety and kindness, or even authenticity.

So, in the end, what's it all for? Here I was feeling like a star, and being treated like a star, but what's important in real life is doing the decent thing. It's like Camus says in *The Plague*: There's an absurdity to the universe, and you can either do nothing or continue to push to do the best you can. And the best you can do is just do the decent thing. There's no payoff. The good people of the world are those who, in spite of there being no payoff, do the decent thing anyway. That's what being human is. That's the example of a human, being.

ART TK

seven

NEW YORK CITY BLACKOUT

am leaning out the window of my soon-to-be boyfriend's fifteenth-floor hotel room, spellbound by the sight of an unlit Central Park at sunset. Dusk is falling, but there are no streetlights illuminating the sidewalks, no traffic signals changing from red to green. Not a single window glows in any of the apartment buildings bordering the vast urban green space. All I see are endless trees and monoliths of concrete. New York City is dark, rustic, preternaturally serene. I feel as though I'm looking out over the Blue Ridge Mountains of Kentucky, not the heart of midtown Manhattan.

I've never seen the city so peaceful. There are no ambulance sirens, no police whistles, no taxi drivers honking their horns. No jackhammers pounding, or angry people shouting in the street. I don't hear a single airplane flying into LaGuardia, or helicopters buzzing back and forth across the Hudson River. The rooftop air-conditioning units stand idle, useless in the August heat.

Instead, I hear birds chirping. I see cyclists and pedestrians cruising beneath the leafy branches of the Seventh Avenue entrance to the park after work, taking their time, moving with ease. These are the rhythms of a bygone era, the pace of life a hundred years ago in the age of horse drawn carriages, steam engines, and gaslight. I'm looking back through time, imagining my location on a map, contemplating the dimensions of this a low-lying island on the coast of the Atlantic. I feel like I can conjure exactly what this area looked like when the early Dutch settlers traded goods with the Lenape Indians in the late 1600s. This will be a night to remember, I think. One for the storybooks.

This pall cast over the landscape is a result of the largest power outage in U.S. history: the Northeast blackout of 2003. From space, it looks like somebody punched America in the electrical face. The blackout covers most of New York, New Jersey, Connecticut, Michigan, Maryland, Ohio, Pennsylvania, and Ontario. Millions of people have been dropped into the technological dark ages.

Desperate though our circumstances are, I have never been happier to be stranded somewhere in my life. I stare out at the rooftops and fire escapes, believing that magic still exists in the world. Whatever transpires tonight, I finally know for certain that my guitar player and I are into each other. For weeks now, our interactions have been laced with subtext—a subtle exchange of caring and affectionate gestures. But the way we both spontaneously assumed we'd spend doomsday together cements it: We're in love. Okay, maybe not *in love*, but definitely heading in that direction. The problem is, he has a girlfriend.

Matt is on the bed, tuning his instrument. He's been joking all afternoon that the city is going to turn into *Mad Max* after the sun goes down. It isn't funny. Nobody knows what's going to happen. Like in another cult sci-fi film, *Escape from New York*, we might wake up as convicts in a Manhattan island prison, with microchips under our skin and a burning desire to kill Snake Plissken. I'm prepared for inconvenience but not for anarchy.

"You'll have to become my property," Matt teases me. "It's the only way I can protect you."

If the city does go to hell tonight and I'm forced to make my home among the psychopaths, miscreants, and hooligans, I know my band and crew would be good guys to ride with. But New Yorkers appear to have adjusted their routines to the new reality and are hunkered down for the evening. It's finally calm out there in the streets. Just a few hours ago, you would have thought the world was ending.

Our tour bus pulled up to my hotel, thirty blocks south, in Chelsea, about an hour and a half before the power died. My band and I stumbled out into the sunshine rested, relaxed, excited to play a sold-out show at the Roseland Ballroom. Normally, New York is everybody's favorite stop on a tour. Booking agents plan the route to ensure artists are at their peak in the Big Apple. My eponymous album is getting a big promotional push from Capitol Records and an equally intense negative reaction from the press. It's a heightened moment for all of us. I have just enough time to check in to the hotel room, spread out my belongings, and change into fresh clothes before the air-conditioning and the lights go out.

It takes a few minutes to realize that something is significantly wrong. I try a couple light switches. Then I notice that the digital face on the bedside alarm clock is blank and the phone charger isn't working. I assume it's a hotel issue and sit back down to wait for somebody to fix the problem. It's the middle of the day, so I read a book and wait. Eventually Aaron, my tour manager, calls to say that the whole city has lost power, that our gig tonight will probably be canceled. He's going over to the venue now to discuss it with the promoter.

I have the option to remain in my room or come with him. I can tell he wants me to stay put. The hotel will bring up candles and snacks, he says. With the elevators out of commission, carrying my bags down eight flights of stairs to the bus doesn't make sense until we know more about the situation. Nothing has changed dramatically. But the thought of sitting by myself in a room in the midst of a big city without electricity freaks me out. There's no telling what we might be facing later, and I don't want to be separated from the group. I will not—*cannot*—be by myself tonight. I grab some essentials and race down the stairwell to the lobby.

Luckily, the stairs in my hotel are well lit. They've propped open the doors at every landing, letting in light from the large prewar windows. This isn't an option in most buildings in the city, and it isn't going to help once night falls. At least I know my son is safe back in Los Angeles with my parents. He's probably having the time of his life, so I don't have to worry about him. In fact, he's been on tour with me so much that it feels liberating not to have to be on my guard, to be able to worry about myself for once. I'm already slipping into primitive thinking. Somewhere in the deepest part of my brain, my survival instinct has kicked in, warning me that the ultimate game of musical chairs has begun—and that, if we're facing Armageddon, I need to be paired up.

The first floor is in chaos. The staff are stressed. The tense smiles on their faces confirm it. People want information that the hotel doesn't have to give. When will the lights come back on? Will guests receive a refund? How can they get a taxi? Are the airports still open? Two bicycle cops ride their bikes right into the lobby to give the hotel manager an update, which amounts to little more than "We're working on it." The word-of-mouth network is in full swing.

It's acceptable to talk to strangers now. TVs aren't working, so anybody with any news is promoted to town crier, repeating what they've heard to the crowd. The dude with the battery-powered transistor radio is king. A lot of people are suffering flashbacks to the traumatic events of 9/11. The attacks on the Twin Towers happened less than two years ago. Watching the city break down again is retraumatizing. No one wants to hear the word "terrorism," but everyone is thinking it.

Matt and some of the other guys have walked down from their hotel in Midtown to meet us at ours.

"Okay, here's the situation," Aaron says. "Nobody knows what the fuck is going on, why this blackout is happening, or how long it's going to last. It's hot, it's humid, it sucks, so, there's that. The good news is we have a tour bus with a generator and a full tank of gas; so we have electricity, air-conditioning, a shower, food, beds, and we can leave any time we want. Maybe just charge your cellphones before you go anywhere, and stay in touch. Those are the main things."

We stand around him in a loose circle, listening.

"I propose that we wait," he continues, "and see what happens in the next couple of hours. This could all change in a second. The electricity could come back on, or not. I think the gig is probably going to be canceled, but maybe not. Nobody knows yet."

We nod solemnly, exchanging glances.

"There are a few things on the schedule that I think are worth doing if possible, like the *Good Morning America* appearance tomorrow. I'm sure those guys are still broadcasting. I think we should stay in the city tonight and leave in the morning after the performance. That's my two cents. But whatever you want to do. It's your call."

He means me. It's my call. But I'm blending in with the group, pretending my opinion doesn't matter. I don't want responsibility for this decision. I want to do what everybody else is doing. I want to be the girl. I want to be saved.

"I mean, I'm down to stick around and check it out," Matt's brother, our drummer, offers. Everybody feels safe, since we have an escape vehicle at our disposal. We're the luckiest people in Manhattan: engaging in disaster tourism, camping in a deluxe RV at the dawn of the apocalypse. Our group splits up, with plans to reconvene later. Matt and I go with Aaron to the venue to check on the status of the show. He can't reach the production office on his cellphone, because the cell towers in the area are overwhelmed by call volume. I'm secretly hoping we get stuck here for a week. I think it would be fun to live like a Jane Austen heroine—fall in love and not have to work. We could probably barter.

My fantasy is short-lived. We step out onto the street and find ourselves in the middle of a war zone. Chelsea was humming along, clean and uncrowded, when we arrived two hours ago. Now it's mayhem. Customers are pulling food and water off store shelves. No one can get any money out of the bank, because the ATMs are frozen. The subways aren't running, and people are standing around or sitting down on the sidewalk, because they have nowhere to go or can't risk the exertion of climbing the stairs again in this August heat. I'm shocked by how quickly civilization's safety net is unraveling. We need to be resourceful. Everyone's going to have to pitch in and help everybody else.

We arrive at the venue and collapse against the wall in the shade. We're standing in front of a building so resolutely closed that there are tables and chairs stacked up against the front doors from the inside, and a heavy chain, looped twice and padlocked, around the outside handles. If riots do break out later, as everyone is predicting, this club owner has nothing to worry about. It's clear that people in the rock and roll business are prepared for catastrophe.

Aaron is a native New Yorker, not shy about targeting well-dressed businessmen on the street and asking for the inside scoop. "Hi there. Excuse me, sir, I can see you're in a rush, but I was wondering if you have any information about when the power's going to come back on? We're in a band, and we're supposed to play a show here tonight"—he gestures toward the Roseland—"and we're just trying to figure out if we should stay in the city, or if it would be wiser to get on the bus and leave."

The magic words come when he admires the person's appearance from head to toe and adds, "I don't mean to bother you; you just look like someone who knows something." The script varies, but once he utters that phrase, everybody stops and reports what they've heard, mostly rumor and innuendo. One man shares a guess that proves accurate. "Two days, maybe. Tonight, tomorrow night. That's what my brother-in-law, who's an engineer, says. Sorry; that's all I know. Good luck." He rejoins the crowd of people, each marching stoically toward one of the city's bridges or tunnels.

Fear of the unknown eats away at us as the sun slides lower in the sky and the traffic starts to dwindle. Soon it will be as dark as it would have been in a pre–Industrial Revolution era. At the height of summer, New Yorkers are facing a long night without air-conditioning, lights, fans, or refrigerators. Nothing cool or refreshing to drink after walking up dozens of flights of stairs. Sweaty and aching inside their stultifying domiciles, they will have no amusements to distract them from the blackout's oppressiveness: no television, no stereo, no video games or computers. Lesser inconveniences—no toasters, alarm clocks, hair dryers, or washing machines—add insult to injury. Modern life is proving hard to give up.

The promoter finally sends a roadie out to confirm that the show is canceled. We're free to call our insurance companies and make our claims. Matt and I walk back to his hotel to rehearse our acoustic set for tomorrow. It's hard to look at the tired and frustrated faces of all the bewildered citizens who can't get home, and who probably can't reach their loved ones by phone, either.

When we reach Matt's hotel, reality hits me like a wet bag of sand. We have to walk up fifteen flights of stairs in pitch darkness. It takes three times longer than normal, because we have to wait behind people of different ages and physical abilities, some of whom shuffle along step by step, unsteady on their feet. I hold on to the railing as invisible bodies brush past me on their way down. I get tweaked by the sound of everybody's breathing, and by the closeness of the air. I smell these strangers' breath, their deodorant, their personal hygiene.

Matt uses his cellphone to illuminate our path, wasting valuable battery life. We need to buy some of those tiny disposable flashlights that hustlers are selling on all the street corners. I pause at the tenth-floor landing to catch my breath. My heart is pounding against my rib cage. I keep thinking about the victims of the World Trade Center disaster, who had to make it down far-more-harrowing stairwells, and in toxic smoke, to escape. I feel like I'm going to have a panic attack.

Once we're safely inside Matt's hotel room, I run straight to the window, sticking my head out and inhaling the fresh scent of twilight. The clouds are pale pink. A hawk soars between two skyscrapers, making slow, lazy circles on an updraft. It's a relief to be hidden away, high above everything. I don't know if I want to go back down those stairs again. I'm nervous about being alone with Matt for the first time. I'm sure he's staring at me. My whole back feels hot. Being with him is what I wanted, but now that I'm here, the bed feels twice its normal size, a looming presence in the room, fraught with meaning, impossible to ignore.

I turn around. Matt's packing up his gear. I take in his broad shoulders, the curve of his biceps, his strong hands and thick, dark hair. When he kneels down to retrieve a guitar pick from the floor, his thighs stretch the fabric of his jeans taut.

I feel paralyzed, like anything I do right now will be the wrong thing. I've been staring out the window so long that Matt gets up and walks over to see what I'm looking at. He stands very close to me, our arms touching. Neither of us moves or pulls away; we stay perfectly still, pretending it isn't happening. Sparks explode in my chest. Something powerful, almost painful, passes between us, a current strong enough to make my toes curl and my spine tingle. There's no other word for it: electricity.

The sensation teeters between bliss and agony for a few more seconds; and then, just like that, it's awkward. We break apart, but the room feels too small now. We need to get out of here. We need to go somewhere else or something is going to happen. Matt's demeanor changes. He becomes businesslike, as if he's disappointed in himself and, in a weird way, disapproving of me. Or maybe I imagine it.

"Listen." I cock my head, smiling. Far below us, a gang of cyclists shouts friendly insults at one another as they speed around a corner, the whir of their spokes pulsing like fan blades as they propel themselves forward. "Let's go out and see what's going on, before it gets too dark." I dance back and forth, feeling like we're missing out on all the action.

Matt checks his phone and says his brother wants him to meet up at a nearby restaurant. It occurs to me that I'm not necessarily invited. A cloud of fear fogs up my brain. Are they ditching me? I can't walk back to my hotel by myself. I can't sit alone in a dark room all night. I don't even know where our tour bus is parked. Somebody has to help me. Someone has to take care of me. I'm not used to doing things for myself.

The truth is, every member of the band and crew is hired by me, including the bus driver, and yet I somehow I feel like the baby of this operation. When you're the star—the role I'm currently playing—somebody is in charge of you at all times. Like animal handlers, they get you where you need to go, make sure you have food and water, anticipate your every need. It's a system designed for efficiency, but it basically infantilizes you.

"Of course you're coming." Matt empties two large handfuls of loose change from his pants pockets, creating a small coin cascade on the night table. "I wasn't going to leave you here." He winks at me.

I don't complain during the unpleasant trip down the stairs. Once we're outside, the tension between us vanishes. We're just bandmates again. We buy a bunch of those tiny keychain flashlights from a guy selling glow-in-the-dark rave paraphernalia. The atmosphere is surprisingly convivial. The sidewalks are crammed with people strolling along in pairs and small groups. It feels like a national holiday. Everybody wants to be together, to spend as little time as possible in their dark, oppressive apartment buildings.

We weave through the crowd, shielding our eyes against the blinding glare of oncoming flashlights. I'm shocked by how many people are planning to stay out overnight. They've made campsites with whatever materials they could scrounge up, stretching out on smooth patches of grass, wide stone steps, benches, and low ledges.

It's a terrible situation. This would be a humanitarian crisis, I realize, if it were storming or freezing outside.

I'm touched to see how many stores and restaurants have stayed open, willing to help out in whatever way they can. At the very least, they provide somewhere safe and reassuring for people in the neighborhood to go. Vendors are generously distributing perishables at no charge. We pass a dozen people eating cheesecake off paper plates, licking half-melted gelato cones, and popping mini-éclairs in their mouths. It's a freaking block party on the Upper West Side.

"Let's go in." I tug Matt's sleeve, tempted by the steady stream of desserts flowing out of an attractive bistro a few steps down from the sidewalk. Votive candles glimmer in the windows. Ironically dressed hipsters slouch around the nearest tables. It takes a minute for our eyes to adjust to the dimly lit interior. Candles cover every surface. I feel like I'm in a cavern or a grotto, everybody cast in silhouette, their shadows dancing across the walls and ceiling. In spite of everything, the restaurant is filled with customers. There isn't a single free table.

While we wait for something to open up, Matt hears his brother's voice behind him. In the darkness, we didn't realize we were standing right next to Saul—our bass player—and Matt's brother, Nate.

"What's up, dude!" They bro-hug. We order drinks from a cocktail waitress and catch up on the surreal events of the evening. The chef is putting out dishes for diners to try for free. The refrigerators stopped working at three in the afternoon, and all the gourmet food is slowly spoiling. The most ubiquitous dish on offer is ice cream. It's safe, refreshing, and also melting the fastest.

The staff are drinking alongside the patrons. There's a feeling of "live for today, because we're all going to die tomorrow" in the air. Some people are singing pop songs to fill the void left by the disabled sound system. It's a socially sparkling atmosphere, reminiscent of Rick's Café Américain in *Casablanca*. Some of the guests are people who have kept their original dinner plans and showed up for dates, regardless of the altered circumstances. It's inspiring.

We're getting plates of food because all of the tables are taken. "Try this." Nate shoves a forkful of pasta into Matt's mouth. "It's really fucking good."

"Oh my God." Matt groans like he's just tasted Aphrodite's bathwater.

I'm getting drunk. We're all laughing. Matt is speaking for both of us, answering in the plural while I stand quietly by his side. I like how he enjoys taking responsibility for me. In this broken-down city where everything is up for grabs, I have a champion. Moreover, I have brothers-in-arms, comrades with whom I work side by side: all of us traveling in our eighteen-wheel pirate ship all over the country. I'm in a band. Don't mess with us.

Matt gets a call from Aaron saying he needs to move the bus. The scene downtown is getting a little crazy. There have been arrests and incidents of drunken vandalism. I'm going to sleep on the bus tonight so I'll be ready for *Good Morning America* tomorrow. I have to wake up at 4:00 a.m. to get my hair and makeup done. Most of the guys are going to sleep there, too. We all put in cash to close out our tab and vow to return to this bar in the future to commemorate our wild experience of surviving the Northeast blackout of '03.

The crowd outside the restaurant has grown considerably. No one is observing liquor laws. Everyone's holding a cocktail and a cigarette. We pass a group of tall, attractive men wearing miner's headlamps and sipping martinis. That's brilliant, I think, a hands-free light source!

"Excuse me." I squeeze between them, intimidated by their bold attire.

"Liz Phair."

The voice is instantly familiar, ringing all sorts of bells. I lean in closer, peering past the bright light shining out from the man's forehead.

"Courtney? Oh my God!" It's Courtney Taylor-Taylor, the lead singer of the Dandy Warhols. We're on the same label, and I was just in a meeting with him back in Los Angeles a few weeks ago. I'm flustered. "What are the odds!"

"Yeah, I saw you guys were playing here tonight. We're in town for a gig, too." He's nonchalant.

"This is insane, isn't it?" I gesture around me, indicating the power outage. I'm acting giddy, puffed up by the attention. I can't get over the fact that the coolest guy on the street has turned out to be a contemporary of mine. I'm pushing a six on the scale of annoying.

Introductions are made. Matt dutifully shakes everybody's hands, but I can tell he's lost a few ounces of confidence in the face of these older, more established musicians. Being around other artists who are my age, my generation, breaks the spell I've been under from hanging out too much with all my young bandmates.

Courtney and his friends are hilarious. They're like the *Ocean's Eleven* guys. They trade comedic commentary under their breath, mocking the self-important people around us. One minute you're straining to hear what they're saying, and the next, they hit you with a punch line so unexpectedly wicked it cracks your ass in half. That's how these guys roll. They wear their ridiculous headlamps with aplomb. Further proof that rock and roll is supremely well adapted to crisis.

"Where did you guys buy those?" I'm edging closer to Courtney, examining the details of his headlamp. Matt doesn't like my casual proximity. He says something loud and laughs, stepping forward so that I naturally step back. But my little bird-face keeps twitching, inspecting. I'm plotting the steps that must be taken in order to get a headlamp of my own. Until I get my hands on this vital piece of equipment, I won't be able to think about anything else.

"A guy was selling them on the corner, a couple of blocks that way." Courtney indicates the direction in which we were already heading, to meet up with the bus.

"Cool. Can I have a sip of your martini?" Without waiting for Courtney to answer, I blithely take a sip of his drink. He clocks my rudeness but takes it in stride. I'm not the first drunk girl he's had to deal with.

He's talking to Matt and the other guys while I stand there tapping my foot. I'm really only calculating the odds of finding this vendor before he sells out of merchandise or moves on, but it seems like I'm annoyed about something. Matt thinks I would rather be with Courtney. I don't have time to explain myself; the headlamp vendor is going to leave the vicinity, and I want to buy a bunch of these for our bus.

All Matt's talk about *Mad Max* and *Escape from New York* is doing a number on my head. In my drunken state, I've begun to think like a survivalist. This blackout could last for days or weeks, or even forever. These headlamps could be the difference between life and death for us. These headlamps might be the most important things we own if we find ourselves running from a mob, taking shelter in the subways, or crossing the river at night. It's potentially a big fucking deal, at least in my imagination. I start interrupting.

The boys are talking about musical gear. Matt's really enjoying himself now. Gear is a subject he knows a lot about, and it's given him a way to be competitive. He's got everybody's attention. They're hanging on his opinions and recommendations. I'm ready to leave; I want to go right now. But all he sees is that while he's talking, I'm suddenly irritated.

I interject something stupid like "I don't understand why rock and roll equipment has to be so heavy. Why can't they make guitars out of graphite?" Nobody wants to explain it to me. They let my non sequitur hang in the air for a beat, then move on. I keep glancing at Courtney's headlamp. Matt interprets this as me checking out another man right in front of him. He's hurt, but he tries to conceal it. He doesn't know me that well yet. He has no idea how hyperfocused I can get when I'm really interested in something.

They're talking about Def Jam, for Christ's sake. I'm frustrated beyond belief. We are in a crisis situation. Does anyone remember that? We need headlamps! I'm certain that this is the best idea I've ever had. I'm already imagining, twenty-four hours from now, the band and crew thanking me, congratulating me for being smart enough to purchase these ultramodern lifesaving devices. I want to be the rock band that makes it into the papers for having come through the emergency against all odds. If the Dandy Warhols somehow make it into the New York City blackout winner's circle and Liz Phair's band doesn't, I will never forgive myself. I finally drag Matt away from his rock-star conversation. Believe it or not, we actually do find the headlamp seller, exactly where Courtney said he'd be, and he still has plenty of headlamps available in a range of colors, for a very reasonable price. It shocks Matt almost as much as it satisfies me. It doesn't end up saving our lives, but I do sleep better that night knowing that if all hell breaks loose, we can go 007.

It's getting late. The streets are starting to empty out. New Yorkers are reluctantly going to bed to spend a fitful night worrying about tomorrow's fresh horrors. Matt and I stroll down the sidewalk, in no hurry, enjoying a silent rapport. After he realized that our safety truly was my motivation, his hackles smoothed down, and his affection flowed toward me again. After every misunderstanding, our trust in each other deepens. I don't know how I would have gotten through tonight without him. He tells me to look up at the sky and points out how many stars there are above us right now. It's a beautiful sight. Very romantic.

It's incredible to think that there was a time on earth when the stars were so visible that they mesmerized our ancestors, the same way the billboard lights on Forty-second Street and Broadway transfix tourists visiting Times Square today. Their distant, twinkling fire is so steady and eternal that you can't help but contemplate your own improbable and fleeting existence. Humans have created their own nighttime light show, and in the absence of it, here before us is the original inspiration. How life arose on earth is still a mystery, but I'm willing to bet that the process has something to do with electricity.

Two cyclists whip by us, so close I feel their wind-drag snap my clothing. It's official. The city belongs to bicycle gangs. The menace on two wheels is growing. Bike messengers act like they've been waiting for the chance to dominate the road for years and their moment has finally come. It's a reminder that when we finally do run out of fossil fuels, we'll still have bicycles.

"Oh, thank God! You guys are here!" Aaron sounds like a worried mother as he opens the door of the bus. He's beaming from ear to ear. He wraps Matt up in a side-hug. "Liz! Matt! See? The family is all back together again!" He checks over his shoulder as some teenagers run screaming down the street. "Heyyy!" Aaron suddenly bangs on the door when some guy drags his backpack along the side of the coach. "As you can see," he says with a sigh, climbing up the stairs behind us, "it was getting a little rough down here." He stops for comedic timing. "Down here"—he wags his finger to make sure we understand—"in *this* part of town." He draws a line under the point. "I'm sure it's fine up by *you* guys, but . . . down here it's *Night of the Living Dead*."

He's teasing, mostly, but he wants to get going, to find a parking spot closer to the *Good Morning America* studio. It's awesome to be inside our climate-controlled, fully operational bus again. We flop down on the lounge couch and bask in the air-conditioning. I'm safe and secure, prepared for anything. I marvel at the luxury of television, dimmer switches, music playing, the cold soda I pull out from the refrigerator. It's only been eight hours since the power went out in New York City, but it's given me an entirely new perspective on what our lives would be like without the grid. I don't ever want to go without electricity again unless I'm camping. Maybe not even then.

"There were some serious nutjobs in the streets who showed up just to be dicks." Aaron fills us in. "Like, 'Hey, we're here. Remember those signs we were carrying, warning you about Armageddon?'" Aaron shakes his head. "Nobody's happier about this situation than those assholes. It's been a long night—let's just say that." He sits back down, smiling proudly. The brakes release and our big beautiful coach rumbles along on its way.

We settle in and shrug off the chaos of the world outside for a few minutes, watching the news on television. They're calling it a butterfly effect, blaming the entire Northeast going dark on a series of small but snowballing errors that had catastrophic consequences—aging infrastructure in America exacerbated by poor maintenance of utility lines in rural Ohio or some such bullshit—likening this national disaster to a situation where one of those pesky little Christmas tree lights goes out and takes the whole strand with it. Officials parrot the explanation at regular intervals to calm the public and dispel suspicions of foul play, but none of us believe it for a second. The disruption is too widespread, too unprecedented.

"That is such bullshit!" Aaron shouts at the television. "There's no way, *no* way, that's what happened. They expect us to believe that some cows or something over in Ohio fucked up the wires and now we've got this?!"

Matt and I shake our head in disbelief. It seems perfectly obvious that the official stance is a cover-up for terrorism. In post 9/11 America, nobody believes we're getting the real scoop from the news anymore.

"I mean are you telling me that's how easy it is?" Aaron continues. "Why doesn't China just attack us, then, if we're so easy to take out. I mean, if the whole grid is that susceptible, a foreign adversary could just cripple us like that." He snaps his fingers. "I mean, I don't know, it just seems really fishy. Is all I'm saying. I don't know."

"Yeah, no, this is the work of hackers, 100 percent," Matt agrees. "This is definitely cyber warfare."

I just want to go to bed and wake up and have everything back to normal again. I get a few hours of sleep, and Aaron wakes me up at four-fifteen in the morning to tell me that the makeup artist is here. "I let you sleep a little later," he has the nerve to say. It's a miracle that this girl showed up, but she lives in Manhattan, and her place is really close by.

"What was I going to do?" She's applying two different types of foundation to my skin while I hold still, trying not to yawn. The corners of my lips are twitching with the effort.

"There's no electricity in my place." She dabs the cream on me with a moistened sponge. "if I'm just going to sit around the apartment twiddling my thumbs, I might as well get paid."

"Absolutely," I agree. But I'm confused. "If you had no alarm clock, how did you wake up this early?"

"I never went to sleep." She grins, enjoying my reaction. She blots my forehead and nose with setting powder. "It's no problem." She shrugs. "If you think about it, would I rather lie there in the dark tossing and turning in the heat, *not* getting paid, or come here and hang out in your air-conditioning?" She laughs. "You know? Plus, I get a *Good Morning America* credit on my resume."

She's so pretty and demure. I would never expect her to have a hustler's attitude. It's inspiring. It makes me wonder why I've been reluctant to take control of my own career. As if looking deliberate about business is unfeminine.

"I love what you're wearing," I say, staring straight ahead as she curls my eyelashes.

"Thanks." She smiles, genuinely pleased.

"Would you mind if I copied you and wore a white tank top on the show today?"

"No, not at all! I think that would be really cute." She cocks her head, appraising her work. "You don't want to look too glam when everybody else has had such a rough night."

"Yeah, exactly." I breathe shallowly as she outlines my lips with a pigment pencil.

The news coming from the television in the front lounge is grim. The anchors list the accidents and injuries that occurred overnight. They describe what happened to people who got caught in the wrong place at the wrong time. People who tried to reach loved ones and had no way to ensure that they were okay.

I feel guilty for having thought only about my own gratification last night. What am I doing pursuing this thing with Matt? Don't I realize I'm playing with fire?

"I think I'm in love with somebody who has a girlfriend," I blurt out to this perfect stranger. I confess it because we're women. Because it's five in the morning. Because we're in the middle of a national emergency with nothing but this bus and each other.

"Do they live together?" The makeup artist doesn't bat an eye. She goes straight to the practical.

"Yes," I admit.

"That's bad." She shakes her head, like she's been there before. She delicately blends bronzer over my cheekbones with the pads of her fingertips. "You can't do that."

"I know." I lower my head, ashamed of being someone who needs love instead of someone who already has it. She cups my chin with her hand, lifting my face up to hers so she can finish applying my lipstick. I can't hide from her gaze. I know what I need to do. As long as Matt and his girlfriend are together, I vow, nothing will happen between us. If they break up, that's a different story.

I wish I could tell you everything turned out for the best. Matt and his girlfriend did break up. He and I did start dating. For two years we had a sweet, fun, erotic, and volatile relationship that ended miserably. Matt's ex called me once, out of the blue, after he and I had been together for a few weeks. I listened to her accusations and answered them as fully as I could. I was admittedly guilty of allowing things to progress, but I thought I was safe, because, physically, we didn't cheat. She thought otherwise.

We show up to the *GMA* outdoor gig on the backs of motorcycles. Once again, rock and roll supremely adapts to adversity. We look freshly showered, happy, and professional. Matt and I play two of my popular radio songs, and everybody wants to know what our secret is. How did we pull off such a sparkling performance on time, and under these difficult circumstances? I want to say, "It's because we're in love." Instead, I act nonchalant, like Courtney Taylor-Taylor.

As soon as we get offstage, I pass out sunflowers to all the little kids in the audience. It is a glorious, spectacularly clear summer morning, and I feel blessed to have made it through the night, to have had Matt by my side as a companion and protector. I'm thrilled to know that he shares my feelings and yet we didn't cross the line. We're safe. But there's a catch The way Matt and I stuck together during the blackout confirmed what everyone had only suspected. Our burgeoning romance is now an open secret. We've made our feelings everyone else's problem.

Coping without electricity for a second day sucks. None of the challenges are novel anymore, and everyone's frustration is piling up. My quadriceps burn as I climb the stairs in my hotel. Twenty-four hours' worth of room-service trays are stacked to the ceiling on eight-foot-tall catering carts in each hallway. The stink of rotting food is nauseating. I think I'm going to puke from the smell. I'm tired and dehydrated. I've walked countless miles around this city since we got here yesterday. In the midday heat, New Yorkers are literally wilting. People slouch down or stretch out on every available surface in the shade.

I can't wait to get out of here. Everything that was exciting about being trapped in the Big Apple last night suddenly sucks, because after our performance, Matt is acting distant and professional again. He feels guilty and under scrutiny from his brother. When I asked him what was wrong, he said he thought I should be the one to put the brakes on our attraction, that men are biologically bound to try things and women are supposed to be the gatekeepers who block their advances. I think that attitude is bullshit and sexist. He's responsible for his part in wooing me. My hopes for us are now just little blobs of mercury swimming around the ceiling of my skull with nowhere to go—like air bubbles trapped in a diving bell.

ART TK

eight

NEW YORK CITY BLIZZARD

I stride the length of the subway platform, moving purposefully, like I know exactly what I'm doing. I'm a grown woman, it's 2010. I don't want the other riders to know how scared I am, or think they need to worry about me. Somebody really should, though. If anyone watching this performance knew the truth, they'd see that I was blithely walking off the end of a gangplank, dropping feetfirst into a roiling sea.

The people behind me aren't talking, although they are clearly together. It's unnerving, just the three of us here in this empty station in the middle of the night, trudging silently along in a pack. There were only a handful of people on the entire train, as far as I could see. I shift my bag over to my other shoulder, pretending there's nothing unusual about tonight, that it's just the end of another long day. Judging by the way I'm dressed, you'd think it was November, not February.

I stop to consult a street map posted above the turnstiles. I don't give myself enough time to memorize the route. I've got a natural sense of direction, and I'm pretty sure I've taken a good mental snapshot. Before I've even gone ten steps, though, I've already forgotten it. I'm running on pure adrenaline. Instead of turning around and checking the map again like a sensible person would, I decide it doesn't matter, that I can figure it out along the way. I've had to fight so hard just to make it this far, I can't risk losing momentum, or I'll also lose my nerve.

This is how I'm adulting now. I throw myself forward through sheer force of will, without the necessary wisdom that's supposed to come along with it. I'm new to this whole "take charge" thing. But so far it's been working. Besides, the grid is pretty straightforward in Manhattan. Avenues run vertically, streets run horizontally. How hard can it be? Back in Brooklyn, when we plotted my strategy, Eliza said to get off at Twenty-third Street and walk west. I can't remember the name of my hotel, but I know it's somewhere in the area. It has a very distinctive shape, like a triangular wedge of cheese or a giant slice of wedding cake. It's famous.

The tunnel splits off in two directions. I take the staircase to my left, hoping that exit will bring me aboveground on the north side of the street. I'm not familiar with this part of Manhattan. I climb the stairs with poise, still a little bit onstage in my mind. It can take hours after playing a show to come down from that high. I'm the star of my own movie, the maker of my own destiny. I can accomplish the impossible.

My confidence at this point is priceless. I'm in denial up to my eyeballs. There's a blizzard raging outside, a full-scale, governor-declared a state of emergency, and I'm that idiot trying to navigate hazardous conditions by myself at two in the morning. You read about people like me, stubborn assholes who blatantly disregard official warnings, thinking they can outsmart a hurricane or outrun a tornado. I'm determined to be reunited with my luggage, sleep in my own bed, and make my flight out of LaGuardia tomorrow morning.

The thing is, I'm on tour. I'm busy and tired. It is crucial to me that I show up for all my gigs, give my fans a performance they love, and collect my pay. Nothing—not illness, injury, or an act of God—is going to stand in my way. This isn't some playground on wheels or bacchanalian circus in the sky. This is business, and I take my job very seriously. I don't have time for the weather to fuck up my itinerary.

I'm also a mother. My son is entering high school. I need to be there for him, to make sure he's supervised and has someone to talk to during this vulnerable transition into adulthood. If I have to be out on the road, I'm going to make sure that my time away from home counts. I'm going to crush it every night and leave the audiences cheering.

We accomplished that goal at our show tonight. We rocked the house, played the hits, unearthed some rarities. People were hanging over the balconies, singing all the lyrics. It was a total madhouse backstage. That was only a few hours ago, and yet it's hard to believe any of it was real now that I'm out here by myself braving the cold, dark night. The rock and roll lifestyle trains you to withstand extremes. One minute you're partying in a mansion, the next you're parked in a urine-soaked alley full of homeless people. But the fact that I'm determined to go through this ordeal to get back on track with our schedule goes beyond dedication. It borders on self-punishment.

I could have avoided this situation. Or handled it differently. We all knew the storm was coming. The news anchors talked of little else over the course of the last twenty-four hours, predicting that a wide swath of the United States would likely be severely impacted. The North American blizzard of 2010 was dubbed "Snowmageddon" and "Snowpocalypse" by the talking heads, who described its size and power with breathless reverence. The beast swirling in the air above our heads was so big it has nicknames.

"Expect to see accumulations in excess of twenty inches in some urban areas," the meteorologists predicted, "with conditions spawning isolated instances of thundersnow."

No, that's not AC/DC's new single about snorting cocaine off a woman's thighs. It's a rare and dangerous weather phenomenon that produces unusually heavy snowfall, gusting winds, and lightning and thunder. Real Metro-Goldwyn-Mayer wrath-of-God stuff. It scared the crap out of me earlier, while we were slipping and sliding our way through Brooklyn on the way to the subway station.

Those innocent flakes I saw fluttering in the air this afternoon were just a premonition of what would become a cataclysmic finish. I was grabbing dinner with the legendary music manager Danny Goldberg before our show at the Music Hall of Williamsburg when I got my first inkling that trouble was brewing.

"Look. It's starting to come down," Danny said, pointing to the fluffy white tufts swirling around the pedestrians as they walked past the window. He apologized for not staying to see our concert and advised me not to delay my departure, to have a car ready to go as soon as I got offstage.

I thought he was overreacting—that success had made him a hothouse flower—but I took his recommendation. I thought I had everything under control, until I found myself standing in the middle of the lobby after our performance with pandemonium breaking out around me. Frantic concert-goers streamed out the front doors, fleeing into the night like they were racing to board the last helicopters out of Saigon at the end of the Vietnam War. Because of all the activity, snowdrifts formed on the floor in the entryway, wedging the front doors open. Frigid blasts of air blew straight into the building. How had conditions deteriorated so rapidly in the hour and a half that I was onstage?

Greg, my guitar player, came running up, his eyes wild. "The car company canceled," he said. "No one's allowed to drive back into Manhattan. The bridges are closed. We're staying out here. Do you want to stay with us?"

"No, I want to go back to my hotel," I whined, feeling blindsided and disoriented. I hate unexpected changes when I'm out on the road. A tour has a predictable rhythm, a daily routine that's the only thing keeping me sane when I have to surrender my life to the music business. "I'll call a different car service," I mumbled, already googling. "Or take a cab. I'm going back to Manhattan."

"I tried. Seriously. You'll never get a cab in this weather." Greg searched my face, hesitant to leave me but anxious to get moving himself.

"Yes I will," I snapped, imagining myself stuffing twenty-dollar bills through the opening of a taxi window, bribing either the passenger or the driver to let me share a ride. I had that flinty, faraway look in my eyes that said I was already disassociating from the situation, traveling in my mind to a happier time in the future when I'd solved whatever dilemma I was facing. I was looking straight at Greg, but I was no longer really there. He knew better than to argue with me when I got like this.

"Okay." He shrugged, heading off to supervise our load-out. "Are you sure?" He turned back, aware that I was being unrealistic but overwhelmed by his own responsibilities. He had six other people to worry about.

"Yeah," I said, staring at my phone screen. "Go do your thing." He'd done all that he could. Technically, I'm his boss.

I wasted precious minutes dialing every car company in town, even hitting up those tacky stretch-limo places that cater to groups of prom-goers. I received the same answer repeatedly: No one was accepting new reservations; there was no way to get back into Manhattan. Tears of frustration welled up in my eyes as I realized our next gig was now in jeopardy. If we didn't play our show in Virginia the following night, I'd lose a lot of money that my insurance would only partially cover, since it would be a first claim. That was unacceptable. There had to be another way.

Other than teleporting, it seemed like my only alternative was to abandon my luggage at the hotel and stay out there in Brooklyn with the band. Tomorrow I'd have to cram myself into the van and hope against reason that the freeways were clear. I'd specifically elected not to make the drive with the guys, choosing to fly on my own instead, because it would be a five-hour slog through heavy traffic on the best of days. I didn't even want to think about how long would take after the mother of all storms dropped a foot and a half of snow on the East Coast. My claustrophobia was already making hives break out on my cheeks, big ugly welts that felt hot to the touch.

Fuck it. I'd just have to suck it up and deal. I made multiple calls to hotels in the area. I even tried the questionable motel chains I would never normally patronize, but it was too late. Every hotel room in Brooklyn was already booked, some with waiting lists. Thousands of people were stranded here in Brooklyn, just like me, and they'd had two extra hours to panic and prepare their accommodations while I was chained to a microphone onstage, oblivious. I regretted calling out an audible spontaneous addition to our set, the song "Help Me Mary."

I'd run out of ideas. I had nowhere to go, and the club was emptying out. I regretted not accepting help from Greg, who was doubling as our tour manager to save costs. I truly didn't know what to do. I couldn't secure a car or cab to take me anywhere. There was full occupancy at all the hotels I could walk to. By the time the club locked up for the night, I could be begging a security guard or janitor to let me stay at their place. There probably wasn't even a gas station or laundromat open that I could stay awake in all night, if it came to that. Everybody had gone home and boarded up their doors, practically. It was a freaking mammoth blizzard.

By a stroke of luck, I spotted Greg's brother's girlfriend, Eliza, crossing the lobby. I was overcome with relief to see someone I knew who hadn't left yet. She offered to let me sleep at their place, on the floor of Greg's brother's studio. She doubted he had extra sheets and blankets, but she was sure they could provide me with some sort of makeshift mattress. At the very least, I'd be safely inside. I imagined myself curled up like a dog at the foot of their bed.

It was an option, but one I would definitely feel weird about.

She also mentioned that the subway system was still running. My heart skipped a beat. Of course! Why hadn't I thought of that? It felt like a stay of execution. I'd be able to get back to the city and sleep in my own room. I asked her to explain exactly what train line I needed to take and give me detailed directions to the nearest subway station. She rattled off a set of instructions, easy enough for a native to follow, but after seeing my worried confusion, she graciously offered to escort me there. It was only a few blocks away.

I slipped my arm through hers, latching onto her like a lamprey eel. We stepped through the front doors of the venue, leaning into the wind like a pair of old biddies. The street was filled with pedestrians and vehicles. Chaos reigned as people vied for the one narrow strip of navigable road space. Snow blew in our eyes, biting into every inch of exposed flesh. Multiple cars spun out in the icy conditions, unable to maintain traction. A BMW accidentally clipped a young man, who jumped out of the way and kept walking, unfazed.

As we rounded the corner onto a side street, we came across a block of abandoned cars, their noses pointing in all directions, ditched in whatever position they'd gotten stuck in, as the snow piled up on their roofs and filled in the gaps under their wheel wells. Wind blew the snow in ugly vortices. The situation was rapidly deteriorating. I cringed, caught off guard by the sudden explosion of thunder and lightning overhead. I couldn't believe this charming neighborhood had become a surreal and terrifying landscape.

We stopped to help some stranded motorists push their sedan off a slippery patch of ice. The four of us dug our heels in against the weight of the chassis, rocking the car forward each time the driver gunned the engine, but it was hopeless. The car just slid backward into the curb again. We apologized and moved on. I had my own gauntlet to run. The most ominous sign came at the end of the block, when we were forced to scatter to avoid a Humvee—one of those double-wide, military-grade, all-terrain vehicles that Arnold Schwarzenegger used to drive—skidding off the road. Its tires burned rubber as the driver tried in vain to back it up—just another casualty in this automobile graveyard.

Eliza and I exchanged glances across the street.

"Can I really do this?" I called out to her. "Do you think I'm crazy to try?"

Our eyes locked, two young women who had probably grown up in similar circumstances, both of whom left home to seek out a more challenging, unconventional life. She'd just seen me rock out in front of a crowd of music fans at our show, singing about personal and painful experiences. In that moment, there was no distance between us because of our age difference. We read each other perfectly.

"Totally!" she shouted back, conveying her absolute faith in me and, by proxy, in herself—and more broadly, in all the girls who'd been tomboys at some point in their lives. "It's going to be fine once you're on the train."

Famous last words.

Emerging from the underground, I find myself on a desolate and windswept tundra. Lower Manhattan is completely deserted. I thought there would be some people still out in the city, or that it would in some way resemble the New York I'm accustomed to, with pavement and sidewalks. But there is nothing, nobody. As far as the eye can see, everything is buried beneath a unbroken blanket of white. I'm standing in a snowy wilderness. I feel as though I've stepped out of Professor Kirke's magical wardrobe, into the wintry kingdom of Narnia.

All the signs are covered in ice. I can't read any of them. I turn to ask the couple who came up out of the station behind me if they know which direction west is, but they've already disappeared around the corner. No one else got off at this stop. I'm completely alone, shivering in the midst of the silent, indifferent Manhattan monoliths.

I could kick myself for being so naïve. Most people left work early tonight, heeding the warnings of meteorologists to get home safely before the worst of the weather hit. Thankfully, there's a lull in the wind so I can gather my thoughts. I tilt my face up to the black sky, shielding my eyes against the heavy flakes drifting earthward between the tall buildings. I feel so small in their shadows.

I look to the left and right, trying to orient myself. The silence is disconcerting, like that eerie hush that falls over the landscape when the birds stop singing ahead of a tornado. There are no cars on the streets, no taxis speeding along the avenues, no snowplows with their rotating yellow lights, scraping the roadways free of ice. It's as if no one has ever lived here or ever will again.

Distant lightning behind the clouds illuminates the skyline for an instant, and I picture the whole, two-thousand-mile-wide storm system slowly spiraling above me, its vast arms reaching out across several states. The low snow clouds directly overhead seem gentle and enfolding by comparison, like a protective canopy, though they stretch on, I know, for unimaginable distances.

I need to make a decision. There's no one I can call in the middle of the night who'll pick up—except for Greg, and I don't want to wake him, considering he has to make the long drive tomorrow with our band and all our gear. He'd have to wait up for me if I rode all the way back to Brooklyn. But I can't stay out here freezing my ass off much longer. With two feet of snow on the ground and more coming down fast, I need to think quickly. I don't want to spend the night in the subway station. It seems stupid to try to get a reservation at another hotel, one I could actually locate if I got off at another stop. They're all probably booked, and I'd only be there a few hours before I had to come back for my luggage anyway. I might as well soldier on.

I start walking, my thin boots making squeaky, crunching sounds as the snow compacts beneath my weight. I have to swing each leg forward with effort to wade through the dense accumulation. Within seconds, my toes are aching from the cold. My plan is to figure out which direction I'm heading by triangulating the street number, avenue, and address outside the station I just left, which should be easy once I reach the first intersection. But by the time I get to a street sign, I discover it's been shellacked with frozen muck. I can't knock off the ice, no matter how hard I bang on the pole or jump up and smack it with my fist. I struggle on, hoping for better luck on the next block. No dice. That sign is illegible, too.

I take a left, thinking maybe one of the side streets was spared the brunt of the wind, but every sign I encounter is mummified, frozen solid. I could be walking north, south, east, or west for all I know. I start to panic, speeding up as I search my surroundings for recognizable landmarks. I pull out my cellphone, trying to remember the name of my hotel. I start googling keywords, losing track of time. All of a sudden, I look up and realize I've gotten completely turned around, and I don't even know how to get back to the subway station. I retrace my footsteps as far as they go, but fresh snow is filling in the tracks too quickly.

A sickening jolt of fear passes through me as the reality of my situation sinks in. I'm really in trouble now. I have no idea where I am. Everything is closed, locked up, the inhabitants asleep. I don't know if the storm is going to get worse, and I have nowhere to take shelter. As far as the eye can see, New York is dark, silent—a ghost town. I start to run, passing imposing doorways, gates, and windows with iron staves. It feels like the city its turning its back on me. I think about pressing a random apartment buzzer and asking a stranger for help, but I know how unwelcome a late-night solicitation would be.

I pull out my cellphone and brush off the snow that keeps melting on the screen. I have only one bar of battery life left. One freaking bar. I'm lost in a snowstorm, I have no other way to find my hotel, and there's no one who can help me. In this moment, I realize—no hyperbole—that I've put myself in a situation where I could actually get frostbite or worse. This is crazy. I'm going to freeze to death in one of the busiest cities in the world.

"Please, please, please," I beg God, my fingers shaking as I type repeated keywords into Google. "Triangle hotel New York." "Wedge hotel." "Cake slice building." "Triangle building new york." Finally, I hit upon the magic phrase. The screen fills up with a picture of the Flatiron Building on a bright and sunny day. My memory comes flooding back: lecture slides from my college art history class. Greg asking me this December if I'd like to try out a new hotel in a famous building downtown. The doorman holding open the door of my cab earlier today as I left for Williamsburg.

Google Maps shows a location a quarter mile from where I'm standing. I follow the GPS, my heart racing. I'm so close. But I'm terrified the battery is going to die.

"C'mon." I beg my phone to live, willing it to keep me company on this bleak and frightening trek. I'm Tom Hanks in *Cast Away*, talking to my volleyball. I'm pretty sure I've memorized the way to my hotel now, but I feel an irrational attachment to this glowing screen, my only lifeline. My shock at my own recklessness has me rattled. I slog through the heavy snow, my legs aching, my pants damp and crusted with ice from the thigh down. What series of catastrophic mistakes brought me to this point in my life? How did I stray so far off the beaten path? It's hard to say.

I'm still recovering from being betrayed by my ex-boyfriend Rory, a year ago. Something died in me at the end of that relationship. It changed me in a fundamental way. If you object to religious terms like "penance" or "purgatory," then I'll describe my state of mind as a self-imposed moratorium on love. I have no interest in dating seriously. My faith in my ability to spot the wrong kind of guy is nonexistent. I survived the blow, but just barely. I got back up and started living again. That's the most positive thing I can say about my recent history.

But I'm proud that I can recognize that this wasn't just done to me, that my choices in life played a role in why I am alone. I kind of like being independent for a change. I've gone from boyfriend to boyfriend, playing the needy-girl part too often. I need to develop as a person.

Almost the moment I have this thought, my phone dies. Total loss of power. It's just me out here now. Me and these imposing buildings. My awareness expands to encompass the eerie, silent world around me. Now that I have no up-close distraction I am forced to perceive myself from afar, to listen to the haunting sound of my footsteps in the stillness. I notice all the dark windows and remember that there are actually people behind those glass panes, some of whom could be watching me right now. I freak myself out imagining someone's face suddenly appearing from behind a curtain. My heart starts beating rapidly. I have to shake the frightening image off.

I look down the length of these dark, snowy streets. It would be easy to believe I am the last person on earth. How fucking scary would it be if a pack of wolves were roaming New York right now? I can easily picture their shaggy gray coats and bowed heads. If they caught my scent and started chasing me, where would I run to? What could I do to defend myself? It's a heart-stopping image, one that feels like it came out of the mists of time, from centuries ago when Manhattan was still a wild island. Trappers must have faced such threats if they were lost out at night, in the winter, alone.

I swap the image of a pack of wolves for one of the gaunt and ravenous hellhounds from *An American Werewolf in London* streaking toward me at unfathomable speed, fangs dripping with saliva, beady red eyes red homing in on its kill. How terrifying would it be to be the object of that bloodlust, to watch your own death coming at you and be paralyzed? I'm scaring the crap out of myself.

I think I hear a noise, and I freeze, my heart pounding, my breath rasping. I stop and listen, mentally mapping the environment around me. All of a sudden, a huge *floomp* of snow falls off a tree and lands right on top of my head. I protest loudly, dusting the snow out of my hair, feeling like an idiot—like nature just threw a pie in my face for taking this all too seriously, for not looking around with an open heart and mind. I'm convinced that the trees and buildings are watching and laughing at me.

But not in a bad way. It lightens the mood. I recognize it as a sign that I need to trust more, that I'm not as alone as I perceive myself to be. I feel like a loved child. This is the way I used to interpret the work of God in my life when I was a little girl. I often believed there was a benevolent presence or a guardian angel watching over me, a divine being with a sense of humor who would teach me lessons in the kindest, gentlest ways. Like the way I was taught not to lie.

When I was eight or nine, I went on a hike with my Girl Scout troop. I was bored by the manicured suburban woods we were tramping through, having grown up running free in much wilder regions. I wanted to break away from the pack, get out from under the noses of the volunteer moms. I pretended to see a rabbit hopping down a side trail and called out to my friends to come chase after it with me. I convinced them to keep following, making up a constant stream of falsehoods about how I saw the rabbit up ahead and how, if we hurried, we'd catch him. They knew it was a game, too; just an excuse to get away from the stupid badge activity and have a real adventure.

So you can imagine our surprise when we turned the next corner and saw a big fat rabbit sitting right in the middle of the path. He acted as unconcerned as if he were somebody's pet; not scared of us at all. He just twitched his nose, stood up on his haunches to get a better whiff, and then hopped away, leaving us to stare, dumbfounded at the bizarre coincidence. Deep in the forest preserve, I knew God was playing a loving trick on me, reminding me he was watching, and that I'd better be good.

There was a time when a small part of this metropolis felt like home. I spent my junior year of college in an apartment overlooking the St. Mark's churchyard in the East Village. I was just a baby back then, barely out of my teens. Navigating the transportation system was daunting. The trains were confusing and crowded, and I was too shy to hail a cab. I often walked twenty blocks or more to get to work, stopping occasionally in the doorway of a random apartment building to consult a shiny gate-folded map.

I have no business being out here in the middle of the night by myself, walking foolishly into the jaws of a massive blizzard. I mean, it's crazy. It's nuts. I'm determined to make it back to my hotel, convinced that I can catch my scheduled flight out of LaGuardia in the morning, despite the fact that four out of the five regional airports are closed due to gusting winds and whiteout conditions. There's no rational basis for my conviction. I'm driven by pure, blind stubbornness.

I stop dead in my tracks, a tiny figure in the middle of a six-way intersection. There it is: the Flatiron Building. I immediately recognize its distinctive wedge shape, a wedding-cake slice in a world of rectangular pasta boxes. I look all the way up, taking in its sheer size, its commanding presence. It's an exquisite piece of architecture, delicate in detail, feminine. How could I have gone in and out the front door this morning and never stopped to appreciate where I was? I stand in front of the famous building and apologize. I say out loud how grateful I am to finally be home.

There is a light on in the lobby, a small, friendly little glow. How lovely it looks in the midst of all this darkness, how heartening. I feel as though my spirit is being drawn toward its warmth, that the whirl of society and gaiety is welcoming me back into the fold. Even though I've made it to my destination, against all odds and after a long ordeal, I'm not ready to go inside yet. Once I cross that threshold, life will start up again, and I'll forget what it was like out here where I've been, and who I was when I was in it. I don't want to abandon my newfound trust in myself, or leave behind this wilderness that has embraced me and whom I have conquered. I'm a different person.

I stand for one last moment in the silence, listening to the sound of my own breath. I will never again have the chance to see New York this way: without any people, without any cars. I can see all the way down Fifth Avenue and Broadway, the wide, white thorough-fares sparkling in blue light, the sidewalks indistinguishable from the streets under deep snow. It's all one groove in an endless canyon. I laugh out loud at my earlier fears. I wasn't crazy, or hallucinating; I was navigating. Just like I always have. I can trust myself. It's a slow process. But I can make time for it.

I cross the plaza reluctantly, stealthily. I've grown accustomed to the way my boots squeak, and I even pivot a little on them, side to side, like a snowboarder. I see the doorman through the glass, list-lessly leaning on the counter, picking at his fingernails. I'm going to sneak up on this guy and freak him the fuck out. My bold animal senses are shrinking back down to normal size, like Alice in Won-derland shrinking back down to fit through the door. Five minutes ago I was talking to my friend the Flatiron Building, eye to eye, soul to soul. Now I've shrunk down to the size of a penny under the Flat-iron's shoe. I am human again.

The guy jumps back a little when he sees me. He instinctively prepares to opens the door, then hesitates. I'm still ten feet away, and he's probably traumatized from having the howling wind blow across his knees all night. He doesn't know the wind has died down. I know what's out there. He doesn't.

He looks good in his hipster bellhop vest. He pushes his face up to the window, squinting, looking left and right, trying to figure out where the hell I came from. I have appeared virtually out of no-where. He holds open the door, and I pass under the thermal lamps, staring at the red, jiggling light it makes on the floor as I stomp my feet. Great soap cakes of snow slide down the side of my boots and float like tiny icebergs in their own puddles.

"Welcome back," the doorman is surprised by the sudden appear-ance in the middle of the night of a woman who has seemingly dropped from the sky.

"Thanks!" I feel my windburned cheeks rise in a genuine smile for the first time since I left the stage. It feels good to be safe and inside. I can't believe I made it.

"I hope you had a nice evening." He automatically performs his duty as doorman, then surreptitiously checks the 150 feet or so beyond the windows again, not sure if he's missing something.

"I did!" I turn around, thinking tonight must have been crazy at the hotel, too. "Did you?"

"A lot of people got stuck, because their flights were canceled." He steps forward, and I realize he is very handsome, maybe an actor or performer. "And then our night staff couldn't make it in, because the snowplows gave up around six or seven, so it's been pretty eventful. I'll probably have to sleep here."

"You should." I nod, walking toward the elevators. I can tell he expects more of an explanation, that there's an unspoken agreement that you don't walk up to the front door of the Flatiron Building at two in the morning in the middle of a blizzard without a story to tell. But I think I should stay a mystery. I don't believe either of our memories of tonight will be improved by my telling him the details. If I explain what happened in a logical fashion, it won't be true to my experience. If I tell him the story the way I perceived it, it'll just sound crazy. That's the nature of a worthwhile secret. It's not that you won't tell but that you can't.

Another guest walks into the lobby wanting information on canceled flights and airports closures.

He sees me. "Hi, how's it going?"

"Good." I step onto the elevator and press my floor number. "How're you doing?"

The doors partially close. Then a second set of doors, hidden within the doors, closes the rest of the distance, locking lip to lip. I'm still in my heightened state of awareness. I understand why this detail draws my eye, and what the symbolism means: You have reserves of strength inside of you that you're completely unaware of until you absolutely need them. Many generations of inherited survival skills still reside within you, thanks to the reproductive success of your ancestors. Then they appear, as if by magic, to close the impossible gap. You're never truly alone. Relatives who faced innumerable trials and tribulations are in you always, ready to come to your aid when the crucial moment arises.

ART TK

nine

SOTTO VOCE

'm in Paris, eating the best lavender-honey duck breast in the world. I have visions of Provence. I have flashbacks of sun-drenched wildflowers on the bluffs of Big Sur overlooking the Pacific. I feel like I'm going to pass out from the delicious richness of the juicy meat and crisped skin. It's melting on my tongue, making me groan with pleasure. It's 2003, but I feel like I could be enjoying a sumptuous and leisurely banquet in la Belle Époque.

"Oh, *try* this." I pass a forkful over to Matt, my boyfriend, who wraps his lips around the morsel and nods in agreement. "Yeah, that's way better than mine."

"Here." I push the plate between us and pass him my carving knife. We eat in silence for a few seconds, luxuriating in the atmosphere of the little bistro on Rue de Je Ne Me Souviens Pas. It's been an incredible day. I had a bit of trouble getting the ladies in the perfumery to understand my idiosyncratic pronunciation of "Helmut

Lang"; after twenty minutes of my guttural yelping, the whole staff crowded around me with quizzical expressions on their faces. Then, when I finally thought to simply write it down, they all threw their heads back in relief and shouted, "Helmut Lang!" Which sounded to me like exactly what I'd been saying. But at least I was able to purchase the scent I'd come for and leave perfectly satisfied.

Now, after this remarkable meal, at a wonderful little restaurant we happened upon by chance, I am quite sure I've had the quintessential Parisian experience, complete with romance. I'm just about to order dessert when Matt suddenly jumps up out of his seat and starts throwing a flurry of francs down onto the table top. "We're going to miss the show! We have to go!" He doesn't mean the theater, or some burlesque extravaganza. He is referring to *our* show—*my* show, to be more specific. We are the performers, and we're supposed to be onstage in twenty minutes.

We run out into the street and try to hail a cab. We have wandered so far afield in our happy daze that we're turned around and can't find our bearings. It's all side streets, with no taxis in sight. We start running. I try out my broken French on every pedestrian we encounter. "Pardon, s'il vous plaît, où est le Paradis? Le rock club?" Most of the natives can't understand me and shrug in sympathy or laugh at us, as we race by in desperation—praying that we're headed in the right direction. We finally run into someone who both speaks English and is familiar with the venue. It's too late to catch a cab. We jog the entire mile and arrive only five minutes late, but with stomachs churning from our rich meal. We have to go out onstage before we can even catch our breath.

I hadn't realized that the music halls in Paris allowed their patrons to smoke indoors. I'm facing a thick cloud of cigarette smog. "They may be thin, but they're not healthy," I mutter, referring to the oft-quoted stereotype of Parisian women. I ask the crowd if they wouldn't mind lighting up outside, or even abstaining altogether, to spare my voice. My request elicits jeers. If anything, in response to my plea, they smoke more. It's awful. I'm in the middle of a song when I feel my left vocal cord, the one I use for all my low tones and thick timbre, give out completely. It simply stops working. The audience can't tell, especially after the audio signal is patched through the sound board and has reverb slapped on it, but I know I need both my vocal cords to get through an entire show, especially in the midst of this toxic nicotine cloud. I keep singing, but I start trembling out of fear. I'm currently on a pop tour, playing some vocally challenging numbers, and I have to be audible above the volume of a full band. It's only our second number. I have fourteen more to go. It's akin to an airplane flying with one engine: I can do it, but it's a nail-biter. If anything goes wrong after this, I won't be able to continue.

Instead of moving around and engaging with the audience, I stay extremely focused and still, planting my feet front and center and keeping my eyes nearly closed. This is not performance; it's survival. At some point I feel a tickle in my throat, and I have to suppress the urge to cough. Tears are streaming down my cheeks, but somehow I make it through the entire seventy-five-minute set using only my weak, reedy soprano. I am incredibly grateful to the muse for supporting me, and fairly impressed with myself.

After we get offstage, the band and I swap our horror stories of the night, and of our individual struggles to overcome the toxic fumes. Someone teaches me how to say "Go fuck a duck" in French so I can use it on the rude crowd the next time I'm here. We feel grateful to be American and are glad we are flying back to the States tomorrow. All in all, we had fun, but I feel a little under the weather later. My throat is sore. I hope it doesn't turn into a bad cold. I have a lot of holiday performances coming up, and I need to be at full power for this season.

My health takes a turn for the worse as soon as we get off the long flight home. The plane's dry air was murder on my vocal cords. Even after a day of rest, I'm sick as a dog, but I have to show up to work. I have a temperature of 103 degrees, and I'm about to go on live television. I'm distracted. I just got a bikini wax in the green room, and now the hair and makeup person at NBC has given me Shirley Temple ringlets for the performance. I look at myself in the mirror, and I want to walk out of the building.

"Do you think anyone will notice?" I whisper to my tour manager sarcastically.

"Honestly? It's not great," he says with a laugh. "I mean, it's definitely a look. It's a bold statement; let's put it that way."

There's no time to fix it. I have to go out on set in five minutes. I'm here to sing "Winter Wonderland" as part of Rockefeller Center's annual tree-lighting ceremony. I'm uneasy about using a prerecorded backing track. It feels suspiciously like karaoke, and I suck at that. Everybody tells me it's going to be fine. They wrap me up in a huge, soft blanket while we wait outside on the plaza for changeover. Despite my covering, the fever is making my teeth chatter uncontrollably. The acetaminophen I took is no match for this flu. Tremors travel up and down my body. I was afraid to take anything stronger, in case it made me delirious.

When the program goes to a commercial break, they usher me into a little open-air booth and sit me down on a stool. Stylists fuss with my hair and makeup. A tech comes in and adjusts the baffling on one of the lights, his crotch hovering right in front of my face. They've got heat lamps aimed up at me from below, so at least I'm not shivering. I'm worried I'll feel disconnected from the music, though, with no instrument in my hands and no musicians around me. Singing along to a canned track feels impersonal. I don't trust it.

Standing just a little bit away, Matt reminds me that there are two bars before the first verse, so I'll know when to start singing. The prerecorded holiday tune sounds roughly the same until you get to the chorus, so it's hard to tell what section of the song you're in without a cue. I have an earpiece, and I nod as the audio engineer inside the building sets the volume level and adjusts the equalizer. He rewinds the track, and everybody steps away while we wait. Now it's just me alone here in the barrel, if you don't count the five million viewers watching the live broadcast at home. I try not to think about it. In the space of thirty seconds, I've gone from an atmosphere of frenetic team activity, lasting hours, to total isolation and absolute stillness out here on the plaza. I listen to the sound of my heartbeat pounding in my ears, feel my breath draw hot and shallow in my sore throat. I'm staring straight into the camera lens, blinded by two huge beauty lights positioned on either side of the crouching cameraman. Everybody is in set position. I feel like one of those ski racers waiting at the top of the mountain for the starting signal.

Through my earpiece, I can hear the broadcast. It's silent during commercial breaks, with the occasional burst of chatter from the station's behind-the-scenes technical communications. Then the anchors chime in, doing their shtick as they banter back and forth. I nod and smile and say something innocuous like "I'll be singing 'Winter Wonderland'" or "I'm excited to be here." The voices respond with encouragement—"Can't wait to hear it!" or "From the artist who sings the song, 'Why Can't I?' Liz Phair!" I don't hear anything for several seconds. Finally the track fades up, and I wait through the requisite two-bar intro, as instructed, coming in on the first line. *"Sleigh bells ring, are you listening? In the lane snow is glistening . . ."* It sounds pretty good. My voice is holding its pitch. When you first get sick, you can usually power through a few nights before the virus affects your vocal cords. It's the tail end of an illness that really kills you. Several days of dehydrating cold medicine takes a toll. But you can sing through delirium, fever, nausea. Once the inflammation travels down into your chest, though, and you start coughing, you're totally screwed. I continue on. *"A beautiful sight, we're happy tonight, walking in a winter wonderland."* Something sounds off about the mix. The chords don't sound right in the turnaround before the second verse, but I plunge ahead, assuming it's an equalizing issue in the studio's audio booth. *"Gone away is the bluebird, here to stay is the new bird. He sings a love song as we go along . . ."* I sing the last line of the second verse over a dissonant chord, aghast at the musical clash: *"walking in a winter wonderland."*

Oh fuck. I can hear that I'm in the wrong section of the song.

That was supposed to be the first line of the chorus. The engineer in the control booth must have faded in the track late, and I am off by a whole two measures. I know this only in hindsight. At the time, I simply have no idea where I am. My brain is too addled to do the math. I'm hopelessly lost on live television, fumbling like an idiot in front of millions of people. There's no live band to switch it up on the fly and follow my lead. This is a prerecorded instrumental arrangement, and it's marching relentlessly on without me. Maybe if I weren't so feverish, or if I were accustomed to working this way, or if I didn't keep glimpsing my poodle curls in the reflection of the camera lens, I could have salvaged the performance. But I'm malfunctioning like a faulty robot. My circuit board is fried. I sing the wrong line over each part of the chorus, until it sounds so bad that even I have to stop and trail off midsentence.

I stare straight ahead, listening intently, trying to find any clue as to what part of the song I'm in. I'm afraid to guess and end up clashing with the music again. Almost fifteen seconds of silence pass before I pick back up on the chorus. Finally, I'm in synch with the arrangement again, but I'm so flustered from fucking up massively on live TV that when I reach the bridge, I can't remember any of the words. My mind draws a total blank. I start mumbling gibberish, singing parts of other verses, humiliating myself like I do when I go to a friend's house for Shabbat and they start reciting the wine prayer. When it is time for an actual verse to begin, I make a hash of that, too. I'm just repeating myself. It's a disaster. I'm blushing crimson, and I look utterly miserable on camera. I *am* miserable, frankly. It's a miserable rendition of a holiday classic.

The song finally ends, but the cacophony is still ringing in my ears. I'm pretty sure all New York City is laughing at me. The anchors grab the reins once more, like nothing happened, but everyone out here on the plaza feels incredibly sorry for me. They all tell me that it wasn't that bad, that the people watching are hardly going to notice that I messed up the words. I know they're lying through their teeth. There's no point in self-recriminations now. Everybody in The United States knows the words to this song.

Bumbling one's way through a high-profile appearance is not the kind of thing you can get away with easily. Just ask Ashlee Simpson. Everybody messes up from time to time, but it's a major drag when it happens to be during a beloved annual tradition.

The next morning, Howard Stern is making fun of me on his radio show for my deer-in-the-headlights car crash of a performance. It's all over the Internet for a while, too, with people speculating that I had a stroke, or that I'm on drugs, or that my brain lost oxygen due to the tightness of my hairdo. The indie press has been waiting for me to fail, and though this is disappointingly low-hanging fruit for them, they weigh in with snarky wisecracks until the dead horse is thoroughly beaten and no one has the heart to take one more kick.

I'm sick as a dog on the fourth day of this illness, but I still have to get up and make the rounds for the holiday season. When you have a hit song on the radio, it means they boosted you specifically throughout the year, and if you want to sell more records, you have to show up for all their Christmas extravaganzas to pay back that support. Their loyal fans expect to hear the songs they associate with the station, and "Why Can't I?" got a lot of airplay in a number of markets.

December is a wild time to be popular. You end up running into the same artists over and over as they too perform for the stations that made them famous. I remember bumping into the Black Eyed Peas, Fall Out Boy, and Hootie & the Blowfish repeatedly that December. The holiday variety shows only want two songs from each artist anyway, so being sick hasn't been a serious problem for me yet. But by the time we roll into Chicago after playing "Winter Wonderland" and "Why Can't I?" for all the East Coast stations, I have full-blown laryngitis.

I wake up on the morning of Q101's Christmas show and can't make a sound. Not a squeak. Not a growl. I have to write everything down on a piece of paper to communicate. I can't even call my manager to let him know we're in trouble, because he wouldn't hear me over the phone. I open my mouth, take in a lungful of air, and all that comes out when I speak is a hiss. Zero tone. Zero pitch. I doubt you've ever had laryngitis this bad in your life, because, when you got sick, you probably weren't also singing two shows a day for weeks at a time.

In my business, you don't cancel gigs unless you are a multimillionaire or a drug addict and pretty much already on a downward spiral. If you're anywhere between those two extremes and have a hit song to play, they will dig up your grave, roll your dead body onstage in a wheelbarrow, and make your jaw move with their hands if they have to. That's not much of an exaggeration. It's 2003, and the music industry is practically a black-market economy, with payola flowing freely and a prevailing mob mentality on the executive floors. Too many back-room deals are struck, too much money is spent, too much manpower is expended trying to cover vast amounts of territory. Radio programmers leverage other assets to get you into the optimal position to launch you even higher in the stratosphere so the labels can finally start raking in the fun money, and they are not going to let you walk away.

Up until now I could disguise my vocal issues by having the band double my parts and using pitch-correcting software at the soundboard, but this morning is different. I don't see how I can possibly play the show when there's just no sound at all coming out of my mouth. Making some kind of noise is a crucial aspect of singing. What am I supposed to do when I get onstage? Clog around like a River Dancer? (Again, see: Ashlee Simpson.)

We explore the idea of lip-synching, but the whole band is here, and we don't have the premade tracks to do it right. For all of us to fake it, the bass, the drums, the other two guitar players, and I would have to jump around pretending to play our instruments, and that's pretty risky. You only perform like that on video shoots. Bands that lip-synch live use at least eight and sometimes up to twelve backing tracks, blended together so they feel slightly out of alignment and thereby authentic. You don't just play the fully produced radio version of the song on a mono mix and bounce around with your amps unplugged, unless you want to wake up to a career-ending press volley the next morning. We're in a real predicament.

When I get to the venue and show my manager how bad it is, he lies right to my face. "It's not that bad, Liz. Come on."

"Russ!" I scribble the words on a piece of paper and push it across the table at him. "There's no way I can sing! I can't produce a single word." I assume he will agree with me, and I'm even throwing up my hands, silently laughing because it's kind of obvious what the move here is. I need to go home and go to bed. I have a good work ethic. It would be one of the first times in my career that I've ever canceled anything. It's clear as a bell that I cannot perform my duty. Surely he can see that.

Boy, am I wrong. My manager tells me that, of all the stations in the nation, adult contemporary in my hometown of Chicago is *the* linchpin, and we can't afford to blow it off.

I write, "You think I'm blowing it off?" underlining my words multiple times, rather severely, and passing the note back to Russ. I wish I had written, "Buddy, you can put a microphone in my face, you can jam the head down my throat all the way back to my tonsils, but you're not going to hear anything. I should mention that a standard live mic is almost the exact size and shape of an erect dick, and the front-of-house guy is always telling the singer to "Put your mouth right on it." And while we're on the subject, please note that an electric guitar is more or less shaped like a stylized and supersized cock and balls. I've given this career all I've got, I think, and I'm sorry it's not enough.

But the show must go on. They push me out on the stage, and with the divine assistance of the cherubic Jason Mraz, I mouth my way through the worst rendition of "Winter Wonderland" ever performed on any stage in the world. A bullfrog has more melody. A weasel has better tone. And you know what? Nobody notices. It goes off like clockwork, and no one's the wiser. I'm stunned, and a little depressed, to be honest. Do I even need to be here?

Live radio events attract a very general type of music fan—somebody who doesn't have a lot of choices, or maybe a lot of sophistication. They are loyal to a specific station, and that's about it. They're often under the age of sixteen and chaperoned by an older sibling or parent. The people behind the scenes don't mind fooling them, and I hate that they are so gullible and taken advantage of. I'm sick of the pop world and all its trappings. I never thought I'd say this, but I miss rock and roll clubs.

I fought my whole life to have a voice, both literally and figuratively. If I stay in this radio realm, I'm not sure I need one. I feel like a prop, a cardboard cutout, a clone, and it is a terrible feeling. I grew up listening to the radio. I'm not a music snob. I never equated broad taste with bad taste. But this past week has left an unpleasant funk on my palate.

I leave the show in a good mood, which my manager misinterprets.

"See?" He slaps me on the back proudly, "I knew you could do it."

"Va baiser un canard, Russ," I quack under my breath. And that's the last time I ever did do it.

ART TK

ten

LABOR OF LOVE

"Whatever you do, don't look at it!" My friends are laughing, but they're serious, too. They've both had babies, so they know what's going on with my vagina. I just had a Brazilian bikini wax this morning. I expect to go into labor any day now, and I thought it would be nice for the hospital staff to have a clean, prepped canvas to work with. I'm embarrassingly naïve about the amount of byproduct that will spew forth from my body during the process of giving birth, but my heart's in the right place.

"Why? What wrong with it?" I shift uncomfortably in my seat, worried about the tender flesh still, stinging from its hot-wax treatment. I haven't tried to look down there since my belly grew so big I can no longer see my toes.

"Just don't." Caroline and Viv are in fits, remembering their own unwitting encounters with their nether regions in the third trimester.

After lunch, I go to the club to swim. The locker room is empty, so I spread a towel down on the bench and reach a compact mirror around the great globe of my stomach to try to get a look at myself. I have to contort my limbs to find the right angle, but as soon as I catch a glimpse of my labia in the reflection, I gasp and almost drop the compact. They're huge, red, and puffy—like a baboon's ass or something. That is not my vagina. I'm shaken and angry. Not because I can't handle the sight, but because it's yet another physical alteration that I have no control over. My body has been changing for nine months now, in ways that are both exciting and alarming, and I'm tired of surprises. I just want to hold my baby in my arms. I'm ready for this construction phase to be over.

They say remodeling a house puts a lot of stress on a relationship. The costs go over budget, and it always takes longer than expected. I relate to this metaphor. My due date has come and gone, and I'm still waddling around the neighborhood like a human lotto ball, almost as wide as I am tall. He's grown so big that there isn't enough room in here for the both of us. If he doesn't leave soon of his own accord, I'm issuing an eviction notice.

I slip gingerly into the pool, relieved to feel buoyant; I'm lugging around an extra forty pounds on land. It was fun to be pregnant, until it wasn't. I can't find a comfortable position to sleep in at night, so I'm exhausted. All the Christmas parties we attend are sophisticated cocktail gatherings where everyone stands in high heels, chatting and laughing, while I sit in the corner at the bar. I am my own snack table, resting a plate on my baby bump and munching away while my husband socializes. I was a veritable Wonder Woman in the second trimester going to yoga, flying to and from Los Angeles, recording my album, hiking in Glacier National Park. Somehow, my energy collapsed in the last month, and I've become Dan Aykroyd's character in *Trading Places*: a bitter, drunken Santa detangling salmon from his fake beard on the city bus, staring dead eyed at the passengers around him. Okay, not the drunk part, but I'm over it.

"How is this worth it?" I asked Vivienne one night last week when we were getting into the car after exercising. It was cold outside, the dark time of the year in Chicago. I no longer go to clubs, since I can't drink. I hate maternity fashion. I'm not into the whole Yummy Mummy scene. I didn't want a baby shower; I'm still having flashbacks to the nightmare of writing 250 thank-you notes for our wedding presents.

"You'll see." She held the door open for me, thinking about the best way to explain it. "When your child looks up at you with pure adoration in her eyes and says, 'I love you, Mommy,' it's the most incredible feeling in the world."

Never having experienced this joy myself, it sounded like a bullshit answer. I'm not one of those women who fawns indiscriminately over children, raising my voice to a ghastly, girlish squeak. I tend to talk to children like they're adults and have had some really good conversations with the ones I know. But I'm having trouble keeping things in perspective. I want to dance. I want to run. I don't want to have any of these symptoms anymore. I have phantom labor pains, my skin itches, my boobs are huge. Silvery stretch marks have started appearing on my abdomen, despite my slavish application of cocoa and shea butters. My baby kicks me nonstop, like an aggressive mid-fielder, and I have to pee constantly. For something so natural, I'd have thought evolution would have arrived at an easier process.

It's possible I have an incomplete outlook on life's greatest mystery. My brother and I are adopted, so they didn't tell pregnancy stories in my family. As far as I'm concerned, you can go to the store and pick up a perfectly fine baby that's already fully cooked. No need to toil all year in the kitchen. At the same time, meeting someone who is related to me by blood is of immense interest. I've struggled my whole life with issues of identity. For as long as can remember, I've pondered the existential questions of who I am and where I came from. The specter of abandonment has waited in the wings, lurking in the shadows, insisting upon acknowledgment.

I never know how much importance to give it. Is it a minor detail in my biography, or does it define me? When I look at old family photographs, do they really pertain to me? Are those my ancestors, or am I playing at nostalgia? However much I wish to belong to any one person or group, that urge is almost always counteracted by an awareness of being different, as though there's a barrier around me, thin as a layer of ice on an eyelash, that prevents full integration. I keep people at arm's length and in their separate categories—even those with whom I have long-term, committed relationships.

I remember when my father sent me the original copy of my birth certificate—for the purpose of gathering passport paperwork, or because I'd lost my driver's license. It arrived in a manila envelope. When I held the yellowed document in my hands and looked at the time and date, punched out on an old-school typewriter, I burst into tears. It was overwhelming to touch the last artifact that connected me to a mother I never knew—a young woman who, for whatever reason, couldn't raise me. I saw a vulnerable infant changing hands, and I wept for the agonizing decisions of everyone involved, for chances lost and new roads opened at a heavy price. It was also a snapshot of a fleeting moment of wholeness, before I carried in my heart this broken piece of glass, which I'm careful not to disturb lest it cut me. I cried because I recognized a feeling I must have had once but could no longer summon, no matter how quietly I sat or how happy I was. It makes for great art, though; I'll say that.

I mean, who cares, right? It isn't a big deal. There are much bigger deals in life. But it's my deal, and I've done my best to adapt. Now, on the cusp of becoming a mother myself, all these emotions that are tied to being secure with or separated from a child swirl around in my subconscious. I vacillate between being blasé and being ecstatic about what's about to happen. Will my child have a different kind of bond with me than I had with my own parents? Will I see traces of my biological mother and father in his features? I'm keen to meet this energetic somebody who looks like a smiling wombat in the ultrasound pictures.

But I'm not impatient to see the inside of a delivery room. Giving birth is something I have a lot of fears about. The thought of having an episiotomy, for one thing, terrifies me. Having my delicate perineum sliced open the way one scores a loaf of bread haunts my waking dreams, and I know it will be necessary. When I entered puberty, a male pediatrician examined me and offered this opinion: "You're very tight. It may be difficult for you to have intercourse." His assessment turned out to be untrue, but I was thereafter convinced I was deformed somehow and even tried to break my own hymen in high school, shoving three fingers up my pussy while I sat on the toilet, violently thrusting until I hurt myself badly. I ended up contracting an acute infection that made urination excruciating. My mother and I had to cancel a weekend trip and instead go to the hospital, where I received antibiotics, a catheter, and some excellent morphine.

I was too humiliated to explain what happened to the attending physicians. I'm sure my mother assumed I'd had sex, but I was still a virgin when I went to college. My high school boyfriend and I discovered all the ways to have fun without full penetration, and I never told him the reason we didn't "go all the way." At that time in America, there was still a lot of shame and negative perception surrounding vaginas. They weren't something you celebrated having, or spent a lot of time musing over. Girls referred to their genitalia as "gross," an orifice better left uninvestigated. I spent years perusing porn sites before I came to appreciate my own lovely seashell. If anything, now I wish it were less ordinary looking and more anatomically bold or quirky. I guess I could bedazzle it.

Nonetheless, even at nine months pregnant I feel very self-conscious fitting my heels into the stirrups on the examination table so that my ob-gyn can check my cervix. Something about seeing her face in rapt concentration above the paper dressing gown spread across my lap, focused directly and solely on my vagina, makes my skin crawl. It's all I can do not to clamp my knees together, sit up, and shove her backward on her little rolling stool. I adore my ob-gyn, but in this context I feel like a farm animal whose organs are the functional property of the state. What I can't articulate is the way my soul resides in my pussy; in my clitoris, to be exact. It's not just biological tissue to me. It's a whole different way of knowing.

I understand that obstetricians see vagina after vagina all day long—and that, as an owner of a vagina herself, my doctor has the ability to differentiate between a person and her parts. Still, I feel like she's peeking into my deepest, most intimate experiences, as if she can see everything and everyone I've ever done with my O'Keeffe iris. My vagina is secretive. It isn't used to presenting itself on command, without coaxing. Women don't publicly spread their legs apart in our culture. I'd love to feel sunlight on my pussy. I think it would be great to get a tan down there, lying on chaise lounge with my knees butterflied, soaking up some vitamin D. But it's not safe to bring out an unprotected honeypot in this Cenozoic era, given the way men accuse us women of "asking for it" every time our hemlines ride a little high. So my vagina luxuriates in darkness like a blind albino cave-salamander that needs constant wetting to keep its skin sleek and pliant. You can't just sneak up on it or you'll startle it into retreating even deeper into its grotto.

But, drilling down (yes!), as uncomfortable as the clinical exposure makes me feel, the real cognitive dissonance sets in when she strikes up a conversation with me while expanding my vaginal canal with her speculum. I'm sure I'd talk with my patients, too, if I were in her shoes, to break the ice, forge a bond, distract from the awkwardness of the situation. What she doesn't realize as she peers into my infinity hole is that I have the distinct sensation that my vagina is looking back at her. Those 8,000 nerve endings in my clitoris are hooked up to some primitive opportunist in my DNA who has survived famine, war, enslavement, childbirth—who has distinct tastes, tactics, and tolerances independent of mine. Normally, my vagina and I work in concert and no one's the wiser, but when she's got it isolated, cordoned off from the rest of me, I don't know what it's liable to do.

Most of the time, my elegant little piece of baby machinery sleeps between my legs unless stirred by something I read or see, or if Prince Charming comes to awaken it from its enchanted slumber. It does not wish to be inspected or measured. I worry that it has no clue what's coming down the pipeline soon, what bulbous protuberance it will presently have to accommodate. But when the time comes, I'm confident it will rally better than I. For now, I've got it stuffed in a bathing suit, submerged under water, bobbing peacefully. I see the lifeguards over by the pace clock eyeing me with equanimity. Pregnant women are a reassuring sight to almost everybody.

Unbeknownst to me, the chlorine I'm breathing right now will give my child asthma in the future. He will suffer major bouts of constricted-airway disease that will see us rushing to the hospital, sometimes in an ambulance, often in the middle of the night, to treat his insufficient lung capacity. If you want to talk about fear, let's talk about watching your son progressively lose the ability to breathe right in front of your eyes. The studies that determine a link between postnatal health problems and pool gasses haven't come out yet, and everyone recommends swimming as one of the best activities for pregnant women to engage in, because it's low impact and won't stress their already loose ligaments. But every generation does something unknowingly terrible to its offspring, and this is my contribution to that fine tradition.

I do the backstroke, following the ceiling panels to make sure I'm moving in a straight line. Once I pass beneath the race flags, I take two more strokes and glide into contact with the pool's edge. I rest with my elbows on the ledge, removing my goggles so I don't walk out of the club with deep indentations around my eyes. Eventually, I wade over to the ladder and get my foot on the bottom rung. Climbing up out of the water is difficult now that my center of gravity has shifted forward. I stop halfway up, as soon as gravity starts to pull on my unaccustomed weight. I feel my wet fingers start to lose their grip on the aluminum poles. I will die of embarrassment if I fall back into the pool. Luckily, a passing lifeguard sees me struggling and grabs me by the wrist, hoisting me up on the pool deck as if I weigh nothing. I feel petite and feminine again for one glorious minute, until I catch a glimpse of my reflection in the locker-room mirror. Best to avoid mirrors from now on, I think.

That night as I lie in bed listening to my husband snore, feeling my baby kick me in the diaphragm, I ask myself again, How is this all worth it? I worry about what's going to happen in the delivery room. I'm frightened.

"It's like wind sprints," Vivienne says, explaining what contractions feel like. "You just have to push through the pain knowing it will be over in a couple of seconds." Viv and I were both on the track team in high school. She's tall and has long legs: a sprinter. I ran cross-country. She has me convinced I can give birth without getting an epidural or taking any pain medication. The baby shouldn't have a bunch of drugs coursing through its system for its first taste of life, she argues. Viv labored for five and a half hours with her first child, and I believe I can white-knuckle my way through anything that lasts only as long as it takes to fly from New York to Los Angeles.

My labor begins the next morning, after my husband goes to work. It's the real thing this time, not one of those false alarms I've been having over the past several weeks. My water breaks, and I know I'm going to the big show, ready or not. I pace back and forth in the kitchen, the cats following me around. They're yowling to be let out, but I can't risk us going to the hospital on short notice and leaving them out in the cold. I call my parents, my doctor, and several friends to tell them I love them, as though we're living in the nineteenth century and I might not make it home. I've opted to take the natural approach, so the nurses tell me to keep track of the intervals between contractions and head to the birthing ward when they're coming five minutes apart. We live fifteen minutes away from Prentice Women's Hospital, which is reassuring.

By the time my husband, Jim, arrives, the cramps are really starting to hurt. I didn't realize my uterus was capable of contracting in all directions at once. My womb seems to be compacted, compressing like a body on a slow descent to the bottom of the ocean, getting crushed incrementally by the increasing water pressure. Jim is lying on the floor next to me, timing my intervals while leafing through the birthing manual for the first time. I'm annoyed, since it's been sitting on his bedside table for months, but pretty soon I too am looking over his shoulder and boning up on the material, because we're that kind of people; we're the type who typically cram for an exam.

It's ten o'clock at night, and I've had enough. I've been in labor for thirteen hours now, and the contractions are roughly six minutes apart. We pack up my overnight bag and cruise on over to the hospital. This is the last time for a long time that I will feel unmitigated joy. It's late December, but I roll down the windows and let the cold air wash over me. It's so much better to go somewhere and do something than to just sit around waiting.

We get checked in to our private room and . . . sit around, waiting. The nurses come in to examine me, then deliver the bad news. After all this time, I'm still only five centimeters dilated when I need to reach ten. How is that possible? I've been in labor for twice as long as Vivienne was, and I'm not even halfway there. What's wrong with my cervix? Is it too narrow, too small? All my insecurities about my vagina come flooding back, and I feel like I'm twelve years old again, in that stupid doctor's office, ashamed of being an anomaly.

My vanity would like to jump in here and say that my vagina is perfectly normal, and that this is a story about what society does to wound a woman's psyche. Okay, no, it's not a story about that. My vanity just wanted to jump in here. Sorry for the interruption; please go on.

The nurse asks me what I want to do. My doctor hasn't even left for the hospital yet. She's aware that I'm in labor, and they're keeping her informed of my progress. They can start me on an oxytocin drip to speed things up. Or, if I still want to try for a natural birth, I can go home and continue laboring. The first word that jumps out at me is "try." The second thing that grabs my attention is the verb "laboring"—as if I'm a workman out in the quarry, swinging a pick-axe in the hot sun; or a prisoner in ankle cuffs and an orange jump-suit, shuffling along the side of the highway, chained to my fellow inmates as we spike trash and stuff it in garbage bags. Neither sounds fun. This is not going to be a piece of cake, I gather.

Everybody is different, the nurses say, and every expectant mother proceeds at her own pace. Jim supports whatever decision feels right to me. Neither of us wants to admit that we didn't read this far in the pregnancy handbook. I hesitate, unsteady.

Then I hear Viv's disembodied voice in the back of my head, cheering me on like she always did at school, challenging me to be the best version of myself. You can do this, she shouts from an imaginary running track. You're almost there! Don't quit!

"I want to try to do it naturally," I say, almost convincingly.

"Okay." The older nurse nods, her face a practiced mixture of neutrality and pragmatism. "Just give us a call when you're ready to come back, or if you have any questions." In retrospect, I should have found it ominous that they were willing to let me go in the first place. They were certainly not worried that I was going to deliver anytime soon.

Back at home, the contractions intensify in strength but not in frequency. I stand in the shower eating spoonful after spoonful of bland oatmeal as the warm water sluices over me, pausing to press my face up to the cool marble every time another cramp debilitates me. This is ridiculous, I think. How is this worth it? Do I really need to be some kind of hippie hero? To forgo modern medical advances to prove a point? Is this all about competing with my friends? What is so wrong with inducing dilation or taking pain medication, any-way? It must be safe, or nobody would use it. Just then, a particu-larly vicious contraction brings me to my knees. I call out to my husband. "Jiiiiiiiiiiiim!"

We're back in our birthing suite at the hospital. I've done an about-face and am now hopping around the room demanding that an anesthesiologist stick an eight-inch-long needle in my spine before one more contraction hits. That's what it's come down to—I don't want to feel anything after this. Nothing. Nada. I want to be knocked out cold, and to wake up like the Virgin Mary with a halo, a suite of lambs at my feet, and a swaddled cherub in my arms. My husband watches all this without being able to do anything to help me. He trusts the doctors, as I do, but his tension has no avenue of release.

Once the drugs hit and I'm pacified, they decide to wait on administering the oxytocin. They want to give me a little more time to dilate on my own. They tell us to rest, to try to get some sleep. It's going to be a long night. Jim settles into a chair, and I'm tucked up in bed, just drifting off, when the door opens and my parents sweep in. They are coming from a black-tie function at the Fortnightly, a club on Bellevue Place a couple of blocks away.

I open my heavy-lidded eyes to the vision of my father in his tuxedo and my mother in a floor-length fur coat—"the Beave," as my brother and I jokingly refer to it when she wafts around the house in it on cold winter days. Underneath, she has on a green taffeta dress with a big black, velvet bow at the waist. She talks and laughs with my husband while my father teases the nurses. He's head of infectious diseases in another department at the hospital, and everybody knows and loves him here. The two of them present a surreal contrast to me in my thin cotton dressing gown, hair disheveled, barely able to put two words together. I feel like the Christmas goose looking out at all the colorful decorations and the happy people around the table, almost but not quite able to forget that they're about to carve it up and serve it.

Almost as quickly as they came in, my parents are gone again in flurry of air kisses and well-wishing, off to the Drake Hotel to spend the night. My doctor is here. She's told them it would still be quite some time before the main event. Watching my ob-gyn roll up her sleeves and feel around in the blood and muck is not really their thing. They're very excited, though, and a lot of people at the hospital are excited for them. "Dr. Phair's having his baby!" "Oh, is it time? That's wonderful!"

I wake up in the morning to see that flowers have arrived. I'm still not dilated, but at least I'm not in any pain. The fetal heart monitor says our baby is strong, and tolerating the mild but sustained contractions well. At this point, it's just a waiting game. I'm twenty-four hours into my labor. We have breakfast. Mom and Dad visit again, this time without their superhero costumes. I hear women in other rooms screaming and swearing as they battle through to the end. Nothing much is happening over here. We're just kind of chilling, doing the crossword. Jim calls out the clues and the rest of us chip in with guesses.

One woman lets out a particularly blood-curdling shriek, and we all pause for a moment to let her anguish pass through and on out of the ward. Is that what's going to happen to me? Is that where this is all leading? I think about the pain I was in yesterday, and my anxiety level shoots through the roof. How is this all worth it? I envy my family. They get to sit around and watch, while I'm the one who has to go through the actual barbarity. When my doctor comes in next, I ask her if it's too late to get a caesarian. I don't really want one; I just need the psychological out. She's seen it all before: the bargaining, the panic, the attempts to control the situation.

She reads the fetal heart monitor and frowns. "I don't love the look of this. The heartbeat is getting a bit faint. I'm going to start the oxytocin. Let's get him out of there."

Now I'm focused like a laser beam on the ticker tape slowly emerging from the EKG. Something finally clicks, and my maternal instincts take over. Up until now I've been somewhat passive, letting the staff do their thing. But now I'm starting active labor, and I am not fucking around. The thought of something bad happening to my child—of this nine-month-long labor of love turning tragic so close to completion—galvanizes me. If I have to reach down there and pull him out by the umbilical cord with my bare hands, I will. I'm his mother, and nothing is going to hurt my child. Even my own body.

Even so, it takes six more hours before we reach complete efface-ment and dilation. People come and go. The day is a blur as they continually tweak the dosage, fine-tuning it, keeping the balance between too much drug and not enough heartbeat. My womb is holding onto this kid, almost as tightly as I will hug him before he goes off to college. At some crucial point, my doctor has had enough. This isn't worth it, she thinks. I'm close to ready, and my child can't wait. The sun is setting on the second day. We are thirty hours into my laboring. Surprise, surprise: The word fits.

What happens next shocks the hell out of all of us. My private room, which has been a simple bed-chairs-and-bathroom affair, suddenly transforms into a full-on operating stage. Doctors, nurses and a resident or two rush in—more people than I can keep track of, an alarming testament to the urgency of the situation. Huge lights and oxygen tanks and other industrial equipment descends from the ceiling. All manner of frightening medieval tools are laid out on cloth-covered trays. My parents are ushered out into the hallway. Only my husband remains, backed into the corner so the profes-sionals have room to maneuver. Stirrups come up out of the foot-board of my bed. This entire metamorphosis takes no more than two minutes, from start to finish.

I'm lost in the center of a storm. I am in the eye: dumbfounded, blinking, watching, as my vagina is the focus of every single person in the room. Not even narcotics have enough power to deaden the force of this blow. I am actually aware of the breezes blowing across my genitalia every time someone moves abruptly or spins around to grab another implement of torture. I, me, Elizabeth, the person I identify as, is helplessly sidelined, playing second fiddle, understudy to my own pussy. There she goes, I think, that brave and heroic *objet d'amour*, ready to give her life for this difficult extraction. You will never be the same, I tell my vagina telepathically, but I will love you forever if you help me right now.

A young man comes in and parks himself on a stool to my right.

He's the person they've all been waiting for. He's the anesthesiologist. This isn't true, obviously, but in my memory I see him dialing knobs and flicking switches on a wall of audio-interface gear: preamps, compressors, DI boxes, all the filters you use in a recording studio. It must be the epidural cocktail making me hallucinate, or just the fact that I'm so scared, and I have to imagine a familiar setting to reassure myself. He's talkative and good-looking, the rock star of this extravaganza, and he knows it. I can tell he has the run of the hospital, is in universal demand.

I'm torn between keeping up with his comments about my career and his love of music and looking down at what the rest of the team is doing between my legs. For a while, at least, the doctors and nurses need me to pay attention to them.

"Okay, now pushhhhhh." I push. You better believe I push. But as soon as I feel that sharp twinge of pain, I back off, remembering that horrible wailing from the women in the other rooms. I'm worried about how thin the membrane is between my vagina and my anus. I'm afraid.

"Dan, can you give her a topper?" My doctor for the win, ever alert to the micro-fluctuations of my emotion.

The anesthesiologist twists the narco-drip dial, bumping up my buzz a smidge. It is a game changer. A flood of serotonin warms my body, and I feel all warm and fuzzy. I push when they tell me to push.

"Okay, I can see his head. Here he comes." Nick, my son, is crowning.

They wait for another wave of contractions, not bothering to ask me when they're coming, but instead, following a seismograph print out.

"Okay, push, Liz."

I push, but not hard enough.

"That's good, but this time, really bear down!"

I sit up straight and make that eeeeeeeeee sound through clenched teeth. Lying on my back with my legs up doesn't seem like the correct or logical position for getting a bowling ball out of your puss, but I don't say anything. Our ancestors certainly didn't deliver their babies this way, and it makes no use of gravity, but this is how it's done these days, apparently.

"One more, Liz. You're doing great."

"Eeeeeeeeeeeeeaaaaaowwww, ooh that hurts! Unhhhh, I don't want to feel that!"

I look over at my buddy with the drugs. "Can I get just a tiny bit more, please?"

"Sure!" He adjusts one setting and cranks the party up to eleven. I don't know how to tell you this, dear reader, but I am now high as fuck. Too high. Wasted.

"I saw you play at the Vic," Dan the Man tells me. "That was a great show! You rock."

"Ok, Liz, we're almost there, give me a big push."

"Unnngggggghhhhhhhhhhhhhh."

"That's good, that's good. Keep pushing. Here comes his head."

"What was that guitar? Was it a Fender? You play a Fender, right?"

I can't believe I'm having this conversation right now. It's surreal. My main problem isn't Dan, though. I feel like I have to hide how high I am from the doctors and the nurses. I start coaching myself. Don't let your head tip over. Keep it together, Liz. Get a grip. Just act natural. I feel like I'm back in high school and I've come home from a party to find that my parents are still up.

"His head is out! Okay, he's inverted. Okay. We're going to need the forceps. Right now. Come on, Anna. *Now!*"

"I brought my *Exile in Guyville* CD. After this is over, would you mind signing it? I could leave it at the nurses' station."

I look over at Jim. My husband has a priceless expression on his face, somewhere between awe and pure animal panic.

"His shoulder is caught. Right there. No, wait until I say." My doctor and another ob-gyn each have hold of one arm of the forceps, and they are leaning back, using their weight to pull my son the rest of the way out. I find out later that they were afraid he had the cord wrapped around his neck. I feel a *whooshing* sensation, and I know he's out. It's over. I hear a sharp cry, and I know he's alive. I pass out.

I come to again, briefly, and have just enough time to see them suctioning his mouth and nose on a warming table, pricking his skin and testing his reflexes, prying apart his eyelids to administer eye drops, and wiping him down with wet cloths. This must be the source of all alien abduction fantasies, I think—some dimly repressed memory of this callous entry into the world. They lay him on my chest for a moment, but I lose consciousness again. I am too weak to tell them that I am dangerously close to death. I have completed thirty-two hours of labor.

The next time I wake up, the room is back to normal, and my mother is holding my newborn, tightly swaddled, in her arms. It's the sweetest and most loving tableau. My eyes are so filmy that the light behind her head makes it look like she has a halo. The two of them are gazing at each other, and I feel the enormous relief of knowing that if I'm gone, he will be loved. He will be adored. I pass out again.

When I wake up for real, it is nighttime. Everyone has gone home—even Jim, who needs sleep after our marathon ordeal. I am totally alone. I have instructed the nurses to bring me my child if he wakes up and cries, and in about five minutes, a lady softly enters my room and places my baby in my arms. She strokes his head and suggests I try breastfeeding. She tiptoes back out again, quietly closing the door, leaving us to get to know each other. All I can see of him under his little blue hat and his little striped blanket is his face. He opens his eyes and stares up at me, perfectly calm. The room is very dim. A soft orange glow from the streetlight outside pours in through the windows.

"Hello there. Hi, baby," I coo at him. He looks up at me with an expression of pure adoration. I feel like I've known him forever, like we've been together throughout time. I am flooded with the greatest, most profound love I could ever imagine. I finally understand that there are true miracles, and we are experiencing one. I feel complete. I feel whole. My God. It is worth every bit of it and then some.

Two days later, we go home to our town house on Geneva Terrace in Lincoln Park. I've had a wonderful time bonding with my child at the hospital, and I am nervous about leaving behind the comforting wisdom and instruction of the nurses. But I'm also eager to recuperate in the privacy of our own rooms. My mother comes over to help us adjust to the new routine. I trust in her guidance. She's a wizard with children, and when it comes to anything I'm uncertain about in life, she always knows what to do. But since she was never pregnant, she can't give advice about nursing. Nick has been snacking on breast milk, back and forth between the two nipples, and my boobs are huge, gargantuan. While I go upstairs to change clothes, she stays on the couch, singing softly to him as she rocks him gently in her arms.

I stand in my dressing room, staring at my naked body. It's been ravaged by pregnancy: a road map of stretch marks and veins, a sullen little pooch where the baby bump was. I'm the kind of person who notices every microfluctuation in my figure. All I want is to have some control back, to feel like I am the master of my own ship so I can focus on caring for my newborn son. Yet on top of everything, I also have to contend with this stranger I see in the reflection. It's going to take a lot of work to put myself back together again. My tits are the size of cantaloupes. All of a sudden, milk shoots straight out of both nipples, like bullets out of the fembots in an Austin Powers movie, spraying all over the mirror. I clasp my hands over my chest, trying to staunch the flow, but it squirts out between my fingers. I am horrified, and I have absolutely no idea what to do. Tears springs to my eyes. I cry out for the one person I depend on above all others. "Mooooooooooooooooooommmmmmm-mmmmmmmmmmmmmmmmmm!!!!"

ART TK

eleven

SHANGHAI STREET FIGHT

wake up on the airplane to severe turbulence. The fuselage is bouncing so much that I become weightless for a few seconds before the aircraft slams down again and we rattle forward on the atmospheric white water. I can feel the pilots searching for a smoother ride—slowing down, then gunning the engines to climb above it. They haven't made an announcement, so I assume that either these conditions are unavoidable or they're acting out of consideration for the sleeping passengers. I close my eyes and do my best to ignore the vigorous shaking. I am incredibly lucky to have this opportunity to perform in Shanghai. The travel group that hired me is providing me with a tour guide and driver for several days of sightseeing, and those perks outweigh any distress I may feel on the flight.

I'm no stranger to air travel. My parents took us everywhere, and I practically live in airports because of my work. Still, I hate flying over large bodies of water at night. My imagination runs wild. I have visions of the aircraft plummeting thousands of feet through the air and crashing into the sea. I'd rather be dead somewhere they could conceivably find my remains. Scratch that; I'd rather be alive. If I have to go down, please let it be in the jungle, or somewhere I have a chance of surviving. Every time the plane pitches and rolls, I feel my adrenaline spike. I sit up in the reclining bed, wriggling out from beneath the seat belt I've fastened tightly around the blankets. I lift the window shade and cautiously peer out into the darkness.

There's nothing to see. The space beyond the windowpane has no dimension, no depth. I could easily believe we're on a movie set and I'm looking at a black drop curtain. I squint, pressing my face as close to the window as I dare without touching the surface. I think I spot something glowing in the distance; the orange lights of a city, perhaps; but when I check our position on the flight tracker, it says we're way out in the middle of the Pacific Ocean. As we get closer, I see that the orange glow is something burning in the water far below us. It's too big to be an ocean vessel. I look around to see if any of the other passengers have noticed the phenomenon, but they are all lying in their cubicles, quietly resting. Something is on fire out there in the night, something hot and bright beneath us.

"Excuse me." I stop the flight attendant on his way back to the galley. "I see something in the ocean that looks like it's burning."

"We're over the Aleutian Islands," he tells me. "Part of the ring of fire. You probably saw a volcano."

I turn back to the window, trying to get another look at the lava, but we've already flown past it. I want to circle back and pass lower over the crater, gaze down into the caldera. When, if not now, will I ever get to witness such a thing? How incredible our lives would appear to someone living in an ancient civilization. They would never understand why we stare at these tiny glowing screens in front of our faces while traveling on an aircraft capable of bringing us to within spitting distance of the most miraculous sights on the planet. We sit there in a bad humor, angry that we're not going to make it to our destination on time, while simultaneously experiencing one of the greatest achievements of mankind. We don't even think about it. We're lost in our own minds.

It's hard to step outside of your frame of reference. That's partly why I accepted this trip to China. I wanted to go as far away from the United States as possible. I'm in a rut, unable to see beyond my own expectations. I need to gain a new perspective, to feel like the world is unknown and surprising again. My mood suffers when I get too comfortable, too familiar with my own opinions. I can't see how my limited perspective blinds me. Even now I'm having difficulty toggling between two incongruous truths: In one sense, I'm looking down an aisle that's two and a half feet wide and sixty feet long, but in another, I'm actually suspended in the middle of the sky, high above the deepest water in the ocean.

It's so much easier to live in denial. We've flung ourselves a seventh of the way to outer space, a feat no Iron Age hero or Mayan queen could have imagined, and half of us up here are grumbling about having to pay for Wi-Fi while the other half are munching on potato chips, laughing our asses off at the latest episode of *It's Always Sunny In Philadelphia*. How is it that we can function on multiple levels of reality simultaneously? I can already tell I'm not keeping up with technology. People are living in dimensions that I'm unaware of. If I don't stay open to nuance and complexity, I'm going to miss out on what's really happening. I'm going to make bad decisions. I'm going to fail.

The cabin quivers and convulses, as if the bumpy air is trying to shake the nuts and bolts loose. I trust that the plane will hold together, but the atmosphere is doing its best to test our stability. It's poetic that I'm halfway to China experiencing turbulence right now. I'm halfway through my life as well, and emotionally, it's gotten pretty rocky lately. I've lived long enough to feel like the past is present and weighty, but the future grabs my attention, and I'm attracted to all its possibilities. It's hard to maintain my balance, or even know what balance ought to look like at this stage. I need a new philosophy. No more of that Judeo-Christian sprawl. I need something lightweight. I need something I can fit in a backpack and take with me.

Nǐ hǎo! I've arrived in Shanghai! I can't believe I made it to the other side of the world. Even the name of the city sounds like a greeting. Driving in from the airport, I ask my chauffeur to teach me some useful Mandarin phrases. I googled a few important words before I left the States, and I try out my pronunciation now, much to his amusement. That's how we pass the time en route to the hotel: as instructor and pupil, with him preparing me for a week of new and unusual experiences. There are so many questions I want to ask, but he thinks it's more important that I master the Chinese expression of gratitude: *xièxiè*. No matter how many times I say it, something about my sibilance is still unsatisfactory to him. I haven't located the middle point between a hard "s" and a soft "sh," and I can't stick the landing. He repeats it, his tone growing increasingly urgent. Soon we're shouting, "Thank you!" "Thank you!" "Thank you!" back and forth to each other in Chinese.

We pass a band of enormous apartment blocks that stand like battlements guarding the jewel of a city within. I fall silent for a moment, awed by their resemblance in size and scale to structures on the Death Star in *Star Wars*. They look like holdovers from the Cold War era, utilitarian housing whose sole aim is to pack as many human beings inside the walls as possible. To me they appear austere and frightening, but my driver shrugs and says that a lot of people are happy to live there. The volume of people who come to work and raise families inside the footprint of Shanghai with its booming economy is staggering. It makes most American cities look like sparsely populated backwaters in comparison.

As we approach downtown, the ultramodern spires of new construction rise up out of the heart of the Huangpu river. Their vibrant rainbow-colored LED displays evoke a fairy-tale realm, fantastical and futuristic. The delicacy of the soaring architecture is as delightful as the other buildings were intimidating. My driver says the pace of development is so intense that contractors routinely erect entire skyscrapers in under a year, using round-the-clock shifts of laborers and a scaffold machine called a "wall-climbing monster." Many people lose their lives on the projects, because they have to work so swiftly. The government suppresses those statistics, he says. It is the price the Chinese have to pay, he tells me, for success in the global marketplace.

None of this squares with the China I expected to encounter: a place of spiritual practices and philosophical principles. I had in mind when I arrived a stereotype that is quickly dissolving as I realize how outdated and uninformed my views about Asian culture are. In my hometown suburb just north of Chicago, you hear the refrain at every dinner party: "China's going to take over everything." There are a lot of businesspeople where I grew up who feel threatened by China's expanding market power. I don't know anything about economics, but I'm a passionate student of the soul. I was hoping to be influenced by a different set of values, to see how people incorporate the Taoist ethos of *wu wei:* living in naturalness, simplicity, and spontaneity. Now I'm worried that I'm merely naïve. We pull up to a stoplight that looks exactly like what you'd find at any intersection in Los Angeles or Chicago, and I mourn the homogenization of urban life everywhere.

I'm just about to ask my driver where I can go to experience something uniquely Asian, when I catch my breath at the sight of a ghost. There he is, amidst all this modernity: an old street sweeper patiently cleaning the road beneath the bridge with a broom made of twigs. He's wearing communist-style work clothes, a pair of cropped navy-blue trousers and a matching smock. What he's doing out here in the middle of the night I can't imagine. It's not like he's going to make a dent in a contemporary city's detritus. He must do it because he likes to. He looks bent and careworn but peaceful in his industrious activity. His slow, even strokes remind me of the rhythm I used to get into when I raked leaves in the fall as a teen.

Of all the chores my brother and I had to do, raking leaves was the one I learned the most from. Clearing the lawn of dead foliage and separating it into large piles in the street on a Saturday was one of my first experiences of mindfulness. I was determined to do a thorough job, but after an hour of struggling to rid the grass of every single leaf my hands were covered in blisters, and it didn't seem like I'd made very much progress. Every time I'd turn my back on a patch I'd recently completed, the trees would drop more leaves for me to collect. It felt like an impossible task.

There is nothing that saps your strength like a challenge you believe you can't win. An uphill battle may be exhilarating at first, but as your prospects diminish, the prize no closer than before, hopelessness replaces enthusiasm, and you give up—like folding a losing poker hand. It's even harder to handle that feeling when you're forced to press on against insurmountable odds. Athletes often talk about falling back on technique, and it's true that, if you can control your own movements, you can relax and let the larger issues sort themselves. It turns that out the only war you need to win is the struggle within yourself.

But I didn't know that as a teenager. Despondent, hating to do a less than perfect job, I would aimlessly swipe at the leaves—bummed that I wasn't hanging out with my friends, angry at my parents for not paying for a landscaper, and resentful of any activity I couldn't turn into art. What was the point? More leaves were just going to fall, and I would probably have to spend the next three Saturdays out in the front yard toiling like a laborer for three dollars an hour. My brother didn't care how thorough he was. He worked his way back and forth systematically, until he could say he'd covered his half of the lawn. I would linger, knowing I would go over his parts after he left, trying to make something beautiful out of the ordinary. He saw his duty as a box to be ticked on a checklist. I was trying to effect transformation.

Just when I'd begun to make headway in the east arm of the lawn, next to Cedar Street, the wind kicked up and scattered my subpiles all over the grass again. Now I was really pissed. I redoubled my efforts, throwing my full weight into it, raking like a maniac to stay ahead of the incoming weather. Sweating, my deltoids seizing up, I persisted—unable to accept that I would never prevail against Mother Nature. I believed with all my heart that if I just moved fast enough, I would accomplish my goal. What I didn't anticipate was the wind dislodging the rest of the undecided, up in the treetops. They came down, ruining my whole afternoon's work in five minutes. I was devastated. I had no strength left, and no hope of making a difference anymore. I wasn't in it for the money. I didn't give a shit about learning the value of hard work. I saw the grass as a green canvas that needed restoration, and I thought I could turn autumn back into summer again for a few more weeks of carefree fun.

I'm not sure why I kept raking after that, but I did, this time only thinking about the space immediately around me, harboring no big ambition, aiming to cross no finish line. I would draw the rake toward me in smooth, light whisks, without stopping each time to see if I'd gathered every single yellow-and-brown leaf. I just moved my limbs deliberately, letting the motion itself be the goal. Each fluid stroke was an accomplishment. Without realizing it, I'd become proficient in this skill I'd been practicing over the course of five hours, and my mastery gave me joy. The elegance of my gestures was thrilling to me. I know this sounds crazy, but when I did it right, I felt hot and beautiful, like raking was something a guy riding by on a bike would stop to admire me for, like, Oh man, you really know how to work that handle!

It was meditative, and that's exactly what I see in this elderly gentleman's movements: an acceptance of a never-ending task that can only be tackled with quietness of heart and attention to the present moment. Breathe, stroke, breathe, stroke, thoughts elsewhere. As I sit back in the rear seat of my town car waiting for the light to turn green, I can't help but feel like I've seen something fundamental to my understanding of Chinese culture, some symbolic embodiment of its ethos.

The hotel is very modern. The toilets—my God, they have toi-

lets in Shanghai that can do absolutely everything. They're full service: a spray, a wash, a blow-dry. When I get to my room, I spend
fifteen minutes pressing all the buttons on the commode, learning
what rhythmic patterns and levels of intensity are optimal for me. I
go to third base with a machine. It's so Asian, so *hentai*. It's my first
experience with robot sex, and it's amazing. I am living in the
future—not just across the international dateline but at the cutting
edge of tomorrow's standards of hygiene.

So much is turning out to be different from what I'd expected.
I've brought modest clothing, based on the recommendation of the
guidebooks, but the women who work in the hotel bar are sleek,
fashionable goddesses. The Insta girls of New York and L.A. can't
compare with a Shanghai model's polish and hauteur. I'm starting to
realize that this city is all about opulence and money. Everything is
westernized. I meet one of the women in our delegation for a drink,
and she tells me that most of the cultural sites I plan to visit are tourist traps designed to bilk foreigners out of their cash by running
them through all of the gift shops. Maybe I'm looking for the wrong
China, she suggests. Maybe I should embrace the modern side.

When I wake up in the morning, I feel like canceling my appointment with the tour guide. I want to spend the day shopping for new
clothes and getting beauty treatments at the spa. I want to exude
sophistication, like those young women on the mezzanine level last
night. I wish I weighed fifteen pounds less than I do. Maybe I'll
work out at the gym later. I spend half an hour trying to combine
the clothes I brought into a passable outfit for this cosmopolitan
neighborhood. I decide it would be rude not to show up for the
prearranged sightseeing, but I will simply say I'd like to finish early.
I'm a performer, and I have to take care of myself. I can breeze
through this one activity, then tell my tour guide I'm jet-lagged.

An hour later, I'm inside a Confucian temple, hiding from an
angry mob. Everyone is shouting and arguing, but I don't speak a
word of Chinese, so I have no idea what they're saying about me. All
I know is that I started this street fight, and it sounds like they're

going to finish it. Or finish me. I glance nervously at the temple gate, wondering if at any moment a horde of furious people is going to come pouring through those doors and take me hostage, dragging me back out into the road. What happens next is anybody's guess. A beating? Public humiliation? I don't know what street justice looks like in Shanghai, but from the readiness of everyone in the neighborhood to join in the melee, I know this theater piece is leading to a climax. My tour guide sees my agitation and touches my forearm lightly.

"Don't worry. It's fine."

How is it fine? She can't believe that. Doesn't she hear the bloodthirsty crowd growing louder by the minute? Where are the police? Why hasn't anybody called the authorities? I can't believe this is happening on my first day in Shanghai. I was so excited to travel, and now I'm going to die here, ripped apart limb from limb, or carried aloft on the shoulders of outraged citizens to be shamed in a public square as a symbol of Western entitlement and carelessness.

It all happened so quickly. We had just pulled up outside the temple entrance. I was listening from the back seat as my tour guide described the significance of the site we were about to visit. I reached over to open the door, an action I've undertaken a thousand times before without incident. I didn't hear any cars so I thought it was safe, but I didn't take into account the scooter traffic in Asia. My door clipped a woman on a moped, sending her tumbling onto the pavement and breaking her side-view mirror. I jumped out to help her, but she was already on her feet, shouting at me and pointing angrily at her damaged vehicle.

I repeatedly expressed how sorry I was, pressing my palms together in the symbol of prayer. She wasn't interested in my contrition. Everyone around us stopped what they were doing and rushed over to referee the disagreement. They'd seen what happened. They were there to support her version of events. Hearing the commotion, people in the shops and apartments flooded out into the street to add their voices to the chorus. Everyone pushed in, forming a tight circle around me, their voices raised in indignation.

Soon, I was standing in the middle of a whirlwind of animosity with no way to explain myself, and no idea how to mollify the outraged residents. I folded my hands to my chest, nodding my head, and pointed at the moped. "I'm so sorry," I said to the crowd around me. "It is my fault. I did this." I was deeply apologetic, but I knew our priority should be to establish the woman's physical condition.

Nobody seemed to care about that—least of all her. She let fly a long stream of animated accusations. Did she think I would somehow try to deny what had happened, that I would attempt to pin the blame on her? Her impressive and throaty delivery made the crowd laugh, and I broke out in a cold sweat, realizing that she was well known and popular.

I was bound to lose a case to this well-spoken woman, who seemed to captivate her audience. I wanted to say, I'm one of the good guys! It was an accident! But they couldn't understand me. They wouldn't even look me in the eye. I spun to the left and to the right searching for an ally but was met only with indifference. Reparations, their hardened expressions seemed to say, must be made. I felt like I was having an out-of-body experience. I saw my life tanking completely. My name would be splashed across the headlines back home and my mug shot broadcast on TMZ. If convicted, I might not be able to travel internationally anymore.

My chauffeur leapt out of the car to defend me. He was tall and impressive, not someone to be trifled with. The woman pointed back and forth between me and her scooter, yelling something with great pathos and righteous indignation. Whatever she said raised another sympathetic cry from the onlookers. No one was paying attention to me; they were speaking directly to my chauffeur, who fired off several angry sentences and then gestured hastily for my tour guide to take me inside the temple walls. She grabbed my arm and pulled me across the street, and now we are temporarily safe— separated from the crowd by the heavy doors.

I can still hear what's going on. I'm surprised no one tried to stop us from leaving. No one seems to think that my presence is of any importance in the discussion, and it freaks me out. I can't understand what they're negotiating if not my involvement. As long as they have our car surrounded, they might think I can't get away, but I could run out the back of the temple and climb over the wall and hide out at my hotel, or even fly back to the United States. There seems to be no expectation, though, that I would do anything as cowardly or shameful as that. In China, it goes without saying, you pay for your mistakes.

I'm punishing myself inwardly, morbid thoughts racing through my head. Why did I fuck up like this and get everybody in trouble? We had such a good time yesterday. My chauffeur was so nice to me. Now he's out there haggling for my life. I'm worried about him. I feel responsible. He's all alone, squaring off against twenty or thirty people. There's no way I can sit here and listen while he tries to shout down the rabble. If anyone should suffer the consequences, it should be me.

My tour guide has been talking throughout all of this. I interrupt her to let her know I'm going back out to the street, but she shakes her head and politely steers my attention back to the serpentine river rock rising up out of the shallow reflecting pond. Confucius, she says, told people to emulate the natural harmony they found in their environment, the way a river rock bends and twists to accommodate the flow of water, allowing erosion to carve holes in its body so the pounding current can pass through easily. I feel like she's speaking in metaphors, that she wants me to allow this chaos to flow around me, to accept the anger of the townsfolk and let it pass through me. I try, I really do, but it's hard to ignore the growing cacophony.

The argument goes on and on. They aren't giving up. I've identified the gift shop as the best place to make my last stand. It looks like it's the most heavily fortified location in the compound. Naturally, because it has all the movable merchandise. If you ran off with a Confucian sculpture or a famous lithograph, you'd have a hard time selling it anywhere but on the black market. On the other hand, you could easily peddle the generic jade jewelry in the display cases and all the jade trinkets lining the shelves to tourists from here to the Great Wall of China. No one would ever suspect their origin. The shop has sliding steel gates and automatic locks, so I'm thinking I go there, roll the barrier down, and scream bloody murder until someone comes to rescue. It just might work.

My tour guide is showing me around the main reception area. I can't concentrate on what she's saying. My eyes keep drifting over to the front entrance, anticipating a breech in the barricade. "It's fine," she says, smiling and waving her hand in front of her face. "Don't worry!"

Easy for her to say. They're not after her. I never got the chance to find out if the lady I hit was really okay. I size up potential champions among the tourists wandering around the courtyard and don't see anyone of the requisite size or strength. I'm on my own here. There is no one to protect me from the wrath of the vigilantes.

What's happening doesn't make any sense. Maybe my interpreter is indeed waiting for the police. Maybe her complacency stems from her certainty that the authorities will be here at any moment to arrest me, and she wants to keep me calm until they arrive and take me into custody. I did commit the crime, after all, and she is a witness. Maybe she's smiling because she secretly hates Americans, and she's happy to see me get what I deserve.

If I go to jail, who do I call? Do I ring up my parents? The American embassy? My hosts for the trip? My entertainment attorney lives in New York, and it's the middle of the night there. This is going to cost me a fortune to fight in court. Isn't China supposed to have a notoriously corrupt judicial system? I could wind up doing time in a Chinese prison alongside drug addicts and prostitutes. I might get lice, or get sick. I may not be able to communicate with anyone for months, or even years. I see myself in the witness box, begging an unsympathetic judge for mercy. I wish I'd never come to Shanghai, never been seduced by the first-class ticket and premium accommodations. What seemed like the chance of a lifetime is turning into a nightmare.

"These are the certificates of the scholars who have recently passed their exams," my tour guide says, showing me a noticeboard plastered in overlapping leaflets. She points to a tree whose lower branches are covered in fluttering papers, hanging from short red ribbons. "These are the prayers of the students who will be taking their tests soon." I am struck by the innocent optimism of affixing a carefully worded wish to a tree. It reminds me of the magic rituals I used to perform as a child, when I still believed in supernatural things.

When I was young, we lived in an idyllic neighborhood in Cincinnati, Ohio. Our street was one half of a horseshoe cul-de-sac bordered by hills and woods. My backyard descended a seventy-five-foot slope through three terrace gardens—each progressively less well tended. I used to play with my best friend, Scott Carroll, at the bottom of the ravine between our two houses. We liked to pretend we were homesteaders making household items out of the soft gray clay deposits on either side of the streambed. One day, Scott was too sick to come out and see me, so I went down to our building site by myself and worked on a set of drinking cups, using the coil method they taught us in our kindergarten class.

I was so intent on what I was doing that I didn't notice the approach of a gang of kids from the rougher neighborhood at the foot of Vine Street. They must have seen our handiwork and been curious about who was making these objects. I didn't know anyone else visited these woods. I thought we were playing on private property, like at my grandparents' house. The boys and girls ranged in age from six to eleven, all bigger than me. They tramped right through our secret spot, staring down at me with sneering contempt. The boys in the back started stomping on all our creations, breaking and flattening everything we'd worked on.

"What's that?" One of the older girls pointed at the irregularly shaped vessel in my hand.

"It's a cup," I answered, extending my shaking arm so she could see.

She picked up my carefully constructed bowl of wet clay and examined it, turning it over before squishing it between her fingers and smacking it onto my forehead, where it stuck for a few seconds before falling off and rolling into the ivy. They all burst out laughing, and I turned and ran up the embankment, feeling them pelt me in the back with my own tea set as I scrambled over rocks and through underbrush to make it to my house at the top of the ridge. I didn't cry. I wanted to, but I didn't. I never told anyone what happened down in the ravine, because some measure of their mockery felt deserved. I hadn't thought that what Scott and I were doing was stupid until I saw it through their eyes.

My tour guide informs me that we have to wait before we go any deeper into the temple grounds She says my driver will explain what is going to happen next, but I can't take the suspense. I beg her to give me some idea of what to expect when he returns. She says she doesn't know, but she thinks I will have to pay a fine of some kind. I steel myself. That is going to be difficult, because I don't have very much money, but I can ask my parents to loan me at least a thousand dollars. Maybe the record company will chip in a few thousand more and deduct it from my next advance. I'm not earning anything for my performance here—it's just an all-expenses-paid holiday—so my hosts won't be able to give me anything.

I can hear the murmur of the crowd rising to a crescendo again. I feel sick to my stomach.

"How much longer will this take?" I ask.

My interpreter shrugs, slightly embarrassed. "Pay no attention."

She's completely serious. She really expects me to tune it out. As far as she's concerned, we're having a perfectly lovely day of sightseeing. We stand silently in the courtyard for a few minutes, at a stalemate. I'm incapable of pretending any longer that this isn't stressful. We've been in here listening to the ruckus for twenty minutes, but it feels like it's been ten hours. With each passing second, I worry, the price of my freedom is increasing. I'm also afraid that they think all Americans are rich. If I can't pay the fine, if the amount is too high, what then? Is that when they call law enforcement? Is this another way to shake down tourists, to take cash in exchange for keeping transgressions out of court? Or is this really how they settle disputes in their communities—maybe because they don't trust their own legal system? Both possibilities frighten me.

My interpreter sees me struggling. "It's a beautiful day," she says hopefully. "I think you will never forget us." She smiles. It's her first joke. Amen, I think ruefully. We stand in the silence a while longer, and I come to some sort of exhausted acceptance of my fate. If this ruins me financially, so be it. She's right. The sky is clear, the birds are singing. What's done is done, and I have to make amends. Anyhow, there's a cap on how much I can pay. You can't squeeze blood from a stone.

Finally, after nearly half an hour, my chauffeur slides through the temple gate and strides over to us, the expression on his face impossible to interpret. I thought I was cool with everything, but I'm suddenly trembling again. Get a grip, Liz. It's only money. Hopefully, it's under ten grand. I can scrape together that much. If it's twenty thousand or more, maybe I can book some shows while I'm here and pay some of it back that way. That wouldn't be the end of the world.

He and my tour guide exchange a few words in Chinese. He's sweating. He looks relieved after his arduous diplomatic mission. He's a lot younger than I realized, now that I see him out of character; somewhere in his late thirties.

"It will cost fifty-four twenty," my tour guide informs me.

"Fifty-four dollars?!" I'm speechless. You could knock me over with a feather.

"No!" She and my chauffeur laugh like that's a ludicrous suggestion. "Fifty-four yuan. If you would please give Li Qiang seven dollars and ninety-eight cents"—she gestures for me to hand the money to my driver—"he will pay the woman on the motorbike now."

Seven dollars and ninety-eight cents! I open up my wallet and pull out twice that amount in order to offer Li Qiang a tip. He seems embarrassed and refuses to take any more than the exact sum he negotiated. I'm still trying to process what all this means. How could they go to that much trouble over the price of a fancy cup of coffee back in the United States? I'm certain that in New York this altercation would have resulted in a lawsuit. I suddenly feel very protective of any foreign visitors to our shores. How can they possibly cope with our litigious capitalist mentality? Clearly, money is not the priority here. No, this was a fight about honor. The victim's honor, mine, and my driver's—and more broadly, the community's sense of right and wrong. This was about restoring balance.

We spend the rest of the afternoon strolling through the gardens. My tour guide promotes the local artisans who display their wares in the tea shop, and I spend as much money there as I can. I understand now that it's not about funneling me through a tourist trap so much supporting somebody's gig here in Shanghai. The dried-up flower they drop into my teacup unfurls into a beautiful blossom. I want to learn everything. I feel so blessed just to be outdoors on a sunny day, here on the other side of the world, alive in the time of easy travel. The golden sun blazing in the sky far above us hits the red-tiled rooftops, but down here in the galleria it's cool and shady. In a way, I guess, living with complexity is as simple as finding the proper altitude. If you don't change where you're flying, you'll never reach the smoother air.

ART TK

twelve

THE DEVIL'S MISTRESS

"I know it feels good, Kelly," I say into the phone. "Like, really good." I dump a box of spaghetti into a pot of boiling water. "But, trust me, it's heroin. It will destroy your life."

I'm not talking about drugs. I'm trying to stop my friend from cheating on her husband. She's having strong feelings for her son's twenty-five-year-old karate instructor, and she's trying to convince me she's found her soul mate.

"I hear you, but this is different." She struggles to characterize it. "I feel like myself for the first time in ages. Like a part of me has been dead inside, and he makes me feel alive again. I think this could actually be good for my marriage. Brian and I had sex the other night, and we really connected, you know? Like, more authentically than we have in a really long time. Being with Mateo makes me able to be more present with my husband."

"Except Brian doesn't know," I point out. "It's not like you have an open marriage and he gets to sleep with other women. You're making the choice for him."

"Hmmmmm." It sounds like she's shutting down emotionally. I think she might be offended. She didn't call to hear a lecture. She called because she knows I had an affair at the end of my marriage, and she wants to talk to somebody who "gets it." Nothing I say will make a difference anyway. She's had her first intoxicating hit of infidelity and she can't believe how intense it is.

"Kelly, you've got two kids and no way to support yourself." I cradle the phone receiver against my shoulder, trying to be there for my friend while also fixing dinner. "I'm not saying you have to stay with Brian, but you need to be honest with him. Tell him what you're feeling. Even if he gets mad, you'll have a chance to work things out in the future. If you go behind his back, there's no way to repair it. And, believe me, it's hard to be a single mother. You don't want to end up like me. Promise me you won't do it."

She reluctantly agrees, but I can tell she's lying. When she describes sneaking out of the house at all hours to call this guy and how she feels a rush of adrenaline every time she hears his voice, I know her soul mate theory doesn't hold water. Those are the actions of an addict. I need to get off the telephone. She's reminding me of my own mind-set when I was willing to jeopardize everything and lie to the people I loved just to get another hit of that mind-blowing buzz.

We hang up, and I walk upstairs and to tell my son it's time to eat. He's lying on his stomach pushing his Lego spaceships across the living room floor. I pause in the hallway, listening to him make softly spluttering rocket engine noises. I look up at the wooden milagro cross affixed to archway above our heads. I'd almost forgotten it was there. My eyes drift over to the small silver cross I hung above the mantelpiece. The tightness in my chest eases. We're protected.

It's just the two of us here in this quiet house by the sea. I don't entertain much anymore. The families we know all want to spend their Saturdays at bigger homes, with pools and backyards. They used to stop by in the beginning, to encourage me to find another husband and rejoin their ranks, but I never found the right fit. Or I didn't think I deserved it. I sit down at the dining table next to Nick and watch as he twirls too much spaghetti on his fork. My son, for his part, didn't deserve any of this.

The demon is scuttling back and forth, manifestly ravenous. It wants to kill me, but it's being restrained by another entity in the room. I can't see this second presence, but I can sense its powerful energy. It's hovering somewhere outside my peripheral vision, alert to any movement. I'm lying immobile in the bed, deep in a REM state. I watch as the demon races up and down the windowsill, waiting for the opportunity to tear me to shreds. I'm experiencing sleep paralysis, a common brain disorder that produces hallucinations during the transition between sleep and wakefulness. I struggle against the lethargy engulfing my limbs. I want to sit up, but I can't move. I can't breathe. Something heavy is pressing down on my chest. Where is my husband? Why doesn't anybody help me? Can't they see I'm trapped here? I feel as though I've come to in the middle of surgery and the doctors haven't noticed it yet.

I can read the thoughts of my tormentors. The shrouded figure is only defending me from the demon because it wants to torture me in worse ways later, extracting prolonged agony, causing drawn-out ill health. I'm terrified by its fixation on me. The demon is merely an opportunist. The evil entity lives here. They see me as a resource to be consumed, a carcass ripening on the savannah, and themselves as the keen-eyed predators, circling.

The Lord's Prayer is on the tip of my tongue, but when I try to recite the words, I lose my breath in the superheated atmosphere. This is a purgatory of my own making, a trap I set for myself. Why didn't I go to church more? I'm responsible for this hell-spawn coming. They're here because of actions I have taken that cannot be undone.

Will they do this to my baby next? I arch my back and cry out silently at the thought—sharp as a knife, piercing my breast. Will they travel down the hall after I'm dead and torture and terrify him, too? My regret is as deep as the ocean.

I sob in my sleep, my chest heaving. What kind of life have I led? Was I selfish? Did I help the people who needed me? Did I ignore the pain I caused others? It's too late to adjust my balance sheet. I am truly sorry for being hardened to God, for rejecting his love.

The demon moves in quickly, swooping down for a side strike. As it lunges, I see its shape as a fluttering ball of negative space, the outline of a creature that exists in another dimension. The unseen entity deflects the assault. It studies my limbs with malevolent intent, twitching impatiently. I can feel its claws extending and retracting—can imagine its razor-sharp teeth puncturing my skin, its rough tongue lapping up the blood.

I jerk involuntarily, and my eyeballs roll forward again. I feel myself waking up. My beloved cat, Shasta, is rubbing his head against my chin, purring like a motorboat as he kneads me with his paws. I'm so relieved to be lying safely in our bedroom that tears run down my cheeks. I smooth my hand over Shasta's head, marveling at the beauty of his jade eyes, glinting in the sun. My arms and legs feel like jelly. I'm exhausted from wrestling with my guilt.

My marriage is not working. A void has opened up between my husband and me. I don't care who started what. We're drifting apart. I'm lonely, and it hurts. I wanted this life so badly. I wanted us to start a family. I was in love. But looking back, I realize that I didn't know what marriage was. We didn't discuss long-term expectations, or parenting. We had fun. Our weekends were romantic. We got married before our relationship had truly been tested, and that was my fault. I pressured him. He was wary of making a commitment, but he didn't want to lose me, and I seemed so certain of myself.

I should have noted the significance of his working forty-five days straight before our wedding instead of enjoying himself or helping me with the plans. He'd been married before; I hadn't. I figured,

Everybody does it. How hard can it be? I didn't realize that marriage isn't just about you and your partner. Marriage comes with its own a semi truck of baggage, including the expectations of your family, your community, and society. Even the traditions of the institution itself start rattling around in your head. Your psyche gets pretty crowded pretty quickly after saying "I do."

My love for my son is unclouded, powerful and all-consuming. Instead of dealing with the problems between my husband and me, I focus on loving him. This is a lapse in judgment. This, more than anything, dooms our union. It's too easy to get along when we rally around the one thing we can totally and utterly agree on: that our kid is wonderful. We coast through many months just making life enjoyable for our baby. Meanwhile, our lives are diverging.

I can remember a time when we'd stay in bed all day having sex, then throw on jeans and T-shirts and meet our friends for dinner. Now when we go out on "date night" (an awful term), I'm anxious the whole time that our son is missing me, that he doesn't like the babysitter, that he's crying for any one of a hundred possible reasons and can't convey his needs well enough yet. Jim is frustrated, but he doesn't criticize me. It's a relief when we come home early.

My husband and I have less and less to say to each other. He's working so hard, while I spend my time going to the zoo, the park, and mommy-and-me classes. Instead of relating to each other, it feels like we're reporting back from two different sectors of the front, and nobody's clear anymore why we're waging this campaign to begin with.

We're not the white-picket-fence type, but we find ourselves marching in lockstep with all the other new parents, getting herded toward the suburbs. You hear the drumbeat everywhere: people discussing property values, school districts, frightening crime statistics in the city, pollution, tax credits, traditional versus liberal styles of child-rearing. We cope with our disorientation and loneliness in our own way. None of this upheaval is visible on the surface, which makes it even harder to fix. Who wants to get into a heavy discussion when you haven't slept, you don't have a lot of time for yourself, and you're hoping tonight you might get lucky?

Should we have our son baptized? Neither of us goes to church, but we're at the stage when everybody is affiliating themselves with multiple organizations. It feels like a game of musical chairs. We have to worry about getting Nick into preschool. We fill out applications. We might be too late. There are sailing clubs, country clubs, private athletic organizations. It feels like everything we do or don't do will have a determinative effect on his future happiness. He's only two years old.

There are several prominent churches in our neighborhood—big, impressive places of worship representing a range of Christian denominations. I push Nick past them in his stroller on our way to the zoo, but what invariably grabs his attention are the decorative gargoyles on several nearby houses. "Look!" He points up at the miniature monsters under the eaves. "Look, Mommy!"

"Yeah." I don't really know how to contextualize their frightening appearance. "Look at that, honey."

One of my closest friends in the neighborhood is devoutly Christian. We moved to this area because of the architecture and its proximity to the lake, but a lot of religious families are attracted to this district because it offers them the opportunity to enjoy the fellowship of their churches. They can walk to daily services. They can volunteer to teach on Sundays and sing in their local choirs. Jane, my Christian friend, came out on tour with me as my backup singer at Lilith Fair when she was six months pregnant. God is everywhere. Which makes the Devil thirsty.

I say I'm going out. My husband trusts me. When you're a trustworthy person, you tend to trust other people. At the age of thirty-one, I'm diligent, but I don't deserve the blind faith he has in me. I'm ten years younger than he is, and immature; I'm used to getting my own way. I feel isolated as a young mother, sidelined in my career, and I'm not handling it well. In the midst of all the sunshine, sandboxes, playdates, and Teletubbies, a darker force is taking over.

When the nanny comes to take care of Nick for a few hours, I go visit some old acquaintances over on Belmont Avenue. It's an odd choice for a social call. We have nothing in common apart from working in music. They're on the Goth spectrum, sweet, smart, but much younger than I am. I honestly don't know what I'm doing here. They don't, either. It's awkward. I feel self-conscious, like my being here at all broadcasts that something is wrong in my marriage. Moms aren't supposed to get high in the afternoon. But I'm starved for artistic company. It's a relief to feel as far away from my normal life as possible.

I journal in notebooks. I buy self-help tapes. I exercise. But none of it works. Sometimes I talk to my friends down by the duck pond while we watch our kids feed the birds and chase one another around the jungle gym. I say things out loud, to test the shock value, but underneath it all, I mean every word. I don't like dinner parties, I say. I think I'd fit in better in Los Angeles. Aren't you bored staying at home with the kids? There's a ghost in my house. There's a ghost in my head. I miss the person I was before all this.

There are homeless people everywhere on Clark Street near the park. They stay in this area because one of the churches runs a shelter. When my friends decide they want a bagel and coffee, we all have to push our strollers down the busy thoroughfare. The vagrants' hollow faces and haunted expressions make me embarrassed to dwell on my relatively minor problems. But I don't feel like there is that much that separates them from me. I can see how a mistake or two could compound and then snowball into disaster. I can see the rejection I will face if I keep recklessly testing boundaries.

"Jesus saves! God punishes sinners! The Devil's got his eye on you, pretty lady!" Those aren't the words the homeless guy ranting and raving on a street corner is saying, but that's what I hear when we pass him. He points his bony finger at me. "Beware! Turn the tide! The end is nigh!"

My neighbors, Rob and Arlene, have just stepped out onto their front porch. They're on their way to dinner in matching wool over-coats. I don't know what it is about our body language, Ethan's and mine, that tips him off; maybe we are laughing too loudly, or maybe we step back abruptly from standing too close; but I see a flash of recognition cross Rob's face. He swiftly suppresses it, hiding it well, but he knows I see. We say hello, and I introduce them to my new manager. We make innocuous jokes about the weather. But Ethan and I have been clocked. Nothing has happened between us yet. All that is still a long way off. But the fact that Rob notices—Rob, whom I barely speak to—is my first inkling that our chemistry is some-thing I need to watch out for.

Rob is a born-again Christian. I'm sure he's highly attuned to any type of temptation. But we don't have a lot in common apart from the fact that we live next door. He doesn't have children, and he's never been onstage. He doesn't know what it's like to be famous, or female. People don't realize what a huge transition I've gone through in the space of a single year. I'm trying to fit in with folks in the neighborhood, trying to follow their habits and adopt their sched-ules. Sometimes I think I will never belong here. My friends are all straight; none of them are artists. I don't know why I'm afraid to embrace my true nature. But I know that repressing my feelings like this is only going to make the pendulum swing back hard the other way.

Gardening is one of the things I do lately that makes me feel like part of the community. Every Saturday, a few of us homeowners in this row of townhouses don our work clothes and get down to busi-ness with rakes and trowels, learning to make art with greenery and flowers. We have an unusually high percentage of green thumbs in this area. It feels like a form of creativity to be outside and up to my elbows in the rich, loamy soil. I plant my wishes, and I bury my sins.

I'm at a restaurant with my girlfriends on a ladies' night out. Ethan sends a very expensive bottle of wine to our table, even though he's currently at his apartment in New York. My blushing pleasure is a dead giveaway, and an uncomfortable glance passes among my friends. I wave it off as "an industry thing," but that's a lie. I know what it means. I can't help softening to this treatment. It's exciting. It makes me feel special. For the first time in ages, I feel like a rock star.

Ethan and I say goodbye at an airport after a gig. I get on the escalator to go up to my gate. He waves at me from the ground floor. We stare at each other as the conveyor rises, taking me further away. All of a sudden he leaps onto the descending escalator and runs all the way up to top just to make me laugh. I watch him ride all the way back down again, pleased with himself, never breaking eye contact.

We're shooting an album cover in a rocky arroyo. It's been a long, hot day. Ethan climbs seventy-five feet up the side of a cliff to get cellular service. It is nerve-racking to watch his progress until, finally, he summits. He stand triumphantly atop the mountain, phone in hand, pacing back in forth while he talks to my label in Los Angeles. He is a ham, and everybody loves it. When he comes back down again, he whispers in my ear, "I knew you wanted to see me do that." At first I'm surprised, thinking, No I didn't. But then I realize he's right. I like watching Ethan's feats of daring. I love that he'll do crazy shit like that. It reminds me of my brother.

I'm calling Ethan to tell him what's happening in my day instead of saving the news for my husband. I know I've strolled too far down the wrong path, but I'm addicted to the attention. It makes all the ordinary things I have to do seem colorful and interesting when he listens to me. He puts a funny spin on it, and I feel like a star in a movie he's directing. He's great with my son, too. He's such a kid himself, and he likes to clown around when I bring Nick to work with me. I am living dangerously off balance, topsy-turvy with my priorities. It's like I've floated out to sea and there's no land in sight. What ought to be a big fat red flag feels like nothing. What shouldn't matter at all feels like everything. Then one day I realize it. I need him.

My husband and I have a fight. I'm arguing with the man I married to, but I'm looking at him from the point of view of someone whose allegiance has switched. Jim can feel it. He doesn't know Ethan is pulling the strings, but he knows we're no longer equally invested in our relationship. I'm acting more and more like I could take it or leave it, and Jim is scared by what he sees in me. He's losing his grip on his wife, and he doesn't know why.

My husband has less and less interest in participating in the fanfare around my career. His withdrawal from my world is in exact proportion to my withdrawal from his. I become jealous, irrationally so, of the women he works with. My burgeoning feelings for Ethan and my guilt for wanting to sleep with him make me project the same motivations onto Jim. I'm sure something illicit is going on when he works late, because that's the case with me. Jim is bewildered, wondering where his mature and loving partner went. We no longer sleep in the same bed.

The nanny notices the strain. Her last job was a nightmare, with her trying to take care of a young boy Nick's age during his wealthy parents' bitter divorce. The ensuing custody battle made the boy's life a misery. She shares her story with me in great detail, and it brings us both to tears. I think she's trying to save me, or more indirectly, warn me. I'm paranoid that she thinks I'm already unfaithful. One day I catch her praying over my son's crib. I don't say anything. I slip quietly down the hall, back to my bedroom, but it disturbs me. She is protecting him from dangers that I myself am inviting in. I keep thinking about the line she always says when we're cleaning: "Idle hands are the Devil's playthings."

It's a gorgeous day outside. I'm talking to another neighbor, a single, middle-aged businesswoman whose house is just south of mine. When she puts makeup on, she's really quite beautiful, but truthfully, I feel sorry for her. She lives alone, unmarried, with no kids. She tells me about the previous owners of my home on Geneva Terrace, a story I never heard from the realtor. All I knew was that an architect had gutted and modernized our townhouse for his own blended family. But before they moved in, his wife had an affair, and he sold it because he couldn't stand to live with the painful memories. It sends a shiver down my spine as I realize that I am more than halfway there myself.

But what my neighbor tells me about the original owners next is even creepier. My house originally belonged to four siblings who'd grown up there and continued to live there as adults. It had a dark, shabby Victorian interior, she said. They never socialized. They were religious and kept to themselves. They grew old together in the very rooms we're living in, and two of them died there. The others might have gone to a retirement facility; she doesn't remember. They were aloof figures in the neighborhood. They hated change and followed a strict routine. I don't know if what she's saying is true or just rumor and inference, but what isn't in dispute is that one brother and three sisters lived together in isolation for over twenty years.

I think about the evil entity in my dream. What if one of the dead siblings is angry about the remodeling and likes to get rid of new owners by making the wife cheat? It's hard to imagine any kind of dark energy in our house. It's too bright, white, modern, and airy. I love how the sun pours down from the skylights and refracts through the glass-block hallway. But what you can't see can hurt you; this much I'm learning. I go back inside and play with Nick for a while. We run up and down the floating staircase, dangling a fishing-rod cat toy for Shasta to chase. He pounces, shooting out a paw while hanging from the underside of a step, sending my son into peals of laughter. It's amazing how life can seem so sweet when, really, you're dancing on the edge of a precipice.

My husband is out of town, and Ethan flies in to see me. The question of whether or not we will sleep together hangs over us. It feels, simultaneously, exciting and as evil a thing as I've ever contemplated. In order to rationalize my behavior, I've started bargaining. Touching is not kissing. Kissing is not fingering. Fingering is not fucking. Pretty soon we're all over each other in my foyer, but I refuse to let him come upstairs. The nanny will be back from the duck pond with Nick soon, and he will want to tell me everything about his midday adventure.

"Come on." I grab Ethan by the hand and drag him out the front door. "We can't stay in there!" We're loud. We are not discreet. I explicitly like the recklessness of it. I'm not myself when I'm around Ethan, and that feels liberating. I think if he said "Flap your wings" I would fly right up to the top of the trees and dive down again like a sparrow, swooping along the telephone lines. When we come back from lunch, Ethan drops me off and continues on in the cab. I'm planning to see him later tonight.

My neighbor Rob has been surreptitiously waiting for the opportunity to speak with me. He comes out of his house and makes chitchat at first, but then it turns serious. "You know me as the man I am now," he says. "But I wasn't always this way Ten years ago I partied, I slept around, I did all kinds of bad things. Everything you can think of. I drank, I fought, I stole money from the company I worked for. I reached as low a point as it's possible for a person to go. I hated myself, and I'd hurt or alienated everyone around me who I loved."

I'm taken aback, uncomfortable with this sudden intimacy. But Rob reassures me that he has only the best of intentions.

"One day this old man, this stranger, gave me a Bible. He told me what I'm telling you now. He'd been through the same thing I was going through, had done all the same shameful things I was doing, but he looked respectable and wealthy. I was embarrassed by my state of affairs and envious of all that he had. At first I tossed the book in the back of my car and forgot about it. But I never threw it away. One day, in desperation, I started reading it. I leafed through and let the words penetrate my drunken fog. I found stories in the Bible of wretched men just like me who, with God's help, transformed themselves. I tried every self-help program you can think of, but only Jesus can make a miracle.

"Eventually it led me to Alcoholics Anonymous and, from there, to attending church. I got sober, turned my life around, and met Arlene. It didn't happen right away; I made a lot more mistakes. But when God acts in your life, He calls you to Him through other people—through me, right now, with you. God loves you, Liz, or He wouldn't prompt me to do this. He loves you even in your sin, even in your deepest, darkest secrets.

"I want you to have this Bible. I've signed it with a dedication, just like that man signed his for me. Let God work in you, Liz. Let yourself find the path, and I promise that once you start walking, it will get easier. You'll never walk alone."

I take the Bible from Rob and thank him. It is very awkward. I don't know what to say. It's one of the most profound and undefinable interactions I've ever had with another human being. I walk back up my front stairs and shut the door behind me, sit down on the couch, and just stay there with the Bible in my lap for a few minutes. I'm mortified that my neighbor knows so much about me, about what is going on in my life. I start crying, because he knows, and yet he still sees me as a good person. Suddenly, all the times I've lied or been selfish or deceived people come flooding over me, the memories engulfing me like I'm standing under a waterfall, trying to catch my breath. So many, many bad things.

I skim through the Bible for a couple of days. I enjoy reading the red parts in particular, where Jesus is quoted directly. But for the most part, I try to put my strange encounter with Rob out of my mind. I make sure I won't run into him when I leave the house. I tell myself he's a weird guy, that this is a weird neighborhood, and decide that eventually I want to move away. But I can't forget it entirely. I used to attend church. I was baptized and confirmed. I sang in the choir, for fuck's sake. At one time in my life, I believed in God and thought that when I talked to myself, He was listening. He was like a playmate or an imaginary friend. It rings true to me that the divine being I knew would reach out after a while and just casually get in touch. Like, I'm here for you if you need me. My God was never pushy. He hung back and waited until you were ready for a hug. And I'm not ready.

I'm planning a trip to Miami to oversee a mastering session. My parents are going to stay with the baby, and my husband is going on a weekend getaway with his friends. We've been getting along better, because we accept our estrangement. We've fallen into a rhythm of Don't ask, don't tell. I've even started sleeping in our bed again sometimes, and we're having sex occasionally. I'm also sleeping with Ethan. It started a week ago, and it is incredible. In an odd way, things are better for everyone now that the tension isn't at such a frenzied pitch. I'm having a run-of-the-mill affair. All that waiting was worse than the actual betrayal. Maybe this is how human beings are meant to be, I think, as I get ready for bed. Maybe if everyone were doing it, more marriages would turn out well.

I look at myself in the bathroom mirror, massaging cleansing emulsion into my skin. I'm a real grown-up lady, a sophisticated woman of the world. I've always loved how the warm marble in the bathroom casts a pink glow on my skin. I feel relaxed and loving, in control. I can't wait to get down to Miami and lie out in the sun next to Ethan. Do a little day drinking by the pool. Jim will have fun doing whatever he's doing, Nick will get spoiled by his grandparents, and everything is going to be perfect. I don't know what I was so worried about before. I bet all the couples around here have the same arrangement. It just makes sense. It's better for everybody.

I rinse my face, dry off with a towel, and turn the lights off in the bathroom. Jim is already fast asleep when I crawl under the covers. I make sure I can hear the baby through the monitor, then settle down next to my husband. My breathing slows. My muscles slacken. I drift off, and my eyes roll back in my head.

In my dream, I'm walking up the side of a mountain. The dense foliage makes the trail ahead hard to see. It keeps winding around and doubling back on itself. I'm starting to feel out of breath as the incline tests my fitness. I see Ethan in a clearing about twenty feet up the hill. I wave to him. He has a strange look on his face, like he's sneering at me. I'm suddenly uncertain, unsure of myself. I've never experienced him making fun of me before. I become shy, hesitant, and I loiter on the trail.

"Hi." Ethan appears right next to me in the path. I jump back. How did he get here so quickly? I look into his eyes and see it isn't him. Whoever this is, he looks exactly like my manager, but he's vile, lurid. He has evil, crazy eyes.

"Who are you?" I back away from him, terrified. Ethan doesn't answer. He keeps creeping toward me with the most sadistic, wicked smile on his face. He's enjoying my fear. He's intentionally prolonging it. I turn and run, going as fast as I can, whipping around corners and jumping over roots. Low branches whip my face, twigs scratch my skin, but I can't slow down. Ethan is the most frightening creature I've ever seen. I have to get as far away from him as possible. I finally stop to catch my breath, bending over and clutching my knees.

"Hi," the foul voice whispers in my ear. I scream, falling backward onto my ass. I scramble away from him, but no matter which way I flee, he is right there beside me again, taking pleasure in my panic. I cannot describe in words the depth of the evil in his eyes. No language can convey such cruelty. The more fear I show, the wider and more psychotic his grin is. I'm crying in my sleep, heaving, because I can't get away, because it looks like Ethan, because I'm too afraid to speak out loud who I think this is.

The Devil lets me take another run for it, lets me think I can get away. As far as he's concerned, we can do this all night. My terror is sexual pleasure for him. His look implies that we're going to be doing this together for a very, very long time. I know thoughts of escape are futile. I know what sin I've committed to bring him here. But I have no choice. I have to continue the cat-and-mouse game. That is part of the punishment. The Devil likes to mete out a little bit of hope and then snatch it away. That is the diversion he's brought me here to play.

So I run back and forth while he pops up and blocks me. I cry out to God. I recite the Lords Prayer, but before I can finish, he jumps right in front of me with a face like a Maori warrior and a voice that seems to come from inside my head. "You're mine, now!"

Cracccckkkkkkkkkkkk! At that exact moment, my husband and I are awoken from a dead sleep by the sound of an explosion inside the house. We sit up in bed for a second, frozen, listening, looking at each other in the dark. I can hear Nick's steady breathing coming through the baby monitor. He's still fast asleep.

"What the fuck was that?" My husband is on his feet, heading toward the hallway door.

"Wait." I jump up after him, too afraid to be left behind. We creep ahead cautiously. He flips the lights on. I'm clinging to his back as we inch forward in tandem. There isn't anything obvious that fell over or could have made such a deafening sound.

"I'm going to call the police," I say, running back toward the night table to get the phone.

"No, wait. Elizabeth, come here." Jim motions for me to come next to him. "Holy shit."

We both stand in the doorway of the bathroom with our mouths agape. The huge floor-to-ceiling glass backsplash for the shower has shattered in place. It's a very heavy pane, two inches thick. The weight of the settling house must have snapped it at the exact moment I was having my dream. It's still breaking, more fissures slowly spreading outward toward the edges, a giant spiderweb consuming the once-transparent sheet. It sounds like ice-covered tree branches tinkling against one another in a breeze. I've never seen anything like it. Jim is mesmerized. I can't tell him what just happened. I can't tell him what it means. He wouldn't believe me anyway.

The aircraft is sitting on the tarmac, waiting to take off. I'm still thinking about last night. I'm on my way to meet Ethan in Miami for our romantic weekend. I know I should call it off. I know I should stand up and demand to get off the plane. I will never receive a clearer signal that heaven and hell are real and I am in danger of losing my mortal soul. But in broad daylight, under these ordinary circumstances, it sounds so preposterous, so impossible to believe—even though I witnessed it with my own eyes. I'm also brimming with lust at the thought of seeing Ethan again, and being in his arms. I can't rise above this. I'm not strong enough. I already know what I'm going to do. Just as the Devil knew. I take a deep breath. "Well," I murmur, "I guess I'm Satan's mistress."

We're in Miami. It's an ocean-front room. I got my period on the way down, but Ethan doesn't care. He gets towels from the bathroom and lays them out on the bed, doubling them up so the sheets won't be ruined. Our precautions are ineffective. We finish our lovemaking in the middle of a crime scene, tiny splotches of bright red blood everywhere. I don't understand how we could spread them so far beyond the boundary of our bodies. I feel terrible for the maids. We put fifty dollars on the desk and ball the bedding up under the sink. I leave my shame and my ecstasy on the art deco tiling.

We're on a red-eye flight to New York. The plane is empty. Ethan and I are under the blankets together, stretched out lengthwise in a row of seats. My hip hurts where our weight presses down against the raised seat rest, but it feels amazing to be intimate like this: bold, secret, tender, and slow. My hand barely moves as I rub myself until I come. We freeze and pretend to sleep when the flight attendant unexpectedly passes by, her department-store perfume lingering in the air around us. In the darkness, Ethan's eyes appear to glow. He whispers something funny in my ear, and I tell him he can come inside me. I have a bunch of cocktail napkins ready to catch any spillage. I sit up immediately afterward and stuff the paper wad inside my jeans. I'm proud that we've been tidy.

It's one of life's great ironies that the unattainable fruit, once in hand, starts to rot almost immediately. Once it's no longer connected to the life-giving vine, it's no longer quite as impressive as before. The same holds true for people and objects you desire. Their context is half their appeal, and once removed from that, they quickly lose their allure. Conquer the challenge, and you may savor your own dissatisfaction. What is meant for you comes easily, so improve yourself if you're dissatisfied with your circumstances. Once you are great, then the great things will naturally be nearby. I didn't know any of that when I was younger. But once I gave into Ethan, I realized I'd become just another woman he now had responsibility for. And that was never what he wanted. He wanted what Jim and I had.

It's a year later. We've both moved to California, but we don't live together. We barely see each other anymore. Ethan had a party at his rental house up in Cold Water Canyon and didn't invite me. He's been acting shady lately, and I suspect he's been cheating. Not with anyone noteworthy, I'm sure; just whatever chick he fell into bed with at the end of the night. I drive up and park in his driveway. His friends are helping him put the house back together, picking up beer cans and stuffing them into Hefty bags.

I wait for Ethan in the living room while his interns rearrange the furniture. Everything had been pushed to the perimeter to create a dance floor, apparently. When it comes time to move the couch back into place, I'm so pissed that I don't bother get off. I raise one eyebrow and, with my arms folded and my legs tucked up underneath me, let them pick up the sofa with me lounging on it like Cleopatra and carry it to its usual spot in front of the fireplace. Some of the guys laugh, but some of them are blushing and sheepish. They know there is going to be a fight after they leave.

It honestly isn't one of our biggest confrontations. I have no control over the situation anymore. Ethan's stopped pretending this is even a relationship. We're both sick of it. It fell so far below our expectations. I wrecked my marriage, and he wrecked his— essentially for nothing. We hurt our spouses, our kids, our reputations, for nothing. Empty lust: a cardinal sin. Adultery. Immaturity. Escapism. They should expand the Bible for our modern age. We both wholly and totally suck as human beings, and we know it. All we're left with are some good war stories, of which you are the lucky recipient. Oh, and eternal damnation. Sorry, I forgot about that one.

After the interns leave, I take him upstairs and fuck him in this strange, territorial "this is *my* man," kind of way. And he loves it. His eyes are glistening. He feels wanted again. I think, for the last six months, he's seen nothing but disappointment in my face.

"Promise me you'll always fuck me like that." He looks so handsome as he says it, dopamine-drunk. I'm going to miss him. I always know when it is really and finally over. It's one of my gifts.

My ex-husband is moving out here next week, and we will co-parent like adults. I'm ready to deal with my life and not run from it. There isn't anywhere to run to anyway. The grass is never greener once you're on the other side of the fence. I still have Rob's Bible, and I study it. I don't know if it will do me any good, but I try to absorb its wisdom, which seems universal, untainted by organized religion's obsession with status and control. Mostly, I just try to get my mind right. The only way I can keep the demons off me is to manage my intentions. I still make colossal errors in judgment, but 99 percent of the time, I mean well.

Nick's kicking his feet under the table. He's almost finished with his spaghetti, and he wants to watch television. He gets an hour and a half every day as long as his homework is finished. We go over the words he has to memorize for his spelling quiz.

Even now, seven years later, the impact of my infidelity reverberates in an ever-widening circle of collateral damage. The cracks are just smaller, less obvious than before. The other day, I heard my son claiming to take responsibility for my divorce. He remembers me asking him if it would be all right for us to move to California, and because he said yes, he thought that the split was his decision. No matter what I say, how I explain the timing, and assure him that his father and I are better friends when we're not in love, and that our separation had nothing to do with him, he refuses to accept that his actions played no part.

I hate how much pain I caused everybody. Ethan and I never asked anyone to lie for us or cover for us, but it happened sometimes, because we were so damn sloppy. Looking back, it was almost as if we wanted to get caught. When you expect to be punished but you're getting away with it, it feels worse than nothing happening at all. You start unconsciously looking for a higher power to step in and restore balance to the world. Otherwise, everything you've been taught and everything you believe in are meaningless. Life is random. There is no justice. And that, as it turns out, is psychologically unacceptable.

So you don't believe in the Devil? That's good. I'm happy for you.

ART TK

thirteen

WHAT WOULD LIZ PHAIR DO?

ext TK

ART TK

fourteen

HASHTAG

Text TK

ART TK

fifteen

BREAK-IN AT BLUE HOUSE

'm awakened in the middle of the night by the sound of strange voices in the house. My bedroom is right off the kitchen, and I can hear everything through the thin walls. It's not unusual for my housemates to bring their friends or dates home this late, but I don't hear any familiar voices. It sounds like three black guys arguing.

I stuff a pillow over my head, hoping they'll go away. I really need to get some sleep. I've got exams tomorrow. They don't seem to have any consideration for the hour, but maybe they don't know there's someone sleeping in this part of the house. Exasperated, I pull on some jeans, and I'm about to go out and tell them to keep it down when the tone of the argument escalates. I freeze, my hand outstretched toward the door. The hair on my arm stands up. I've gone as rigid as a statue, listening.

This is not some collegiate debate or drunken disagreement. These guys are angry, threatening violence. There's real teeth behind their words. I don't understand what's happening. Do they even go to this school? What are they doing here? Who brought them, and why are they so pissed off? The loudest one is cursing and pacing back and forth, shouting that he's going to fuck somebody up. The other two are riffling through our kitchen drawers. What are they looking for—a knife? I'm afraid to move, in case a floorboard creaks beneath me. Only a few feet separate us, but I don't think they know I'm here. I don't think they realize they're being overheard.

They stride boldly through the house, unconcerned about the noise they're making. I jump when I hear the sound of glass breaking in the living room. My mind races, trying to identify the object. Then I hear more glass being deliberately shattered. Every high-pitched, splintering crash goes through me like a shock wave. They're smashing all the art on the walls. They're moving through the downstairs rooms with some kind of bat or club, systematically demolishing our property. I start shaking like I've never shaken before, my whole body vibrating from head to toe.

At this point I know they're not students. Nobody enrolled at Oberlin would destroy those pictures. The Allen Art Museum has an art rental program, low-cost, $5 a piece, that signs out authentic Picassos, Renoirs, Matisses, Monets, Warhols—you name it—to students, to hang on their walls for the semester. It's mostly sketch work and minor prints, but they are actual, irreplaceable, hand-of-the-master creations. It's a revelation at nineteen to be entrusted with the output of artists you are currently studying in art history class. My housemates and I have at least four or five pieces hanging in the common area, as well as several more in our bedrooms. These guys aren't here to rob us, though. They're here to break shit and fuck us up.

I hear them coming back toward the kitchen. I panic, backing away from the door. It's too late to run. I search around for somewhere to hide. I consider covering myself with blankets or crouching down in the closet, but it's pointless. They'd find me, and then

I'd be trapped. When they smash dishes against the wall, I feel it reverberate through me. I've never confronted a truly ruthless aggressor, and I can't think straight. The tremors are so intense that I can barely coordinate my movements. If you've never experienced shaking like this: It's qualitatively different from shivering or trembling. It's faster, deeper, and totally beyond your control. It's the body's response to imminent injury, and it freezes you, interfering with your fight-or-flight instinct.

Standing there in the middle of the room waiting to get my ass kicked, I keep hoping I'll hear police sirens. I can't get to the kitchen phone, but I assume someone on the second floor has called them already. Where is everybody? They can't possibly be sleeping through this noise, but I don't hear any of my housemates moving around upstairs. Nobody is coming down or challenging the intruders. How can all six people I live with be out at the same time in the middle of the night? I feel like I've woken up in the Twilight Zone. It doesn't occur to me that they might be in their rooms, frozen in place like I am.

So this is how I die, I think. I'm not ready. I hope they don't rape me, too. That's when I remember last fall's demonstration to protest violence against women. Hundreds of students and townspeople marched through the streets of Oberlin carrying candles and chanting, "Take back the night!" We gathered in the town square to listen to the accounts of sexual assault survivors and domestic violence victims, and to decry the way women are conditioned to accept fear as a normal part of living in our society.

The administration responded by installing a dozen telephone boxes all over campus so you could call security if you felt threatened, or thought you were being followed. I have a stalker at the college, so I'm grateful every time I pass a little blue light, glowing in the darkness. One of these emergency posts is clearly visible through my bedroom window, less than fifteen yards away.

I tiptoe to the other side of the room and brace my weight against the wide window frame. Placing my fingertips beneath the brass lifts, I pull upwards, grimacing as the old wooden stiles squeak in their grooves. The voices outside my door go silent. I hold my breath, praying. My hands are shaking; my legs feel like rubber bands. I'm expecting the intruders to burst through the door behind me at any minute. In a herculean effort, I heave the heavy sash upward, causing a terrible, scraping squeal. I scramble out the window, drop five feet to the ground below, and run barefoot across the wet grass to the emergency phone.

"Please help me." I crouch behind the narrow pole as though it could conceal me from view. "Some men broke into Blue House. They're smashing everything. I'm scared they're going to kill me." The officer asks for my address, but I don't know it. Maybe I never did, or maybe I do and I'm just too frightened to recall. "It's Blue House. It's down Main Street. . . ." I'm racking my brain, looking around desperately. "It's by the stream and the bridge." Nothing I say is helping, but they already know my location.

I expect the attackers to come bursting out the front door at any moment and chase me down the sidewalk, but the neighborhood is absolutely quiet. No lights are on in any of the houses, no cars are out in the streets. Not even the crickets are chirping on this moonless evening. It is a perfectly still night. I hear sirens coming from a long way off, and my panic subsides. Then I feel something brush against my leg, and I nearly jump out of my skin, tumbling backward onto the ground. It's a sleek, sinewy black cat with apple-green eyes, purring ferociously as it paints its shoulder back and forth across my thigh.

The vandals have vanished by the time campus security searches the house. The patrolman asks me to describe the suspects. I tell him that I never saw them, that I only heard them. I can't decide if saying they were black is valid or racist. "I think they were African American," I say finally, after recounting every other detail of the incident. As soon as I hear the words come out of my mouth, I feel like I've stepped over an invisible line. I feel white, in a way that I didn't at the time of the break-in.

Linguistic profiling is potentially a big deal anywhere, but at Oberlin College, it's a powder keg. This is a progressive liberal-arts school, and they don't let any form of discrimination slide. It's the 1990s. If you throw race into the mix, the whole ship tilts. If the police start questioning only black guys because of something I said, it could affect the whole community. In small-town Ohio the headline might read, "Three Black Men Break in to Student Housing, Causing Property Damage, Distress to Occupants." Racial bias in crime reporting is commonplace. Editors get their copy straight from the police sheets.

Even though I'm white and middle class, I don't sit in the lecture halls thinking history is my story. I don't feel like my future is in any way guaranteed. I expect to work twice as hard to be acknowledged in the art world simply because I'm female. How does that make me the oppressor? Why shouldn't I say who I think the assholes were who broke into my house? They broke the law, but now *I'm* feeling guilty? I have this knot in my throat again, worrying that I shouldn't have said anything I couldn't prove. I know a lot of white guys who sound black because they love gangsta rap. The truth is, in 1989, I still expect blacks to be more violent than whites. That comes from living in segregated cities. That comes from my grandmothers. That comes from a lot of places it shouldn't.

The Spike Lee film *Do the Right Thing* came out in the summer of 1989. I went to see it with a friend at a theater in Evanston, just north of Chicago. The audience at that showing was mostly white, and the movie had a profound effect on the viewers. They stared at the screen in rapt concentration. Lee's colorful portrayal of a Brooklyn neighborhood at a cultural flashpoint was Shakespearean in the scope of its social commentary. Even the obviously funny parts only got subdued laughs out of this audience. They were overawed by the message, and alert to any hint of accusation. Their bewildered faces after the movie ended confirmed for me that we'd just witnessed something extraordinary.

A month later, I watched the same film at a midnight screening in

Times Square and had a completely different experience. This audience was entirely black. My friend J.P. and I were the only white people there, as far as I could see. The crowd roared with laughter from start to finish—calling out and engaging with the action on screen, responding to the dialogue as if they were cast members. Every so often I would look over at J.P. in the dark, my eyes widening, cracking up along with everybody else. My expression was like, Can you believe this shit? It was such a wild, joyous feeling. It's amazing how differently the two groups reacted to the same story.

After a brief investigation, police establish that the men who wrecked our house are indeed students—members of Oberlin's basketball team. I'm dismayed, because it doesn't seem like the college or the police are going to do anything. No one will be formally charged. The administration wants to keep the matter private—and, incomprehensibly, the disciplinary board is making us, my housemates and me, pay for the broken picture frames. Insurance will cover the cost of the art restoration, but we, the residents of Blue House, will split the bill for repairing the drywall, repainting the rooms, and replacing the art frames.

I don't understand how this was the committee's decision. I wasn't even there at the hearing. How am I going to get stuck with the bill for an event in which I was traumatized, and that I had no part in instigating? It feels incredibly unfair. My housemates aren't contesting the decision—partly because, as it turns out, they know what provoked the midnight sortie, but also because everyone in this house apart from me is wealthy, and they're accustomed to using money to insulate themselves from conflict. This semester, my roommates are a bunch of trust-fund babies. I like them all, but I was grandfathered in after spending the fall semester away in New York City, working as a studio assistant and living in Alphabet City—on Eleventh Street, behind St. Mark's Church.

The first year I lived in Blue House, I was the lone female resident, a visual artist in a group of male athletes. I'd gotten the room because I knew one of the guys from my sophomore dorm, and I was desperate to live off campus. After one of their gang dropped out, he called to ask if I wanted to fill the vacancy, and I said yes. That strange arrangement lasted a year. They would have these raging keg parties where they blasted Talking Heads and Led Zeppelin. It reminded me of the movie *Animal House*.

I hadn't been a great housemate. Over the winter term, I'd let the dishes pile up in the sink until they were stacked higher than the faucet. I think the jocks had hoped I'd be a mother figure, cooking and fussing over my boys, but I turned out to be the angry punk-rock sister—good for music recommendations and not much else. I was in a rebellious phase, having returned to Oberlin after dropping out to attend classes at Northwestern University and the School of the Art Institute of Chicago. I'd found four years of college in Ohio to be unworkable without breaks.

Now, coming back after spending a semester in New York interning for the visual artists Nancy Spero and Leon Golub, I'm surrounded by these sensitive, haughty private-school kids who throw high-concept dinner parties and serve mixed drinks and wine. Being gone so long, I lost dibs on the best rooms and ended up living like the servant class, in cramped quarters off the kitchen at the rear of the house.

Just to give you an idea, one of our housemates wears bespoke clothes and, when at home in Taipei, is driven around by a gun-toting chauffeur in a Rolls-Royce with a locked briefcase full of cash in the trunk. Then there's Helena, our Renaissance patroness, who is testing recipes for her eighteenth-century cookbook in our homely kitchen. But none of them typifies old money quite like blond, blue-eyed Whitney, whose milky skin, slender build, high-pitched voice, and mid-Atlantic accent make him stick out like a sore thumb among the grungy, opinionated hippie kids of Oberlin.

He's the cause of this whole wretched debacle, it turns out. I'm incensed that I'm going to have to pay for Whitney's idiotic behavior, especially since I'm the one who was the most traumatized. I can't ask my parents for another subsidy. I've already spent enough of their money taking an academic tour of North America, accumulating credits which may or may not apply to my degree. In some ways, when I find out what really took place that night, I feel like I have more in common with the home invaders than with my housemates.

The guys who broke into Blue House live in Afrikan Heritage House, one of the identity-based off-campus housing units. Before I confront my roommates about the bill, I need answers. I corner Whitney in his room and demand an explanation. He sheepishly admits that he was sleeping with the forward-center's girlfriend on the night of the break-in. He confesses that he and this girl were upstairs in his bed, listening the whole time, while the three men went on their rampage. He knew he'd get his ass kicked, so he never called the police.

"What is wrong with you?" I ask him, staring into his unblinking jasper eyes.

"I thought they were going to kill me," he whines.

I'm disgusted. "Uh, yeah. Me too." My first thought is that I'm wasting my time talking to him. What's done is done. But my second thought is how odd it is that the basketball players were willing to risk expulsion and arrest for breaking and entering and destruction of property when they could have just marched upstairs and dragged Whitney out of bed by his boxer shorts. They made all this noise and broke all this shit, but it seems they were afraid to touch him physically. They wouldn't cross that invisible line. Not that Bennett is in any way intimidating. I could probably take him in a fair fight. But they, too, know that race is such an incendiary issue that a single transgression could have disastrous consequences.

They're right to be worried about Bennett's lawyers. But I also suspect they were thinking of the minefield of covert bigots of all stripes, in all walks of life—in the police precinct and the courts, on the committees, waiting to pounce on just such an incident. That's a fight nobody wins.

"Why would you do it?" I ask Whitney, shaking him gently by

the shoulders. I'm trying to get him to understand the predicament he's placed everyone in. He never offers to cover our portions of the bill, even though I know he can afford it.

He shrugs, sheepish. "I've never slept with a black girl before."

Like the basketball players, I lack the guts to file a complaint against him. I'm amazed that I'm going to be left with the short end of the stick. But deep down, I know that this is how it works. I don't have the kind of power he does.

Nobody from Blue House will come with me, but I'm going to confront the basketball player whose girlfriend Whitney slept with and ask him to chip in. I don't know if I'm doing it to prove to myself that I'm not afraid of him—if, by putting a face to the voice, I can heal some of my lingering trauma—or if I truly need justice in this bullshit situation. Maybe I'm still trying to convince myself that I'm not racist by treating him the same way I would a white guy. The truth is, I don't know why I'm going. I am drawn instinctively to the confrontation. Whatever my motives are, I'm still pretty scared.

It's Saturday night. Afrikan Heritage House is throwing a party outside. I'm one of the few white people milling around on the lawn. I ask a nerdy-looking dude which guy is the one I'm looking for, and he points out a tall, broad-shouldered young man. My heart is pounding as I approach him. I tug on his sleeve. He turns around, frowning when he sees me. He's at least two feet taller than I am.

Everybody in our immediate vicinity stops to watch what's going on. His friends close in a circle around him. My friends are standing a little way off by the parked cars. I'm sure he sees the fear in my eyes and hears the quaver in my voice, but I plainly and calmly explain the situation as I see it. I ask him to help me pay for the damage he did to our house.

At first, he scoffs and says we're all rich. "I'm not paying," he says, laughing. But I'm focused, and I can tell that he's putting on a front for the bystanders. I insist that my housemates are rich but I am not. I tell him what it was like for me that night while they were breaking everything. I describe what I thought was happening, and how frightened I was. It's at this point that our body language shifts. It's fleeting, and probably only perceptible to the two of us, but we each take a small step closer together.

"I'm sorry that you had to go through that," he says. His expression softens slightly as he rubs his chin. "I'm sorry I lost my temper. But I'm not paying for the damage." He looks at me, but it isn't a cold stare. He's showing me where his line is.

I hold his gaze, trying to convey that I, too, am aware of the line. I know I deserve better. But for some reason his apology and acknowledgment are enough. Maybe that's what I came for. My heart feels lighter. I'm not sure what currency he just paid me in, but I think he offered me respect. And I can live with that.

ART TK

sixteen

THREE BAD OMENS

'm driving down to Oak Park to pick up my misanthropic friend
Peter. We're going on a road trip, heading back to college for our
one-year reunion. I'm surprised he wants to party at our alma mater
so soon after graduating, but I guess he misses his friends. He should
have come with us to San Francisco. We all fucked off to the West
Coast for a year. Peter went to write scripts in L.A., and my other
friends and I settled in NorCal doing basically nothing. The Bay
Area was even more progressive than Oberlin, and certainly a lot
more fun than any rancid alumni weekend. Still, I'm up for anything
that gets me out of the house for a few days.

I love my parents, but he and I both agree the worst part about
living at home again is the boredom. I'm used to staying out late,
roaming all over the city, and spontaneously meeting new people.
My parents would like to see me take concrete steps to support myself, and that's hard to align with on a daily basis. I want to be an

artist. I've known I was destined to be an artist ever since I was a little girl, and according to everything we learned in art history class about the miserable lives of great painters and writers, that means hedonism, poverty, and ragged, raw brilliance. It's not my fault that my profession reveres lunatics. I was enjoying a carefree bohemian existence in San Francisco until the money ran out. Now I've been recalled to Winnetka to do the thankless work of growing up.

I've been looking for employment, but there isn't much that I'm qualified to do. I stare at the Jobs section in the morning paper, inwardly recoiling at the descriptions. "*Must* have computer skills." "*Must* own a car." "*Must* be able to type 50 wpm." Anxiety pools like a acid in the pit of my stomach until I no longer have an appetite. "Art major" and "artist's assistant" sound like items on a dilettante's résumé in any city, and Chicago's economy isn't exactly roaring in the creative sector. The same disruptive thoughts keep getting me off track: How do I escape? Where can I escape to? I feel like I'm living in the wrong place, raised by the wrong people, born at the wrong time in history.

Sometimes Peter and I meet up downtown and write jokes together. We're supposed to be dropping off résumés and going for job interviews, but we end up sitting around all day in a café laughing our ass off. We want to put out a comedy fanzine, so we think up funny scenarios. We walk through the galleries at the Art Institute people watching. He tries to get me all flustered by threatening to touch a painting or knock over a sculpture. I pretend to be a docent leading a tour; I explain works of art to people who don't know why I'm talking to them. We dress up and take photo sequences of ourselves acting out the skit. I'm supposed to cut out our figures and place them into illustrations, like the media mash-ups in avant-garde magazines. Instead, I've been using them as covers for my Girly-Sound tapes, cassette recordings I've been making since I returned from the West Coast. I live off the money people send me to make copies of my music, but it's nowhere near enough to rent my own place. If I live at home much longer, I'm going to go crazy.

Traffic is light, and I'm moving at a pretty good clip. I hate these stretches of nothingness on the sides of American highways. I think about all the people who live in the brown brick apartment buildings, how they'd all rather be somewhere else. I try to picture myself moving into one of the rear units with the fire escapes and small balconies. At my age, conformity feels scarier than failure does. My goal is to stand out from everybody. I don't care what distinguishes me, as long as it's in the creative arts. I need to express all the emotions and ideas that are tumbling around inside of me or I'll be angry forever. I have so much to say, but nobody's listening. That's my motivation—morning, noon, and night: to show others the world the way I see it. I'm having all these deep thoughts, probably because we're on our way to Oberlin. I think I might need further closure on my whole college experience.

I get to the part of the freeway that is under construction, and I need to pay attention. I'm driving in the left lane, close to a concrete divider. They're doing roadwork on the median, so they've moved this barrier to the outside of the emergency lane. If I roll down the window and reach my hand out, I can probably touch it. It seems incredibly dangerous to leave no margin for error at such high speeds. I'm doing about seventy-five miles per hour, the same as everyone else. I put both hands on the steering wheel at the ten-and-two-o'clock positions, and feel the bumps in the road testing my grip. We're coming up on a long, curving bend to the right. It feels like the concrete divider is closing in on me and I need to outrun it.

I have a split-second thought, one of those random ruminations everybody has throughout the day. I wonder why nobody ever gets into a car crash traveling in the left lane. It still seems incredible to me that all these drivers of average ability pull off semidifficult maneuvers every day and nothing goes wrong. Millions of people manage to successfully navigate to their destinations without dying, despite the potential danger, especially in this inner lane where we go faster and make tighter curves. Just imagine the damage I'd do to all the other vehicles on the road if I lost control right now. That would truly suck for everybody.

About ten seconds after I have this thought, a town car that's coming toward me in the opposite direction starts to spin out in its lane. Time slows down, and I watch the rear of the sedan swing all the way forward and continue moving through the spiral. Because of our relative speeds, I only catch glimpse of the accident before I've passed it. I'm flowing along with the rest of traffic, as if nothing happened. I can still picture the back of the driver's head thrown against the window as the car revolved 360 degrees. I realize I may just have witnessed someone's final moments. I want to stop the car, get off the freeway, and take side streets home, but I can't. Peter's expecting me. This is just the kind of last-minute flaking out he always worries I'll do.

I met Peter on the first night of freshman orientation. We were in the same dorm. Neither of us liked breaking into little groups and telling strangers who we were. He teased me because I wouldn't wear my name tag. I'd written my name on it, but I waved it around on the tip of my index finger for anyone who wanted to know my identity. As if my name explained anything. I could be friends with someone for months and not care what their name was. If I could look it up, I didn't want to make space for it in my brain. I'd memorized data my entire life and never found it to be useful.

Peter and I ended up in very different social circles, but in those early days at Oberlin, we bonded over our mutual discomfort with the progressive atmosphere. We were both from conservative Chicago suburbs and had never experienced anything like what we saw on campus. Everybody had hair in places where we would have shaved it. Everybody took their clothes off in front of one another shamelessly. The books, music, and films we knew seemed unsophisticated next to the cultural references other students made in class. We both spoke less and listened more that first semester, even though we'd been gregarious, outgoing people where we came from. It was a relief to be able to laugh privately with someone, without worrying about being politically incorrect.

When I get to Peter's house, I'm excited to tell him and his friend John what happened to me on the drive down. It doesn't sound as astonishing in the recounting as it felt while I was experiencing it.

"Maybe you're psychic," Peter says, anticipating what I want him to say, but in a tone that conveys his skepticism. Peter's father is the pastor of their church, and he is mistrustful of anything that smacks of religious self-importance. His manner is devilish, impish, in reaction to his upbringing.

"I *am* psychic," I sniff, miffed that I bothered to tell anybody. Legitimately strange things do happen to me, but because I also have an overactive imagination, I have no credibility with my friends.

"I believe in that stuff," John says. He's being nice, but Peter scoffs, wadding up a paper towel and throwing it at him. He doesn't want John to encourage me.

"What?" John says, dodging Peter's missile. "I do! I had some weird things happen to me. Sometimes things are just too coincidental to explain any other way."

We're all hanging out in the kitchen waiting for Peter's mother to call. They locked a frozen pizza in the oven when they accidentally triggered the self-cleaning mechanism, and now our only hope is for her to tell us how to get it out before the pizza burns into a disc of charcoal.

"You don't fucking believe in that shit." Peter wads up more paper towels and throws them at John.

"Yeah, I do," John's diving for the paper balls, trying to hit them back at Peter. "You don't know what I believe."

I'm listening to the two of them spar, reflecting back on the happy holiday gatherings my family had when I was young. I was the only girl in an extended family full of older boys, and I almost feel like I'm at my uncle's house on Grandin Avenue again, standing on the sidelines in my Polly Flinders dress, knee socks, and Mary Janes, watching the boys roughhouse—jealous that I can't join in. I spent a lot of family occasions hanging out by myself, playing with the pets or wandering around the grounds with my grandmother Winnie. It turned me into a tomboy for several years, until puberty brought me back to myself again.

I walk over to the sink to pour myself a glass of water. I can't say what spurs this impulse—maybe I just want to insert myself into the action—but I dig around in the stack of dirty dishes and pull out a wooden meat-tenderizing mallet; one of those block-headed hammers you use to pound filets. I pass the old-fashioned utensil to Peter, who takes it from me, bemused. I stare at the heavy mallet resting in his hand.

"That would suck if that hit you in the face," I say, apropos of nothing, and go back and standing in the entryway to the dining room, leaning against the doorframe as I sip my drink. I can't take my eyes off the meat-tenderizing mallet. I'm thinking how weird it is that we still use technology that wouldn't be out of place in a medieval kitchen.

"That would definitely suck." Peter uses the meat hammer to knock the paper-towel balls at John, who searches around for something he can use as a racket. He tries out a flashlight first, with limited results, then rolls up a magazine, which is infinitely more effective.

We're all having a good time, ignoring the faint smell of burning pizza. I'm fixated on Peter's swing. He's having trouble timing his serve. He tosses the paper wad in the air but misses connecting repeatedly, because of how slowly the paper falls. Wind resistance. I'm about to offer coaching advice when another thought pops into my head.

"Wouldn't it suck if that hammer flew out of your hand and blinded me?"

"What?!" John laughs at my non sequitur. I turn to look at him standing by the stove. At that moment I hear a loud crack, and my vision shrinks to a pinpoint. It's like watching a black-and-white television set turning off. I feel my limbs crumple beneath me. I muster every ounce of strength I have to keep from passing out completely. When I come to, I'm slumped in the doorway with blood pouring out of my nose. I look down at my shirt, which is quickly turning crimson.

"Holy Shit!" Peter yells.

"Oh my God!" John's mouth is hanging open.

Peter and John are so shocked that at first they don't move. When they see me start to slip down further, they rush over, supporting me so I can stand. I have one thing on my mind.

"You guys heard me say that, right? You witnessed that."

"I can't believe you just said that." John is right with me.

Peter looks miserable: guilty and frightened. "I'm so sorry," he says, showing me the empty handle in his hand. "The head flew off. It just detached from the handle. I'm so sorry, Liz. Should we go to a hospital?"

"No." Adrenaline is animating me. "My dad is a doctor. I need to go home."

"Do you think you should maybe stay here?" John's worried I'm reacting too quickly. I'm still shaking. I go check out my face in the bathroom mirror. The bridge of my nose has swelled up to twice its normal size. The skin beneath my left eye is taut and pink, infused with fluid, and you can distinctly see the indentation where the corner of the mallet head hit my face. It missed the inner curve of my left eye by centimeters. If I hadn't been looking at John, I would be blind. Then again, if I hadn't called out the freak event, would it have happened in the first place?

"That doesn't look so bad." Peter is squeezing into the powder room behind me, peering over my shoulder. We both laugh. "I'm really sorry," he says for the third time. He's finding his emotions difficult to express.

"I know. It wasn't your fault." I believe this almost more than he does. I wonder if the car spinning out on the highway was meant to warn me that danger was coming for me, head-on and fast.

Most of the bleeding stops within five minutes. The inner membranes have swollen up to such an extent that blood is now trickling down my throat. On the upside, now that I'm not gushing, the guys will let me leave. I want to get out of Peter's house as soon as possible. The last six hours have been very upsetting. I've already ruined most of his mother's dish towels, and Peter has no qualms about handing over the last of her set with a bunch of ice wrapped inside—for the road. I'm sure they think I'm crazy as I wave goodbye. I barely turn around; I'm literally running out of there. It's the end of an era. I'm sad to say this incident estranges Peter and me. On my part it's all tangled up with my fear of omens and organized religion. I don't like the idea of something invisible holding sway over me. For him, wrecking the face of a girl he liked was devastating.

Everybody thinks my song "Fuck and Run" is about sex, and on one level it is. But it's also about these moments when real connection and feeling is abandoned in favor of self-preservation. We come together and fly apart like colliding billiard balls because, for whatever reason, we sense annihilation.

When I get home, my dad examines me and concludes that nothing is broken. He gives me some codeine and sends me to bed. Mom is out of town, or I'm sure she would have intervened. I check the swelling obsessively over the next forty-eight hours, increasingly concerned that it's crooked. Finally, after three days, Dad looks at me across the breakfast table, bites into a croissant and. without apology or remorse, says, "You may be right. That might be broken."

I'm making him sound heartless. If anything he's too sensitive. But not about medical diagnoses. Any doctor's kid will tell you that, unless your arm is fucking hanging off your shoulder by a thread, they always think their children are fine. They hate bringing their work home with them. Doctors see so many extreme cases at the clinics that your problem looks insignificant by comparison. It's a heart-numbing job. Day in, day out, everybody's got something wrong with them. They don't just think you're fine; they *need* you to be fine. Home is the only respite from illness, injury, and the fragility of mankind. Doctors need to come home to a house full of winners and survivors.

He drives me downtown on Tuesday to see a friend of his. For me, going to the doctor means getting a one-off appointment with the head of some department, some friend of a friend, or a colleague of someone in our social network. I haven't seen a regular doctor since I went to a pediatrician. Doctors will do anything to stay out of the hospital themselves. They know better than anyone the limitations of their profession. Our close friend, a GP, got up the day after open-heart surgery and went home. Think about that the next time you're obsessively trying to get an appointment with your physician because you have a cold.

I lie on the examination table, staring up at a very nice plastic surgeon as he holds my cheeks in his hands and eyeballs my bone structure.

"Mmmmm, that's a little off." He runs his finger over the indentation, calculating the angle of the fracture. "You're very lucky. A few millimeters to the left and you would have lost that eye." I know, I think. But I don't tell him the story. "When did it happen?"

"Friday night."

"Eh, that's too bad. This would hurt less if you had come in right away. But I think if I just apply pressure, I can snap that back for you."

Before I can protest, he leans his weight into his thumbs on either side of the bridge of my nose and pushes down. My barely healed flesh wound shrieks in protest, and my skull is pissed at him, too. He's jamming my head down against the table, smashing my face into the plastic pad in a very unpleasant manner. My eyes are watering. My teeth are gnashing, and my face is twisted in a grimace. We're at a stalemate: force and resistance.

"Just about there." He readjusts his grip, and I hear an earsplitting crack as the barely-fused bone breaks apart again and the whole apparatus locks back into place, more or less. It's still crooked, but as our GP friend comments at a dinner party several months later, it's given me a more distinguished profile. Whatever. I'm not going back unless my obstructed breathing really starts to bug me.

I have to wear a very embarrassing splint on my face for a week. Two long pieces of tape, running horizontally from the splint all the way over to my left ear, supply the torque to keep my nose from drifting out of position. It's not subtle. People stare when I walk by. Worse yet, I have to go to Florida to visit my grandmother. She's my father's mother, and she is not doing well. She's all alone down there, apart from her nurses. My father can't leave work, and my mother is still out of town.

I board the plane, comforted by the thought that everyone will just assume I got a nose job, which is more on-brand for me—less threatening to my ego. A flying meat-tenderizing mallet just doesn't have the same ring to it. I have to make a connection in Georgia. As we're on the final approach, I see that we're flying very close to a nuclear power station. I react immediately to the iconic spindle shape of the cooling towers. Anyone old enough to remember the Three Mile Island nuclear accident remembers that silhouette with dread. It's emblazoned on my consciousness as symbol of invisible, relentless, slow-moving death. Wouldn't it suck, I think, if you happened to be making a connecting flight right when a nuclear reactor was melting down? To have the misfortune to be in the immediate vicinity and get fatally irradiated, for no better reason than that your airline carrier had to make a pit stop?

Right as I have this thought, the plane pulls up shockingly short of the runway—only fifty feet from the ground. The pilot guns the engines, making a steep climb. We bank sharply to the right, away from the towers, and everybody gasps. This is it, I think. I'm psychic, and we're all going to die of radiation poisoning.

My seat mate turns to me. "What's happening?" she asks, her face contorted with fear.

"Maybe something's wrong with the power plant." I lean back so she can see past me out the window.

Her eyes widen as she takes in the Three Mile Island–style cooling towers. "Oh God." She looks at me in startled disbelief. "You don't think?"

I shrug. I'm not committing either way; I'm just angling for credit in the event that I'm right. I need a witness. She's going to be my ringer when I get my picture in the paper. She will breathlessly tell reporters that she was sitting next to the girl who predicted the incident. She'll say she doesn't know how I did it—that I "just knew." I can see in her eyes that she's factoring all the horrible ways in which radiation kills you—the same litany of horrors that was just going through my mind. We all know that whatever dose we receive incidentally, the government will lie about it to try to minimize the lawsuits. We'll live, maybe for decades, knowing there's a ticking time bomb in our DNA.

The pilot comes on over the passenger address system to make an announcement. "Ladies and gentlemen, I'm sorry about the detour, but we got word from the airport that there was a flock of birds in the vicinity, so we are going to make a second approach as soon as they clear the area and get you safely on the ground in ten minutes. Unforeseen events can sometimes happen, and it's better to be safe than sorry. Thank you for your patience, and for flying American Airlines."

My seatmate rolls her eyes, exhaling. "Wow, that's a relief."

I smile politely, but I'm irritated. I think we could have survived an indirect hit of radiation from those towers, and I was about to have my psychic powers validated. An unnatural glow under certain lighting conditions seems like a small price to pay for proof of the divine.

Years later, after my second album had just come out, I did a DJ stint at the popular Chicago punk bar Delilah's. During my set, Peter's brother showed up with the infamous meat-tenderizing mallet asking me to sign it as a surprise birthday present for Peter. I don't remember if I signed it. It's almost a better story if I refused. Either way, I was offended. His brother didn't understand that not only had that accursed object nearly cost me an eye and permanently marred my features, it had cost Peter and me a seven-year friendship. Peter wouldn't like to be reminded of that, either, I felt sure.

Some things heal, some things don't. I don't feel any bitterness toward Peter. I never did, apart from resenting the odd bad angle in a photograph. But if it weren't my nose, I'm sure I'd find something else about my looks to fixate on. We were just two billiard balls that got knocked to opposite sides of the table; that's how I frame it. I got a letter a few years ago from one of our mutual friends, complaining that I had dropped my long-term friends now that I was a rock star. He laid on the guilt pretty thick, but it took no deliberation whatsoever for me to toss the letter in drawer and forget about it. I still have all my long-term friends. They're just mostly women. What he should have said was that he wanted to be a famous actor, and that it was hard to watch my success and not get to share in it.

I doubt Peter would have agreed with the letter's tone. Peter and I helped each other through an uncertain time between college graduation and the beginning of our careers. It lasted for less than a year, but while we were living it, that time felt interminable: a lifetime of self-scrutiny and alienation, packed into eight or nine idle months under our parents' roofs. He influenced my sensibility and my humor, and I hope I was helpful to him in some way.

It would have been nice if things had turned out differently and we'd stayed friends, but we didn't. And this outcome is fine, too. It's much more memorable than some of my other past relationships. He holds an honored place in my personal history. He's been enshrined in the folklore of my life. None of it is difficult to understand if you think like a pagan. We were the victims of three bad omens, and they were real enough to scare me. I await the next cosmic turn of events and wouldn't be surprised if we accidentally wound up in the same retirement community someday. Peter and I would pick right back up where we left off, laughing at all the other old folks wearing their stupid name tags, getting to know one another out by the shuffleboard deck.

ART TK

seventeen

CUSTOMER EXPERIENCE

'm doing it again. I hate myself in a way, but I'm also excited. I took extra time this morning getting dressed, applying my makeup. I tried on several outfits, settling on a feminine bias-cut slip dress and sweater. Am I going to a fantastic party? An important meeting? Is this a radio station visit? Nope, I'm going grocery shopping. I'm going to Trader Joe's.

I know perfectly well that the staff at Trader Joe's is instructed to make friendly banter with the customers. I know that the atmosphere in the store is informal and convivial by design. I know that what I am doing is utterly pathetic and a little unhealthy, but I am currently in so much psychic pain, that going to the grocery store and flirting with a guy who looks like my ex is better than sitting at home crying in my pajamas. This is like training wheels, I tell myself. This is just you practicing getting out of the house and doing things normal people do again.

Ever since my boyfriend, Rory, and I broke up, I've lost all confidence in myself. His betrayal was so devastating that I don't want to leave the house. I feel transparent. I'm so self-conscious that I think everyone who looks at me can see exactly what he did, and I imagine that I must look pitiable to them. Every secret fear I have about myself feels like it's written on a big sign over my head:

I WASN'T PRETTY ENOUGH TO DATE A GUY LIKE THAT.

I'M THE ONLY ONE LEFT WHO IS SINGLE.

IF I WERE SUCCESSFUL, I WOULDN'T BE DOING MY OWN SHOPPING.

THINGS THAT ARE REALLY HARD FOR ME SEEM TO BE EASY FOR OTHER PEOPLE. I WILL NEVER FIT IN ANYWHERE.

IT'S TOO LATE TO FIND LOVE.

I'm lonely every day, and I don't want to be. I don't want his actions to break me. I want to get out and engage with the world again, but I'm too shaken up to risk it. If I were to run into friends or acquaintances that I haven't seen in a while, I would feel obligated to lie about what's going on in my life, and I don't lie very well. There's no way I could put on a brave face and admit what happened. I would burst into tears on the spot. I'm that emotionally fragile right now.

My close friends call to check in. They try to get me to join them for dinner parties, but that inevitably means hanging out with couples, and my singleness feels like a scarlet letter emblazoned across my chest. Rationally, I know that everyone is ultimately self-centered, and they couldn't care less what's going on in my love life. A few women I know might even take some satisfaction in seeing that, indeed, you *can't* have it all. You don't get to be a rock star and have people clap for you, have magazines photograph you, go to awards shows, and still have a happy homelife, do you? You don't get to sing about sex and call men out and still be part of a happy, committed relationship. I wonder sometimes if my own mother agrees on that point. You make choices, and those choices have consequences. Maybe love is not something that is destined to come my way, after the things I've done and the person I've been in the world.

If you think this sounds self-pitying, you're right. This latest heartbreak solidified a fear of mine: I was too far outside of society to ever crawl back in again. I would have to live out the rest of my life on the fringes, always being the odd one out. I was too straight to be deeply enmeshed with the artists' communities I knew, and too bent to settle down with the mainstream suburban crowd I'd grown up with. And now I was alone. Again.

I was a sham, a fraud. The world saw me as a renegade, a fearless maverick, and here I was nervous about making the one big jaunt of my day to the grocery store to flirt with a checkout clerk. This Trader Joe's guy was paid to be friendly. It wasn't even a challenge. I didn't care. I needed something to make the pain disappear for half an hour, and this worked. The pot didn't work, the booze didn't work, but this did. I would come home from Trader Joe's on the days I'd seen him feeling happy and attractive, like I had something to look forward to in life. Where was the harm in it? In the grand scheme of things it seemed like an innocent if embarrassing indulgence. What could go wrong?

When you exit a long-term relationship suddenly, you go a little crazy. The ripping away of someone you love leaves your heart hungry and your arms empty, and you at a loss as to which way to turn. The only thing you know for sure is that you can't go back the way you came. You must go forward, or sideways, or up, or down; anywhere except home again, because that's not your home anymore. You are temporarily homeless.

Losing love can turn you into a ghost in your own life. You go to all the same places, do the same things, but you're not really there. You're surrounded by friends and family, people with whom you intimately belong, but because your heart is broken, you listen to their laughter and conversation as if from a great distance. You're physically present, but emotionally, you're in some parallel dimension from which you cannot escape, no matter how hard you try. Time will refasten what's come unmoored inside you. In the meantime, you exist in the netherworld, with your face pressed up to the glass—wishing you could be like those happy people again, so oblivious, seemingly secure, and self-satisfied.

It could be worse, I tell myself as I drive to the store, feeling foolish. I could be home drinking. This is better than that. I park the car and feel like the poster child for low self-esteem as I walk toward the entrance. I know I look good, in that way that turns heads and has no business pushing a grocery cart around. Being in the entertainment business has taught me how to shine when I want to, and I do it so well that I almost consider it an unfair advantage. It is too effective. I can feel it working already as I wipe the cart handle down with the disinfecting wipes. I look lovely; I smell like somewhere you would want to vacation. My perfume floats on the breeze. It's all superficial. It signifies nothing. It's just a way to present myself that garners a reaction.

I push the heavy cart up the brief incline and through the doors, annoyed that I got one with a bum wheel that perpetually sticks. I can't go back and exchange it for another, because that wouldn't fit with the effortless, happy-go-lucky image I'm working so hard to project, so I smile and force the damn thing forward. I feel my long skirt flutter around my bare legs. I scrutinize the produce, my face carefully composed in a mask of equanimity and sweetness, with just a little bit of vulnerability thrown in to make me approachable. I frown in the cutest way as I gently squeeze a mango, taking a quick sniff to assess its ripeness. A man tips his hat at me, and I light up—as if this is the most relaxing and enjoyable experience. But I am stealing surreptitious glances around the store the whole time, scanning the checkout lines to see if Mr. T.J. is working as a cashier. He isn't.

I float down the aisle, checking my shopping list. I stop in front of the refrigerated section where the milk and butter are displayed. I stay there for an extra minute, knowing that the staff in the back can see through the slats. Sometimes when you open the door to reach for cream or yogurt, you see disembodied hands reaching out, restocking the shelves. I'm trawling myself through the store like angler bait, a shiny and tasty-looking morsel that's hoping to get a bite.

He's not working today. I've made sure to waft around the premises several times, but it's clear I've gotten all dressed up for nothing. I'm disappointed, and also angry with myself. I can't pretend that this isn't a ridiculous waste of money and time. What is it that I want to have happen, anyway? I don't really want to date a Trader Joe's cashier. I want my boyfriend back. But not the person he actually is; I want the person I thought he was—a person who doesn't technically exist. I can remember one day in the car, close to the end of our relationship, when he looked at me and said, "You don't really love me. You love the person you wish I were." I told him that wasn't true. I assured him that I was in love with him. But it turns out he was right. I was in love with a made-up man; involved, once again, with my own imagination.

I see one of the women who works the same shifts as Mr. T.J. She recognized me from my music career, and we've said hi a couple of times. She's definitely noticed my uptick in shopping habits, and I wouldn't be surprised if she knows why. I decide to take a chance and strike up a casual conversation. I ask her about Mr. T.J. She says he's super sweet, goofy, and almost childlike in his naïveté. I've noticed that from our brief interactions. That is part of what is so appealing about him to me, I guess: that he looks like my ex but in a completely nonthreatening form. A declawed version of the body I'm pining for.

Do you remember that movie where Michael Keaton clones himself so that he can have more free time? *Multiplicity*. The first iteration he makes is a tough guy, a real, all-American male. The second clone is effeminate, a sensitive, gay version of himself. The third is a simpleton, a replica that came out wrong in the most cheerful, idiotic way. That's what Mr. T.J. reminds me of: a soft-minded stand-in for the guy who broke my heart. I guess, in some weird way, I'm trying to find closure with a look-alike, because I can't ever reach out to my ex again.

The moment I latched onto this crazy notion was swift and unexpected. I was in the checkout line with my son after school. We were waiting for our turn at the register and I said, "Hey, doesn't that guy look like Rory?"

Nick glanced up briefly. "Kind of. I guess. A little."

But I was struck by the similarities. He really looked like a gentler, friendlier, slightly heavier doppelgänger of my ex. I couldn't stop staring at him as he chatted affably with the person ahead of me, whose groceries he was packing. His voice was loud. I think he liked showing off. He seemed so unselfconscious and eager to engage. My wounded heart started to beat a little faster. I missed the way my boyfriend had completed me. I missed having his strong presence around, protecting me; the way our personalities balanced each other out.

When it was my turn at the register, Mr. T.J. chatted loudly with me, too. I can't remember what we talked about. We just made casual conversation. But there was a moment when I was pushing an item forward on the conveyer belt, and he was reaching back for it, and our hands touched. I swear to God, I felt electricity shoot through my whole body. I pulled my hand away quickly, but it left an impression. My interest in him went from curiosity to full-blown attraction. It didn't matter what my logical brain told me anymore. The injured, hurting side of me got a hit of what it was missing, and all of a sudden I had a hankering for the Trader Joe's dude.

This has to be a common occurrence. I can't be the only one who falls for these affable hipsters who work half the year and travel the rest. There are a lot of lonely people out there— stumbling through the daily grind, moved to the point of tears by somebody's unexpected interest in them. It feels like a cold world sometimes. We can go days without anybody touching us or noticing how we're feeling. Seeing a familiar face in the neighborhood, particularly a young, nice-looking one, and having that person ask you about yourself is intoxicating when you're low, and the next thing you know you're stopping by the store too often. Smart business plan.

But now I'm taking the ill-advised step of trying to make the fantasy real. I've run out of things to say to the woman who works with Mr. T.J. I know this is my one chance to broach the subject before I think better of it and run away. I finally muster the courage to let her see my need. "Do you know if he has a girlfriend?" I ask, like I'm the kind of person who inquires about men all the time; like I'm someone who behaves in totally the opposite way from how I actually do.

"Yeah, I think he does." She winces sympathetically, which is about the best reaction I could hope for.

"Oh well," I say, shrugging. I am grateful that she doesn't register any judgment, any tiny glint of mocking superiority.

"But I can ask," she offers helpfully.

"No, no, please don't," I beg. "Don't say anything. Don't even say I asked."

"Of course not!" She's very understanding. I feel a kinship between us now. A simple human gesture of empathy can mean so much when you're out of alignment. I head toward the checkout line, strangely relieved to know that my interest will never turn into anything more. I guess I know deep down that I won't find what I'm looking for in a Trader Joe's store. But I am confused as to why he gave such special attention to me. In the past few weeks, he's been very solicitous. When we bump into each other in the aisle, he tells me about his travels—how he works part of the year to be able to take the rest of the time off, visiting places all over the world. I listen, nodding, staring at his face trying to see a better, kinder Rory in it.

One day when I came in, he brought out a painting from the back storage area that he'd purchased for me somewhere in Indonesia. It was a hideous example of its genre, one of those dark, acrylic tourist items depicting palm trees in front of the ocean at sunset. I felt really weird leaving the store with a big painting in my cart, but it was so nice to have something a man carried half way around the world to give to me.

He told me he was one of those guys who brings presents to all of his friends, so I didn't read too much into it. Still, now that I know he has a girlfriend, I think its a bit shady. I've seen this dynamic before. My career has this effect on people. Celebrity, however minor, turns people's heads. I try to be the person that I am, but my public image hangs around me like a fog. I can see it in people's eyes as they're talking to me. Once they figure out what I do for a living, they start working out how they can benefit from knowing me, calculating how much access to other celebrities having me in their life would bring them. I don't get mad or feel exploited; I usually just feel dismayed and sense a gap widening between us. It's not their fault. Celebrity is like a disease. It has a predictable pathology, and it's catching.

I leave Trader Joe's knowing that whatever unhealthy impulse took me down this road has reached a dead end. I'm sorry not to have the distraction of my crush anymore. I start shopping at Whole Foods instead. The next time I go to Trader Joe's, I'm back in my sweats and T-shirt like a sane person.

One day about six months later, around Christmastime, I'm in the store with my friend Tracey. Mr. T.J. comes bounding up, glowing with excitement. He says he has something special for me. "You haven't been here for a while, and I was afraid I wasn't going to see you before the holidays!"

Tracey and I glance at each other. What can he mean? He runs off to the stock room and comes back out carrying a giant gift basket with an assortment of gourmet foodstuffs that he's assembled for me. He's carrying it over his head, obviously proud of himself, and everybody's watching us. Seeing this interaction through my friend's eyes is mortifying. She instantly knows that I must have been doing something I shouldn't have to warrant this lavish display, but I assure her that I'm as surprised as she is. In fact, I'm so embarrassed by my earlier state of mind that I'm almost dismissive of my part in starting this madness. I want to erase any of my own responsibility in getting this guy all agitated.

In my defense, his gestures are always outsized to the circumstances. It's just the way he is. I've probably only ever talked to him at the store four or five times. He told me when we met that he's generous, that he likes to do things for people. But still, this whole basket delivery is odd. I take my enormous basket and try not to blush crimson. I feel ridiculous walking toward the checkout. My mind is racing. What does this mean? Why would somebody act like this? What does he want? Tracey is smirking. She thinks he wants to sleep with me. I wish I had never flirted with him. He asks for my number, and out of obligation, I give it to him.

"Maybe we can go get coffee sometime," he says. I say sure, and he looks satisfied. There's something in his eyes at that moment, something much harder and more calculating, that snaps me back to attention. He's not the innocent goof that he pretends to be. I've gotten myself in way over my head. Once again, I've zeroed in on the guy who's presenting a false front, a personality trait that I apparently find very sexy.

He calls to ask me out to lunch later that week, and I accept. I don't know why, whether I'm still in thrall to my crush or feel like I owe it to him. After all, I'm the one who started this mess.

We meet at the Northside Cafe. We sit out on the sidewalk, dining al fresco. The conversation is awkward. He tells me way too much about himself, about his family and his abusive stepdad.. His childhood doesn't sound happy. I listen, but I am very uncomfortable. I'm acutely aware that I should not be having coffee with him. I'm trying to think of how to get out of this situation, of how to prevent things from going any further. He's telling me about his motorcycle.

And then here comes the kicker: He pulls out his cellphone and, with an excited look on his face, formally asks me to attend his wedding in Mexico. "It's going to be great," he enthuses, showing me a picture of his fiancée, and another one of their wedding invitation. "If you give me your address, I can send you a proper paper copy."

I'm stunned. I thought he was trying to hook up with me. Is this guy crazy? Why on earth would he think I would want to go to a stranger's destination wedding in Mexico, let alone to the marriage ceremony of a man I've just been flirting with?

The threads of our interaction are unraveling fast, and he can feel it. He tries to keep my attention focused on him, but I'm calculating how much longer I'll have to remain seated before I can get up and flee. He natters on about his fiancée and tells me that they live over a mortuary on Sepulveda Boulevard. This detail strikes me as particularly morbid.

"Aren't you scared?" I ask him. "Doesn't it creep you out to know that dead people are lying in coffins right below you?"

"Not at all," he assures me. He loves their place. It's cheap and big.

And haunted, I think, but I don't say anything. I thank him for the invitation but very firmly decline to attend their nuptials. He looks crestfallen. How could he have thought I would come? I'm suddenly scrutinizing my own behavior over the course of this ill-conceived romance, looking for clues as to why I find myself in these absurd circumstances.

I stop shopping at Trader Joe's altogether. It's too bad, because it was convenient, but I'm glad I can exit the situation so cleanly. I really have no one but myself to blame. This is why, I tell myself, you have to stay in your own lane, try to do things properly. After a while, I forget about Mr. T.J. I still have issues to work through about my ex, but I'm past the excruciating phase of the break up, and I don't feel so lonely or needy anymore.

About a year later, I stop by Trader Joe's to pick up some quick necessities. I don't even think about Mr. T.J. while I'm there, but I do run into the woman who worked with him, the one I'd spoken to. She pulls me aside, a concerned look on her face.

"I don't know if you heard what happened," she tells me, "but I know you guys were close."

I feel all prickly with anticipation, and defensive, too. How could she think Mr. T.J. and I were close? What has he been telling everybody?

"John committed suicide."

I stare at her. She can't mean the same person. She can't mean that friendly, happy-go-lucky, handsome young man. "But he just got married . . ." My voice trails off.

"I know." She checks to make sure I'm handling the news okay. "It's really sad. He killed himself about six months ago. I just thought you should know."

We look at each other for a while. In the silence, we both communicate our understanding that, beyond the formalities of social norms, people who shop or work or live near each other know a lot more about one another's lives than they let on.

"We weren't close," I feel compelled to state. It's a stupid, petty, vain thing to say in this moment, but I need her to know this. "We just saw each other at the store, and had coffee once."

"Yeah, but you guys were friends," she insists.

I stop myself from correcting her. There's no point. I roll the cart down the aisle in slow motion, trying to imagine how someone so alive and engaging could be dead, gone, buried or cremated. He doesn't exist at all. I'm in the world and he's not anymore. What problems, what issues, was he hiding behind that happy exterior? I flash back to that first touch of our hands. I can see his blue eyes clearly. I can see better now that he was reaching out from a place of pain, just like I was—only I was too wrapped up in my own misery to notice. That must have been the electricity, the spark of connection between us. We were both among the walking wounded. It's terribly sad to contemplate.

I realize that this guy whom I barely knew is now permanently part of my story. I have no choice but to remember him. I'll bet a million bucks that was part of the logic running through his mind when he decided to take his own life, the assurance that every person he'd ever helped or tried to get close to would be shocked, would reevaluate him after he was gone. We would all have to carry him with us in our memories forever, whether we wanted to or not. I pass the canned tomatoes and pasta, the olive oil and the spices. I hear the bell above the office ringing, and the checkout people laughing and calling out to one another in that affable, warm, uniquely Trader Joe's atmosphere. The sun streams in through the windows and the flowers outside the doors burst in a profusion of color, little honey bees buzzing around the blossoms. What a world.

The next time I see the young woman who worked with Mr. T.J., she's manning the check-out line, bagging my groceries. She looks drawn and tired. I ask her how she's doing, and she tells me her mother's been in the hospital with a serious illness. She's been going to visit her every day after she gets off work, sometimes staying with her all night, and she isn't getting any sleep. I read between the lines that her mom may not recover. I listen and try to comfort her. I'm glad to be able to return the caring and empathy she showed me when I was at my lowest. And I'm touched that these human connections can be made out of barely any interaction at all. It just takes a sensitive and perceptive outlook. In the end, we're all going through the same shit, trying to make it through the day with our own private struggles. The stranger next to you is so much more like you than you think.

I start shopping at Trader Joe's again. There's a new Mr. T.J. who's even better looking and more socially adept than John. He and I have a light, flirtatious rapport, but I know not to take it any further now. Sometimes when I see him, he does outrageously cute things, like blow me kisses from his bicycle when he's riding home from a shift. Once, I bumped into him at Vons, a competing grocery store, and he accused me of cheating on him. He definitely makes my heart beat faster, and it adds a sparkle to my day, but the specter of the former Mr. T.J. hangs like a curtain between us.

It may not be fair or ideal, but these arbitrary divisions in society—customer versus worker, older versus younger, established versus just starting out—they exist for our own protection as much to maintain the social order. Without meaning to, we sometimes scrape the safety layer off and end up penetrating one another's lives more deeply than we intend to. Certain collisions, it turns out, are just too hard to take. I'm not saying you should abide by the rules society lays out for you all the time, but I sure as hell recommend not flouting them heedlessly. Just do your shopping and go home and cry in your pajamas like a winner.

ART TK

eighteen

GOODBYES

clean my closet in an attempt to build a better life for myself. I run my hand across the row of fabrics, removing any items that feel scratchy or stiff. I imagine the guy I'm dating wrapping his arms around me, and anything that doesn't feel good to the touch has to go. I think about what I'd take with me if he asked me to move in with him. I think about what kinds of clothes he'd like to see me in if he came home and saw me walking around the house. Garments that fail to pass this test are tossed unceremoniously into a lavender-scented trash bag, then stuffed into the trunk of my car to be driven to Goodwill in the morning. It's like murder: killing the outfits that once served me well. But they have too many memories clinging to them, and I'm ready to start over.

By the time I'm finished purging, half my previous wardrobe is gone. What I keep looks great on the hangers, the racks spacious and sleek like an art installation. Decluttering feels like rebirth, as if

I'm inviting in the future rather than dwelling on the past. I'm scared of winding up as an eccentric old lady living alone in a big dusty house. I deliberately sought out a life in which I would never feel lonely or isolated. I work in a hectic, crowded environment. Yet when I go home and there's no one there, the empty rooms feel even lonelier in contrast. Sometimes I can see that old lady in the mirror looking back at me, waiting for her chance to burst out.

My friend Mallory had to clean out her grandmother's apartment after she died. Mallory's mother was undergoing chemotherapy in another state and couldn't expose her fragile immune system to a flight. Mallory drove down from Winnetka to Evanston every day for a week and bagged up all her grandmother's mementos and keepsakes, her costume jewelry, books, letters, and clothing. She kept a porcelain jewelry box and some dishes, setting aside some other sentimental items for the rest of the family to choose from, but nobody wanted very much. At the end of the process she had to leave her grandmother's whole life, essentially, out in the hallway in bin bags, like so much trash for the garbage truck.

She sobbed as she drove home that Friday night, helpless to shield herself from the realization that this could happen to her one day. All the objects she'd gathered around her, everything she cherished, all this stuff she'd accumulated over the course of a lifetime, was essentially meaningless.

"I saw myself, Liz," she wailed on the phone as she was driving. "I saw us as old ladies with a bunch of crap that nobody wants. Olivia, Adam, Paloma, and Nick are going to have to shovel all our belongings into trash bags and throw them out someday. I don't want have things anymore! I don't want to buy anything, and I don't want to own anything. I don't want any material possessions at all. I want to go somewhere really beautiful and live in a tent.

She'd looked into the abyss, and now she couldn't turn away from the nothingness we all become in the end. For a while, she felt like everything she did was a struggle against the headwind of her own insignificance. Roman emperors carved their names into everything.

Pharaohs commissioned monuments. Presidents have their libraries. Everybody's afraid of annihilation. And whether you walk toward it or run away from it as far and as fast as possible, it's coming for you.

I watched an incredible movie called *Ruth's Journey* about a wealthy woman whose life was ruined because of her attachment to things. Her granddaughter, a young woman from the North Shore of Chicago named Melinda Roenisch, wrote and directed the documentary. Ruth had once been an attractive, outgoing woman who married happily and raised a loving family. She began buying antiques as a hobby, a way to occupy herself while accompanying her husband on business trips. She'd been born into good taste, and supplemented it with further education. She loved to sift through rural estate sales looking for undiscovered treasures. Soon, she was known and respected as a savvy collector.

But in her old age, after her husband passed away and her children were busy with families of their own—deprived of stimulation and suffering from the early symptoms of dementia—she clung to her objects like a life raft, cleaning them obsessively, jealously guarding them when anyone entered the house. It became her all-consuming passion to catalogue and count her precious artifacts. Soon, she shunned visits from her family for fear that they might break something. She followed the maids around like a shadow, occasionally accusing them of mishandling important pieces. Several quit under the strain.

I think about the pleasure I get from arranging my closet; how I like to return to look at it several times in the evening. I imagine Ruth wandering her halls, touching and shifting her antiques slightly to the right or left. Moving a piece to a different room. Changing her mind and returning it to its original place. It must have felt like a puzzle she could never solve; like striving for an elusive perfection. She wouldn't leave the house for fear someone might break in and rob her. She lived in a grand mansion overlooking Lake Michigan, but she was essentially a prisoner of her mental illness. It was hard to say which came first, the hoarding instinct or the pressure of owning so many valuables.

After she died, her grown children had no interest in preserving her collection. It had become a symbol of what had separated her from them. Some vases and historically significant furniture were donated to museums, but the bulk of her estate was sold at auction, mostly in large lots. It was the only way to remove such an enormous cache of personal effects at once. The dealers and collectors gathered in the living room, surrounded by her massive inventory. Everything you could think of as being of use in a household was present in triplicate: silverware, table settings, chairs, sofas, fire irons, table lamps, oil paintings, vases, pedestals, breakfronts, carpets, kitchenware. There was barely any room to move in the house, no quiet place for the eye to land. Her collection was madness materialized—a portrait of a sick woman who tried to heal herself with beautiful things.

It was hard to watch the auction. The spectacle of someone who had lived so privately being exposed in such a public way was painful, like seeing a dignified old lady stripped naked and paraded through the village. Even after she was gone, her objects told the story of her loneliness. It didn't take long before the grand house was emptied of every last belonging as the parasites picked clean the bones of her corpse. All her time, effort, discernment, and devotion had been converted instantly into cash. All the hundreds of Saturdays spent traveling to sales, all the time she spent perfecting her haggling skills, all her dedication to completing those cup and saucer sets—all for nothing. Her life's work had been undone in an afternoon.

In the documentary, Roenisch takes us through the empty house one last time, passing from room to barren room. The sun, streaming through curtainless windows, exposes ripped-up floors. Workmen in cranes and bulldozers remove the fireplaces, doorframes, decorative lintels, and garden statuary to be sold, too, until the house itself is an uninhabitable ruin. The metaphor is so heavy with implications for our society that it physically hurts. You feel like you're watching violence, but it's only the natural order of life here on earth, which we're constantly fighting. The body dies, the body decays, eventually nothing remains. Lover, beware! Be careful of clinging too tightly to anything that isn't eternal lest you lose everything in your quest to keep it.

When my beloved grandmother Winnie began to fade, I didn't want to face what was happening to her. In the beginning, I ignored her limitations. I identified with her deeply, and what was happening to her felt very threatening to me. I used to look at senior citizens as if they were frozen in time at whatever age they happened to be, but after watching Winnie deteriorate both mentally and physically, I saw older adults as being on a slow, inexorable slide into oblivion. I could no longer be around them without thinking about the process.

I worked as an art therapist at my father's hospital one summer during college. I loved commuting downtown with him in the mornings. It was exciting to see what his life outside our home was like. As we crawled along through rush-hour traffic, we played a game where I would select a sports car to follow and he would try to keep up with it. Nobody was moving very fast, so our maneuvers weren't dangerous, but I would cajole Dad into switching lanes and passing cars to keep our "team leader" in view. I think he enjoyed getting a little wild and crazy, too. It reminded him of his youth. With Lake Michigan changing colors on our left and the Chicago skyline looming, the windows of the skyscrapers glinting pink in the dusty haze of dawn, we raced at a snail's pace, and I cheered every time Pops snuck his way around another one of the lethargic commuters.

We'd part company as soon as we arrived at Northwestern Memorial Hospital. I was assigned to different wards throughout the week, rotating between substances abusers, girls with eating disorders, pediatric patients, psychiatric patients, and the geriatric population. I was exposed to a lot of disruptive and unsettling behavior, but nothing depressed me like the aging. They had so little energy. A lot of them looked like they'd given up on life already. I tried to interest them in painting, drawing, or making collages, but it was hard for them to hold the brushes, pencils, and scissors. When I thought about their options, I just felt hopeless.

I vowed that I would never die in a hospital. I would get eaten by a shark or killed by a bear, thrown off a cliff or drown in the ocean, but I definitely wouldn't wither away in the sterile, cheerless atmosphere I witnessed there. Later, I didn't want that for Winnie, either. My experiences with her were so rooted in nature, in gardening and the ocean. It killed me to see her move into a nursing home. When I was growing up, she was always by my side pointing out a delicate flower I'd missed in the grass, or a rare seashell tumbling in the surf beneath my feet. She was so observant. We would sit on the dock in Clearwater, Florida, and gaze into the green water until we could make out sparkling fish lurking beneath the planks. It felt to me like she was always making wonderful things appear as if by magic, but what she was really doing was teaching me how to see. Mystery is all around us, she explained, but it's hiding.

Right before I released my first album, I went with my parents to visit Winnie at her retirement home in Cincinnati. Things were coalescing in my career, finally. Under the moniker Girly-Sound, I had recorded a cassette tape of songs that had caught on in the underground music scene. I had an offer from Matador Records in New York, which was a dream come true on paper, but nothing in my personal life had significantly changed. I was frustrated, waiting for something to happen, needing money. I was hungry to be recognized, and also worried about performing my songs live. I'd never been onstage before. Everyone was telling me I should start playing out, but I had terrible stage fright. I needed to be visible in the music scene, to connect with the community of songwriters who were as ambitious and striving as I was. The last thing I wanted to do was hang out with a bunch of older adults who were no longer working and had spent all their drive.

I was a brat. My parents didn't know anything about my life at the time, and they couldn't understand why I was behaving so badly. We stopped at a Starbucks on the way to the nursing home, and I kicked the wall because I felt like no one was listening to me. Then I walked outside and smoked a cigarette in plain view of my parents, who sat in stunned silence—no doubt imagining the kind of life I'd led in San Francisco. They'd never seen this side of my personality, and it frightened them. My mom didn't even mention the cigarette when I came back inside, which meant we were at DEFCON 2. In fact, they said nothing at all. My mother looked at me archly, as if to communicate: We are going to see my mother. Pull it together, young lady, or there will be consequences.

I couldn't explain that every nerve in my body was screaming, Run, run, run! I was having an anxiety attack, but I wasn't mature enough to articulate it. From her point of view there was nothing for me to resent about our visit apart from its inconvenience. It hurt her deeply to think that I wouldn't repay Winnie's devotion to me for all those years. She didn't understand that it killed me to see my grandmother like this; that it felt like being complicit in her death, in a way that I wasn't prepared for. In my mind, it was a lie to smile and pretend that everything was all right, to persuade her that she should be happy living here when, if it were me, I'd want my family to break me out and take me as far away from this death factory as possible.

We sat in Winnie's lovely apartment eating hors d'oeuvres and sipping cocktails. It was about 108 degrees in the retirement home. We'd peeled off our sweaters, unbuttoned our collars, and rolled up our sleeves. Winnie had her feet up on an ottoman and a cashmere blanket spread across her lap. I was dizzy from the heat and the way the sound was dampened by the plush wall-to-wall carpeting and chintz upholstery. Every once in a while, one of the caretakers popped her head in the door to get a look at us. They wanted us to know that they loved Winnie, and to say how popular she was on this floor. Each one of them seemed to think they were her favorite.

It didn't surprise me. But I wondered if she had any real friends in this nursing home anymore. Two of the women she moved there to be close to had died—one recently. There was a little condolence wreath tacked to the woman's door.

Winnie saw me looking bored. She pointed to the window and said, "Look, Elizabeth." She had that familiar twinkle in her eye.

I got up and peered out into the blue night. Snow had started falling, big, fluffy clumps of it. "Can I go outside for a bit?" I asked. "I want to be in the snow."

My mother frowned. She probably thought I was going outside to smoke.

"Yes," Winnie said. "That's a good idea." She nodded, encouraging me.

"Just don't go too far," my father warned. He thought I was going out for a cigarette, too, and probably wished he could join me.

Downstairs, the residents in the main lounge watched as I walked out the front door, their eyes eagerly following everything around them. I wished I could restore their strength and lead them like a troop of scouts, out into the brisk azure evening.

Once I was in the fresh air, I felt better. It wasn't too cold. I could see a path going around the side of the building, which looked like a good place to light up. I followed the cement tiles into the shadows, stepping gingerly, dodging cobwebs. I leaned against the brick wall and sparked up a Camel Light. Tilting my head, I blew the smoke up toward the trees, feeling like Lauren Bacall: all hips and elbows.

Winnie's nursing home sat at the edge of a steep ravine, just like the one I grew up playing in on Interwood Avenue. I decided to scramble down to the bottom and check out the white ribbon of frozen water meandering along the ravine floor. It looked magical under the moonlight, like a fairy-tale illustration. The ground was harder than I'd anticipated, covered in a layer of ice, and I fell and slid most of the way down, snagging my dress pants on the underbrush. Great, I thought. Now I'll never get back up. A dog in one of the houses on the far side of the ravine started barking.

I stood up and brushed myself off, admiring my new perspective. I tested the frozen stream with my toe. I could feel the pressure cracking the waxy surface, see the black water sloshing below the crust. I could have been five years old again, playing in the woods behind Winnie and Granddad's house. I needed to believe that the past was not gone forever, that even when Winnie died, we'd all get another chance to be together, to do it all over again somehow.

I was staring into the distance, looking at the cheery lights in the houses across the way, when I heard twigs breaking and footsteps trudging through the snow on the slope behind me. I spun around to see a herd of deer walking slowly through the forest. It was a mother and two juveniles. They were traversing the hill on a secret path that had been invisible to me, halfway between Winnie's building and where I was standing, down in the cut. I held my breath as they got closer, unsure if they were aware was there, not wanting to startle them. They plodded along, the snow accumulating on their shoulders—the epitome of sure-footed grace. I couldn't believe I was within spitting distance of these wild creatures. They were so big and soulful. Normally, I only saw deer when they also saw me, or when they were on TV. This was like standing in line behind a movie star at a coffee shop in L.A. You got a totally different sense of the person whom you think you knew so well already.

Winnie died ten years later. We watched her slip away by degrees. First, she lost her mobility, then she was plagued by confusion, then it was breast cancer, then it was Alzheimer's. She'd outlived three husbands, and had a full life until her last decade. I got a call from her care facility while I was eating Easter brunch at a friend's house.

The nurse was a poor communicator. She said Winnie had pneumonia, and she was going to pass away shortly. "I've seen a lot of them like this," she said. "She doesn't have long."

I thought, What the hell are you doing saying that in front of her? I was irritated. I heard her say, in her Ohio Valley drawl, "Winnie? It's your granddaughter. It's Elizabeth. Say hi." Then, to me,

"Well, go ahead, honey. Tell her that you love her."

She put the phone up to Winnie's ear, and I could hear my grandmother's raspy breathing over the phone. I started saying whatever popped into my mind; just stupid stuff, like "How are you? I love you. Can you hear me?" She didn't respond. I finally realized she was unconscious.

I took the first flight I could get and made it to the nursing home before any other family members arrived. I had some cousins in the area who visited Winnie regularly, but this acute crisis took us all by surprise. We'd gotten used to her slow, steady decline, and now everything was happening quickly. No matter how long you anticipate it, I don't think you're ever ready for the finality of death. The no-more-chances of it.

My parents weren't due until later, so I had Winnie to myself for a couple of hours, just the two of us in a room alone. I had no idea what to do for somebody who was dying, so I got some lotion and started massaging her hands and legs, conversing with her like a chatty masseuse. I recounted all my favorite memories of her, describing the great times we'd spent together. I recalled the way the women in our family stayed up until 3:00 a.m. on Christmas Eve, sipping sherry and wrapping presents until the fire died out. I reminded her of the time in Clearwater, Florida, when I tried to save the lobsters she was getting ready to cook by throwing them back into the ocean with their claws still pegged. I talked about the tractor rides, and the sunflowers she grew, and our amazing Fourth of July celebrations when my uncle and my dad turned into pyromaniacs for the day.

I kept watching to see if her limbs moved or her eyelids fluttered, but she was basically gone. Sprouting from her jaw were a couple of seven-inch-long chin hairs that quivered every time she exhaled. I wanted to pluck them so badly. She'd always been very vain about her appearance, even walking in a local fashion show at age seventy-five. But I wasn't about to cause her pain in her final moments. Let the mortician deal with that, I thought. To me, it seemed like evidence of neglect, and I was much chillier the next time one of the nurses came in to check on us. I booted her out of the room before she had a chance to waste any more of my precious time.

Winnie never woke up again. By dinnertime, everyone had arrived. We ordered food and stayed up late, talking and laughing in the next room. If she could hear anything, I imagine it sounded exactly like one of those joyful gatherings in the past when we ate sumptuous meals together and took drinks in the living room, reveling in one another's company. Those were the days when her first husband—my mother's father—was still alive, as was her son. I would say we did a pretty convincing pantomime of some of the happiest times in her life. We all went back to our hotels at about 1:00 a.m., and she passed away sometime between our departure and dawn. I can easily believe she waited to slip away quietly, not wanting to bother anyone.

On the flight back to L.A., all my emotions bubbled up unexpectedly. The in-flight movie was *Finding Neverland*, a tearjerker about the inspiration behind the book *Peter Pan*. I was overcome watching Johnny Depp's character, the author J. M. Barrie, encourage the imaginations of the young Llewelyn Davies boys, who have just lost their father. I thought about how Winnie cultivated my imagination, and how it was an integral part of who I became. She was responsible for so much that I'd been able to do and express as an artist. Her property in Indian Hill was my Neverland, and I hadn't made that connection until it was too late to thank her.

I started bawling in my seat, crying silently. My shoulders heaved, and my face was wet. I kept dabbing at my eyes with cocktail napkins. I put my sunglasses on in the darkened cabin and sat there, a wreck, blowing my nose every two minutes. I was helpless to staunch the flow of feelings that poured out of me. The other first-class passengers were unnerved by my outburst. Somebody passed me more napkins. The other passengers in my aisle kept their gazes deliberately forward, but I knew they must be thinking I was taking the picture a little hard.

Something had gotten jostled loose in me with Winnie's passing, something that had been blocked, and now I couldn't stop crying. In the days after, I became emotional at the drop of a hat. Sentimental. Regretful. In awe of the power of love. Horrified that I couldn't have Winnie back. It became a joke between my boyfriend and me, because I was not sad, I was just *feeling*. He would come over and find me crying while I was cooking. Or a TV commercial would set me off. I knew in my heart that what I really couldn't accept was the act of dying itself. I was crying over the fact that everyone I loved had to die. I was crying because dying had to be a part of living.

One night, about a week later, I had an intense dream. I was kneeling before an altar, looking at Winnie on her death bed. She was swaddled in a blanket, but sitting up, drinking a glass of fizzy Airborne cold medicine that my mother had just poured for her. I heard Mom say, "Mother, you looked so good! Even in death, you were adorable." Winnie seemed pleased, but I felt separated from them, like I was watching this tableau from another reality. The sheets from Winnie's bed extended all the way down to the floor and flowed over the altar, spreading beneath me like a field of snow. I wished I could share in their happiness.

I felt a presence over my left shoulder, a wise and spiritually enlightened being. I was not allowed to look at him, but he said four words to me, and just like that, I was cured. He used simple language, something a human could understand, to describe a much more complex and nuanced truth about the universe: "There is no death." I didn't cry the next day, or the next, or ever again in the same manner. Since then, I have trust in my bones that Winnie's okay, that we're all okay.

My own parents are aging now. They're the ones who need help crossing icy patches of sidewalk and getting in and out of cars. They're preparing to move into a retirement community soon. I'm the one who's urging my grown son to spend time with them on the weekends while he's at school in Chicago. I can't make him understand, any more than my parents could make me see at his age, what an opportunity and a gift the opportunities to soak up the presence of your grandparents, while they're still here. He loves Mimi and Poppy, and he spends a lot of time with them, but he doesn't yet relate to the profound forces of love at work within these intergenerational relationships. He's not supposed to. He's young.

I go with my parents to hear a lecture on North Korea at the Fortnightly of Chicago. I'm in town for the week, staying at a hotel in the loop near my son's dorm. He's already tired of seeing me, so I find myself at loose ends and invite myself to tag along with Mom and Dad. I love the old Lathrop House on Bellevue Place. Nick's father and I were married there. The Georgian-style mansion was built in 1892 as a private residence and sold to the Fortnightly in 1922. It has an old-world glamour that is increasingly rare in the modern age.

When I arrive, the pre-lecture cocktail party is in full swing. Men in sport coats and women in colorful suits and scarves are milling about downstairs. The library reeks of Scotch. I spot my elderberries amongst the sea of white-hairs and join their conversation. I talk with a very interesting couple about 3-D printing, and their grandson's inappropriate attire in this year's Christmas card. I tell them he's my hero. I'm the youngest person present by at least twenty years, and certainly the only one wearing black fishnet stockings. The bartender and I exchange glances every so often to keep it real.

When it's time to take our seats in the ballroom, I notice how many people are having difficulty walking through and finding their seats, including my father. I've reached an age when I don't see older adults as a separate category anymore. I see them as upperclassmen with motility issues. They're distinct people to me now, some awesome, some annoying. I do notice my own strength in comparison, though. I'm aware that my muscles are full and smooth, that my hair is shiny and thick. We are all destined to fade, but tonight, I admire the fortitude and the level of engagement it took some of the people around me to come downtown on a cold winter's night—to hear a talk about a part of the world that is more germane to America's future than its past. It shows interest in a geopolitical reshuffling they may not live to see.

Indeed, when I look at them, really look, I can imagine the women in ponytails, bobby socks, and saddle shoes, the men with their hair slicked back and their shirtsleeves rolled up—all of them going to a dance at a local gymnasium. They were young once, too. And though they may not have come here tonight for the sex, it's clear that they still care what they look like and enjoy being seen and, more importantly, being known by one another. It's so beautiful that it makes me want to cry. We do our best throughout our lives with our ever-changing bodies, but we're always the same people inside, whether we're eighty-two, forty-nine, twenty, or five.

The lecture is disappointing. I can tell the speaker thinks of himself as a hard-hitting journalist, à la Christiane Amanpour, but he's really one of those guys who will tell you he's a spy when he gets drunk enough. He's probably been working on the same "explosive" book for a decade. It's plain from his lack of preparedness that he thinks he can phone this one in and collect an easy paycheck. He's grossly underestimated his audience. The caliber of their intellect is entirely lost on him. He sees a bunch of rich old geezers who've been out of the game for years. I see a group of people who still care about a world that rarely cares about them. As one professional gigger to another, I'm thinking he can go fuck himself. I'm not even sure he's sober.

My dad starts coughing. He snuck his bourbon into the ballroom, and he's accidentally inhaled some. His face turns purple as he tries to suppress a cough. The speaker is droning on at the podium, and Dad is stubbornly refusing to deal with his problem. We offer him sips of water, which he turns down. A woman in front of him offers him a stick of chewing gum. He takes it, unwraps it, pops it in his mouth, and keeps on coughing. Soon, lozenges are passed down the row of seats. These Dad also declines. He's actually enjoying his sudden celebrity, oblivious to the fact that other people aren't enjoying the noise. After two minutes of his intermittent hacking, both

Mom and I give him dirty looks and suggest, separately, that he might want to step out of the room for a second, but he takes our orders for suggestions and waves us off.

"No, no, I'm fine." He shakes his head, grinning and crossing his arms like a ten-year-old, slouching jauntily in his seat. Mom rolls her eyes. I can see I'm going to have to take one for the team.

"Dad," I whisper under my breath, "go outside. You're bothering people."

He gives me a look of wounded surprise, as if it never occurred to him that that would be the polite thing to do, and storms out like we've voted him off the island.

"Jesus Christ," he mutters on his way out. "I just inhaled the wrong way."

Dad is adorable, but he cannot handle criticism.

Seeing my father exit, another tall gentleman decides to make a break for it, too. He gets up out of his seat and walks shakily down the aisle to the back of the room. He probably only needs to use the restroom, an urge as unassailable as any, but forgets that he's no longer the master of his own ship. He's terribly unsteady on his feet and, within three steps, has snagged his toe on the carpet and pitched forward, landing face-first, sprawled out on the floor in front of us. Several women gasp and clutch at their chests. The lecturer stops speaking, and in the ensuing silence, we hear the beseeching wails of this poor man, who cannot get up from the floor by himself.

"I'm so sorry. I'm so embarrassed." He lies collapsed and helpless on the ground in front of everyone. "I'm so embarrassed."

My heart is in my throat as I watch two of the staffers rush over to help him to his feet. He can't even look us in the eye. He hangs his head down in a palpable display of shame that's agonizing to see. This is someone who had likely been an executive, who might have started his own company or been a partner at a law firm. Judging from his frame, he was once handsome, too. I'm suddenly fiercely angry at the way time robs us of our dignity. I want to help, to change his perception about what had happened. Nobody here thinks he's foolish.

My brain is racing a million miles a second trying to think of what I can do or say. I want to stand up and speak. I feel myself rising out of my chair, hesitating, then sinking back down again. I wish I had the timing of a comic. I wish I could get a laugh—to defuse the tension, but also change our collective takeaway, to restore his ego. Funny people have such power to heal others in difficult situations. They can acknowledge the foibles while reminding us all that we're the same. They can change what we remember about a moment. They can redirect our history with a few well-chosen words. But I'm not funny, so I sit and watch as they practically drag him up, one man on either side, holding him under his arms. As luck would have it, they choose to deposit him in the empty seat next to me. They bring him to me, right on cue.

"I'm so ashamed," he whispers. He is trembling, and I can see tears pooling in his eyes.

"Don't be!" I shift my body, recrossing my legs toward him and tilting my head in his direction. "You fell like an athlete! Were you an athlete in school?" I look straight into his eyes, a flirtatious smile on my lips. If my career has taught me anything, it's how to hold the gaze of someone I barely know and meet them exactly where they are, emotionally. I can't count the number of times I have hugged and greeted fans who were trembling and overcome, or had disabilities of some kind that made communication awkward. I can withstand the fires of embarrassment and stay right with you, locked on target for a brief time. So that's what I do.

He and I whisper to each other for the rest of the lecture, getting to know each other like we're on a first date. I lightly touch his arm and throw my head back and laugh. I surreptitiously stroke my skin through my fishnets and wobble my foot in its high-heeled boot. We're two conspirators in the back of class, having a good time. Soon he's smiling, and I bet all the other men wish they had gotten to sit next to the prettiest girl in the ballroom. And that's how you do magic.

"You're parents are selling their house?!" Mallory yells into the phone. She is stunned.

"Yeah, they've been talking about it for a couple of years." I walk through the house looking for the iced coffee I just had in my hand. I adjust the phone, going upstairs to try to remember where I last set it down. Maybe I was in the closet? "You have to move into assisted living before your health deteriorates, or they won't take you."

"Yeah, I know," she says with a sigh. I can tell she's gutted. We grew up together and lived four blocks apart for forty years, if you count my frequent returns as the prodigal daughter. She and her husband bought her parents' house, so anytime Nick and I come home to visit, it's as if nothing has changed in the neighborhood. I still walk over to her place and let myself into her mud room like I did when we were in fourth grade. Our kids have grown up wearing the same grooves in the sidewalks that we did—taking the same routes to the park, to the lake, uptown, to each other's houses. When my parents leave the home I grew up in, it will truly be the end of a long and happy era. I have already done my grieving. I've come back as often as I could these last five years, soaking up the quirks and joys of a community where we put down deep roots. Nothing will ever be the same.

I like the woman who's buying our house. We all do. She will make the improvements it so desperately needs. She will smooth its rough edges and hopefully knock out a wall or two to modernize. I think we will leave behind good vibes for her and her family. But my heart aches to think of never coming home again, never seeing that specific light in those specific rooms, never looking out at the same views again. When you live in a house long enough, you fill more than its walls. Your reputation and your lifestyle anchor your place in the community and your presence on the map becomes part of their daily drive from one side of town to the other. "Oh, there's the Phairs' house. I like what they've done with the planting this year."

I experience it, too, every time I jog along the Green Bay Trail, or when Mom and I take long walks through the beautifully landscaped

lanes in the village. That's Elizabeth Ebert's old house, I say to myself. That's Mrs. Wilson's place. That's where Chris Beacom lived.
That's where I went to that sleepover at Debbie Oberman's and they
had soda pop you could pour straight from a fountain in the sink.
That's Penny Rusnack's mansion. And Lara Chase's modernist mas-
terpiece, where we weren't allowed to go in the living room for fear
of damaging the art. The list goes on and on. When the Phairs leave
Winnetka, we will be doing more than detaching our memories and
belongings from their moorings. We will be detonating a brief, nostalgic seismic wave throughout the whole North Shore.

The decluttering began in earnest several years ago, when we
made room for my brother's family to move back to the United
States for a spell. I tore through closets, organizing, feeling like a
samurai. I didn't fear death during the process, nor the loss of our
past—not even when we began emptying the house in earnest, in
advance of my parents' move. I kept my mind empty and used ratio-
nality to tackle the job. Despite what my mother may tell you, I
absolutely made room for keepsakes and sentimental objects, photographs, school art projects and postcards. But not in duplicate and
triplicate. This was a paring down of items, a selection of what was
truly important, evocative, meaningful, or irreplaceable. Anything
in poor condition was discarded. This was hard for Mom at times,
and though she'd asked me to do it, she found the process emotionally disruptive.

The thing was, I still believed in my parents' future. I knew that
memories we got rid of she and Dad would soon replace with new
ones. If there was one overarching message I got out of cleaning my
parents' house, it was that Nancy Phair abhors a vacuum. She'd
squirreled away so much stuff. Every available nook and cranny was
filled with a bewildering mix of scrapbook ephemera—such as
matchboxes, incomplete decks of playing cards, vintage buttons, and
bookmarks—and rather valuable pieces of jewelry, ivory letter-
openers, Brussels lace, and gold cuff links. If there was a filing system, I couldn't make it out.

Mom followed me around most days, delighted about the extra space and the relief of having her belongings sorted, how it cleared the junk not only out of her drawers but out of her mind as well. On other days, we fought over decrepit, moldy paperbacks she and my father had read when they were newlyweds. "You can buy another copy," I argued. "You can read it on your iPad." I wasn't opposed to keeping meaningful items if there was something rare or singular about them, but these books were decidedly commonplace, and their bindings were manifestly rotten. She grabbed them away from me, in tears, and stormed out of the house. I admit, I can be hard to live with.

You see, for her each thing represents a trip, a friend, an occasion, or an era that she will never have back again. She doesn't have decades ahead of her. She can't travel to all these places anymore. Her life is shrinking, not expanding, and every bit of her past that I throw away, however insignificant, is like a withdrawal from the dwindling bank account of her time here on earth. She's wealthy in receipts. These things are tangible proof that, however little time she has left, she once did have a great deal of time to spend, and she spent it well. She'll need physical reminders of it, now more than ever, if she starts to forget.

When the painful process is complete, she will be starting a new chapter. I truly believe that. They are both healthy and busy. The furniture, art, carpets, dishes, and table linens we've decided to keep might look even better in their freshly painted, meticulously maintained new bungalow. They are certainly the best pieces from their collection: refined, coordinated. Not too much, not too little. We're renting big storage units, in case they want to swap something out or move somewhere else. There are no real endings yet.

But I am experiencing the sorrow with her, in my own way. Even in California, a wave of bittersweet memories will overwhelm me unexpectedly. I love our old house. I will miss the secret place on the roof where my brother and I used to smoke joints. I will miss seeing squirrels racing along the telephone lines with crabapples in their mouths. I will miss the sound of the Northwestern train bringing commuters home at dinnertime. I will miss the peal of real church bells from the tower of Christ Church, where I once sang in the choir, and the gold and purple leaves that plaster the sidewalks in the fall. I will miss everything I can never have back again, like my youthful obliviousness. From now on I will feel the movement of time on a grander scale.

"Ah, there it is!" I left my iced coffee in the bathroom, although for the life of me I can't remember why.

"You're having a senior moment," Mallory says in commiseration.

"Shut up! I am not." I peer at my face in the mirror. Still relatively line-free. I fuss with the hair at my temples, where white strands mingle with the golden-brown locks. "Remember when the kid at Little Ricky's thought you were my mother?" I say.

"Ohhhh, low blow! Fuck you!"

I smile, glad to see our relationship is still intact. I stretch a piece of hot-pink KT Tape along the inside of my left knee where an old injury is acting up. I crack my knuckles while we talk, bending my fingers back to keep them nimble. I think I can feel rain coming, because my joints are a little achy.

"Well, you can always stay at my house when you're in Chicago."

"Thanks, Mallory." The gesture means a lot to me. I may not show it, but I feel a little rudderless.

"Although . . ." She laughs softly, munching on a piece of celery. "Alberto and I just put it on the market."

acknowledgments

TK

ABOUT THE AUTHOR

LIZ PHAIR is a Grammy-nominated singer-songwriter whose debut album, *Exile in Guyville*, has been hailed as a landmark of indie rock. She began her career in the early 1990s in Chicago by self-releasing audiocassettes under the name Girly-Sound. The intense viral response to these early tracks led to Phair's signing with the independent record label Matador Records. She has been a recording artist and touring performer for over twenty-five years, paving the way for countless music artists, particularly women, who cite her among their major influences. Phair is also a visual artist who majored in studio art and art history at Oberlin College. Her writing has appeared in *The New York Times* and *The Atlantic*. *Horror Stories* is her first book.